Puerto Rican Families in New York City: Intergenerational Processes

Lloyd H. Rogler

Rosemary Santana Cooney

WATERFRONT PRESS
Maplewood, N.J.

Published by:
WATERFRONT PRESS
52 Maple Ave.
Maplewood, N.J. 07040

Copyright 1984 by
Hispanic Research Center
Fordham University

This is Monograph #11 of the
Hispanic Research Center's
Monograph Series

ISBN: 0-943862-24-8 (Clothbound)
      0-943862-25-6 (Paperbound)

Printed in the United States of America, 1985

DEDICATION

To the Puerto Rican families in this book and all others like them who in uprooting themselves from their native soil have faced adversity in order to seek a new life for themselves and their children.

Preface

Most of us are born and die as part of a family. A great many of our daily activities are carried out in fulfillment of our roles as members of a family. Members of a family assume different roles within a system of interrelationships comprising the family, and these roles are influential in the way the family copes with both the internal demands imposed upon it by various members and the external demands imposed by society. This book deals with families and how the members of the families experienced social change from the time of their birth in preindustrial Puerto Rico to their lives at present in the neighborhoods of greater New York City. As members of families, they have confronted many vicissitudes associated with their migration from one culture to another. Two features make this book unusual: one, its focus upon a little-known and -understood minority group and, two, its intergenerational approach to the study of migration-induced changes in the family.

To study the families, we went to their homes and interviewed mothers and fathers, one of their offspring, and the offspring's spouse. Each of the 400 persons we interviewed knew that he/she was participating in a research project. We took great care in explaining to them the sort of information we needed from them and why we were seeking this information. We also told them that the findings of our study would be published. To protect the privacy of the families, we have assigned fictitious names to the persons in this book and have changed a few details which might otherwise serve to identify them. However, essential facts have not been altered in any way.

We spent one year in developing and pretesting the study, and two years in conducting the interviews. We experienced many problems while conducting the interviews in the different neighborhoods of greater New York City. For this reason, it is appropriate to recognize and thank first the persons who worked diligently night and day, weekends and holidays, under difficult circumstances, to interview their Hispanic compatriots: Elizabeth Ospina, who coordinated the interviewing team, and who helped in numerous other ways from the inception of the study to its completion; and the interviewing team composed of Vivian Acevedo, José Sanchez, Nydia Vazquez Farinacci, Osvaldo Barreras, Dulce Ureña, José Manuel Rivera, José Diaz, and Carlos Maldonado. Together these persons composed a cohesive, motivated, and congenial field team.

A study such as this one requires the cooperation of numerous organizations and persons. Indeed, we succeeded in our efforts because many community leaders and organizations saw the value of the research. We were well received by churches, tenant organizations, senior citizen centers, schools, clinics, compatriot organizations and many others. Although these organizations remain unnamed, we wish to thank all of them for their unflagging assistance in helping us to contact families and secure their cooperation. Of the many persons who rendered us invaluable aid, we especially thank Roberto Redinger, Pedro Ruiz, Humberto Martinez, Carlos Da Graca Lobo, and Idalia Maldonado.

We wish to thank the following persons who coded the data from the interviews: Gregory Rainone, Ann Renker, George Gabriel, Marta Valentin, Helene Smith, and their supervisor, James McEleney.

A number of highly skilled research assistants participated in the data analysis. We wish to thank them for their contributions: Vilma Ortiz, Rose Marie Hurrell, Anna Veglery, Leonard Correale, Edna Schroder-Guerrero, Kyonghee Min, Michael Vaccaro, Alice Colon, Kevin Colleran, Evelyn Laureano, Emily Klass, and Rena Blumenthal.

Elizabeth Collado enthusiastically undertook many assignments which materially contributed to the book. We are indebted to her for her help.

We wish to express our appreciation to Eneida Welch, Marjorie O'Connor, and Nelida Malave for their secretarial assistance. Mercedes Rivera had the main responsibility for typing and retyping copy, a task which she performed with unending patience. We owe her a debt of gratitude.

Stasia Madrigal assisted in the editing of the manuscript, constructed the index, and gave us the benefit of her generous and sound professional advice on a number of issues. We are very thankful to her.

The main responsibility for editing the final draft of the manuscript was expertly carried out by Janet Turk Cohen. We are indebted to her for her knowledge of what constitutes clear prose and the professional skill and competence she brought to the effort.

The main consultant in the research was Reuben Hill. We learned much from his valuable advice which improved the quality of the research. We thank him for his wholehearted support of the project. Some of the items in the interviewing schedule were taken from Hill's studies. We also wish to thank Dale Nelson, Gerald Gurin, and Melvin Kohn for their sensible and pointed advice on a number of research issues.

Parts of this book have been published as articles: sections of Chapter I have appeared as "Help Patterns, the Family and Mental Health: Puerto Ricans in the United States," *Intergenerational Migration Review*, Vol. 12, No. 2, 1978, pp. 248-259; sections of Chapter IV, with Vilma Ortiz as co-author, have appeared as "Intergenerational Change in Ethnic Identity in the Puerto Rican Family," *International Migration Review*, Vol. 14, No. 2, 1980, pp. 193-214; sections of Chapter II, with Osvaldo Barreras as co-author, have appeared as "Coping with Distrust in a Study of Intergenerational Puerto Rican Families in New York City," *Hispanic Journal of Behavioral Sciences*, Vol. 3, 1981, pp. 1-17; sections of Chapter V, with Rose Marie Hurrell and Vilma Ortiz as co-authors, have appeared as "Decision Making in Intergenerational Puerto Rican Families," *Journal of Marriage and the Family*, Vol. 44, August, 1982, pp. 621-631. (Copyrighted 1982 by the National Council on Family Relations, Fairview Community School Center, 1910 West County Road B, Suite 147, St. Paul, Minnesota 55113. Reprinted by permission.)

The analysis of the data presented here was done at Fordham University's Hispanic Research Center where the book was written. The research was supported by a grant from the William T. Grant Foundation and by Grants #R01 MH28314 and #R01 MH30569 from the National Institute of Mental Health, Center for Minority Group Mental Health Programs.

This monograph is the eleventh in the Hispanic Research Center's series which is designed to stimulate interest in Hispanic concerns. The Hispanic Research Center was established at Fordham University in 1977, under a grant from the National Institute of Mental Health, renewed in 1982, to work toward five major objectives: (1) to develop and conduct policy-relevant epidemiological-clinical services research on processes relevant to Hispanic mental health; (2) to increase the small pool of scholars trained in Hispanic mental health research and to upgrade their research skills through the provision of apprenticeship training and other mechanisms; (3) to provide technical assistance to organizations and individuals interested in the mental health problems of Hispanic populations; (4) to provide a clearinghouse function for the publication and dissemination of mental health materials relevant to Hispanics; and (5) to develop a research environment for scholars from the mental health disciplines.

Lloyd H. Rogler
Albert Schweitzer Professor of Humanities
Fordham University
August, 1984

Rosemary Santana Cooney
Associate Professor
Department of Sociology
Fordham University

HISPANIC RESEARCH CENTER
FORDHAM UNIVERSITY
BRONX, NEW YORK 10458

MONOGRAPH SERIES

The Hispanic Research Center is supported by Research Grant 2PO1 MH 30569-06A1
from the National Institute of Mental Health,
Center for Minority Group Mental Health Programs.

Contents

List of Tables

PART 1

THE RESEARCH PROBLEM AND PROCEDURES, AND THE HISTORICAL BACKGROUND OF THE FAMILIES

I

The Research Problem

Immigration has played an important role in the history of the United States, beginning with the early large-scale movement from Northwestern Europe and extending to today's influx from Latin America and Indochina. The integration of immigrant groups into American society has been widely researched, but little is known about the relationship between a migration-induced change in the sociocultural environment of parents and their children and intergenerational processes within the family.

This book examines the lives of 100 intergenerationally linked Puerto Rican families. Each family consists of two generations: the mothers and fathers in the parent generation and their married child and spouse in the child generation. Thus, the 100 intergenerationally linked families represent 200 married couples, making a total of 400 persons. In 56 of the families a daughter of the parent generation is the link between the parent and married-child generations; in 44 families a son represents the link. At the time we met and interviewed them members of the parent generation were in their mid-fifties; the majority had come to the continental United States as young adults in their midtwenties and had lived on the mainland for nearly 30 years. Almost all of their children either were born on the mainland or had arrived during their preschool years. When interviewed, the members of the Puerto Rican child generation were young adults in their late twenties. Practically all of them live in New York City, mostly in the borough of the Bronx; a few live in the outskirts of the city. This book examines the experiences of the immigrant parent generation in their island-home, their migration and settlement in metropolitan New York City, and the experiences of their children, the child generation, raised in the United States. In addition, we investigate the impact of the two generations' different life experiences upon the transmission of sociocultural characteristics from parents to their children and upon the structure of the relationship between the parent and married child. Our research is premised upon the importance of examining the adaptation of immigrant groups from the perspective of generationally linked family units.

THE FRAMEWORK OF THE RESEARCH PROBLEM

To examine the adaptation of Puerto Rican immigrant families, we have used, as the conceptual framework of the study, Reuben Hill's intergenerational family development paradigm.[1] To paraphrase Hill, the paradigm conceives of the nuclear family as an intricately organized small-group system composed of the paired positions of husband-father, wife-mother, son-brother, and daughter-sister. The reciprocal relations between the paired positions are governed by a system of norms which change with the increasing ages of the occupants of the positions. As an intimate small group, the nuclear family undergoes a developmental sequence of stages which, as Hill states, "begins with the simple husband-wife pair, becoming more and more complex with each additional position, then becomes less complex as members are launched into jobs and marriages and the group contracts in size to the husband-wife pair once again" (p. 9). The expectations attached to the positions change with the age composition of the family, as does the quality of interaction among family members. Hill's conceptual framework identified an important focus of this research: intergenerational differences and similarities between the Puerto Rican parent families who have reached the developmental stage of decreasing complexity and the married-child families who are still at an earlier developmental phase once experienced by their parents.

When first developed by Hill and Stanton,[2] the approach was applied to the study of intergenerational change and continuity in families living in five separate geographically based subpopulations in Puerto Rico. The geographic areas had been differentially exposed to urbanization, industrialization, and influences emanating from the mainland. Whatever the setting of the research on the island, it is understandable why Hill and Stanton made the assumption that the family is a critically important institutional locus for the study of social change in Puerto Rico: the family is central to the island's system of stratification, to its social mobility patterns, and to the transition from an agrarian to an industrial society[3]; it mediates between the economic base of communities and socialization patterns[4]; it shapes the social experiences which accrue from socialization[5]; it is the main context of economic consumption[6]; it is an important repository of modernizing impulses to social change[7]; and it binds together the reciprocal patterns of help in facilitating rural to urban migration and adaptation.[8] The family mitigates the implementation of middle-class rules in urban public hous-ing developments[9]; it extends itself into the ritual coparent system of *compadrazgo* to enlarge the scope of its social security function.[10] It is the object of devotion in an overarching system of cultural values[11]; it is the primary setting for the care of the mentally ill[12]; and it shapes the character of entrepreneurial activities through its system of paternalistic relation-ships.[13] Despite rapid social change, Puerto Rican society at the root cultural level still centers upon the family and its functions. In brief, Puerto Ricans come from a society in which the family is multifunctional and plays a funda-mental role in the governance of its members.

Yet, whether in the context of intergenerational linkages or not, little is known about the Puerto Rican family in the continental United States, in particular, in New York City which has the largest concentration of Puerto Ricans in the world. Few, indeed, are the field studies based upon systematic methodological procedures and clearly articulated concepts. Although the findings of research conducted in Puerto Rico provide valuable baseline data, they do not warrant extrapolating the life circumstances of Puerto Ricans in New York City as a linear continuation of life circumstances on the island, or even of the circumstances experienced at the point of embarkation, San Juan. The new setting creates a set of life circumstances never before experi-enced by the immigrant Puerto Ricans, and New York City's immense size and structural complexity impose upon them new and unfamiliar patterns and demands, such as the need to learn a new language and relegation to the status of a minority group.

In the study of intergenerational change among Puerto Ricans, it is com-mon strategy to focus upon differences across unrelated generations, for example, among those ethnic-group members born in a foreign country (first generation), those born in the United States of foreign or mixed parent-age (second generation), and those born in the United States of U.S.-born members of the ethnic group (third generation). An implicit assumption underlying these comparisons is that the generational differences observed reflect changes occurring within immigrant families. Such differences, how-ever, do not necessarily reflect dissimilarities between parents and children because there is no reason to assume that differences between generations unrelated through kinship are the same as the differences between genera-tions within kinship units.[14] Therefore, we decided that the assumption must be tested by direct matching of lineal members of the parent generation and the child generation, as we will be doing in subsequent chapters.

We believe differences between the parent and child generations could be rooted in the developmental stages of their respective life cycles. Therefore, an important advantage of using the intergenerational family development framework in comparing the characteristics of parents and children is that it sensitizes us to both the life-cycle stage and the historical context as factors affecting differences between intergenerationally-linked family members. This approach makes explicit that dissimilarities observed at one time between parents and their children may have been caused by differences in the developmental stages of their life cycles.

In addition, observed dissimilarities between the parent and child generations could derive from the difference in the historical periods in which the generations were born and raised. The intergenerational family development approach sees the conduct of family members affected by historical changes as refracted through the prism of the respective life-cycle stages. It is one way of examining the relationship between broader social change in the society and changes of persons with family linkages. For example, the parent generation in our study was born a few years before the Great Depression; they have been married for more than 33 years and are at the stage of diminishing parental and increasing grandparental responsibilities as most of their children have grown up, married, and left the household; the husband after working for almost four decades is now approaching retirement age. The child generation in our study was born in the immediate post-World War II period of increasing prosperity and massive migration from Puerto Rico to the continental United States; they have been married for almost 10 years and are at the stage of building a family; they are in the process of procreating and rearing children; the husband is still in the early stages of establishing himself in New York City's occupational system. Thus, socialization experiences acquired in historical periods reflecting very different educational and occupational opportunities and social climates undoubtedly have shaped differently the individual characters of the two generations.

Our examination of intergenerational change is limited, therefore, by a problem common to analytically oriented intergenerational studies: in the absence of large-scale historically oriented longitudinal studies, most intergenerational studies cannot separate with analytical precision the causes of dissimilarity between the parent and married-child generations. Time cannot be set back to look at the parent generation as young married adults — in the same stage of their life cycle as their married children in the present — in order to examine the impact of the different historical periods of their birth and upbringing. Nor can historical periods be held constant to examine the impact of generational life-cycle differences upon intergenerational differences. As Troll and Bengtson[15] recognize from their analysis of methodological problems of intergenerational studies, the effects of life-cycle developmental stages upon intergenerational continuity are ". . . neither general nor obvious." They recognize, too, that the developmental effects of stages of the life cycle cannot be separated from the effects of historical periods with the data currently available (p. 149). Nonetheless, since generations are an inextricable part of their own historical periods, it is important to describe the historical context of the lives of the persons portrayed in this book at different stages of their life cycle. This will be done in Chapter III.

To our knowledge, the intergenerational approach has not been systematically applied to the study of continuity within immigrant families. There is, however, a large and growing body of research studies conducted in the United States that provides a valuable point of departure for comparisons with our own work on Puerto Rican intergenerational families. Reflecting largely upon the popular and academic literature produced during the social unrest of the 1960s and the subsequent decade of the 1970s, Troll and Bengtson[16] identify three major positions characterizing intergenerational studies: first, the "great gap theory" which sees marked discontinuity between parents and children, separated from each other by conflict and rivalry; second, the "nothing really new" position which sees deeply ingrained underlying continuity between generations, the observed differences between them a reflection of other social contrasts; and, third, the "selective continuity" position which recognizes that some characteristics but not others may be intergenerationally continuous. To understand the concept of intergenerational continuity as used in this book, presently we shall stress the importance of distinguishing between intergenerational differences and similarities, on one hand, and intergenerational discontinuity and continuity, on the other hand.

One of the issues discussed in Troll and Bengtson's critical review is which of these three positions is most consistent with the accumulated research findings. The weight of evidence from the methodologically sound studies they reviewed suggests that data are more consistent with the "selective continuity" approach, and there are heuristic advantages favoring it. This position leaves open to empirical documentation the possible unevenness of familial transmission across the factors being considered, such as the structure of social relations, values, belief systems, and socioeconomic attributes. The thrust of intergenerational research has stressed the description of this unevenness. By explicitly recognizing continuity as well as discontinuity, the selective continuity position also issues a challenge to family researchers: Why is familial transmission selective? What are the underlying dynamics of familial transmission that explain "selective continuity"? With the exception of the recognition given to historical periods and life-cycle developmental stages, the literature, thus far, has scarcely begun to address this challenge. The research reported in this book attempts to meet it in the context of the migration experience of Puerto Rican families.

While research focused on familial transmission is growing rapidly, the parent and child generations studied have almost exclusively lived their lives in one society, the United States.[17] There is, however, nothing in the "selective continuity" approach which uniquely and necessarily ties it to the study of intergenerational change and continuity among families who live their lives in one sociocultural system. The study presented here is of persons who have experienced a move from one sociocultural system to another, from Hispanic Puerto Rico to the Anglo-dominated mainland of the United States. Intergenerational data on immigrant parents and their children raised in New York City provide a unique opportunity to examine an important question which has received little attention in the earlier studies: How does a migration-induced change in sociocultural environment relate to intergenerational processes in the family? More specifically, one may ask: Is the pattern of "selective continuity" documented in the general literature characteristic also of familial transmission within immigrant Puerto Rican families? To our knowledge, no other study of immigrant groups has brought primary data systematically to bear upon this question.

BASIC DISTINCTIONS IN INTERGENERATIONAL PROCESSES

Before introducing the specific topics of our research, it is important to define intergenerational continuity and how it is empirically evaluated. For illustrative purposes, we focus upon the educational level of the generations. Intergenerational continuity in education involves comparing the education of the individual parent in relation to other parents and the education of his/her child in relation to other children. The greater the congruence between the relative positions of the parent and child, the greater the intergenerational continuity. The concept of continuity does not require that the parent and child be in absolute agreement, i.e., have the exact same level of education. Rather, the focus is on relative congruence. If, for example, the educational level of an individual father is high in relation to other fathers of his generation and the educational level of his child is high in relation to other children of that generation then there is congruence, which is to say there is intergenerational continuity with respect to education. *Continuity* in education between fathers and children means that fathers who are relatively advantaged in their educational achievement pass on this advantage to their children. Conversely, it means also that fathers whose educational achievements are relatively low pass on this disadvantage to their children. *Discontinuity* refers to the absence of a correlation between the educational level of the parents and children. If there is no correlation, then the relative educational achievement of the father is neither an advantage nor a disadvantage to the educational achievement of his child. Thus, correlations are used to determine the degree of intergenerational continuity between parents and their married children with respect to the characteristic chosen for evaluation.

Although the focus of our interest is on intergenerational continuity, we will present also descriptive information to document general similarities and differences between the parent and child generations. To return to our example above, the average educational attainment of the parent generation may be less than completion of grammar school, while the average educational attainment of the child generation may be graduation from high school. Such comparisons may well reflect broader social historical changes in the expansion of educational opportunities and are of interest in their own right, especially in view of the scarcity of intergenerational studies of immigrant families. However, comparisons between the parents as a group and children as a group do not tell us anything about intergenerational continuity, which, in terms of the example just used, would be the process of transmitting educational advantage or disadvantage from parents to their children.

Intergenerational research becomes confused if a distinction is not consistently made between intergenerational continuity and discontinuity, on the one hand, and intergenerational similarities and differences, on the other hand. Measures of the two concepts can and do vary independently. Although the two concepts are rooted in intergenerational measures and issues, they have substantially different meanings. Yet, it is important to understand that the demonstration of intergenerational discontinuity in families does not lead to the conclusion that the parents have been irrelevant to the lives of their children or vice versa. There can be discontinuity even though the parents have profoundly influenced the lives of their children. This can occur because intergenerational continuity or discontinuity refers to the presence or absence of significant correlations between intergenerationally linked generations with respect to the *same* characteristic. Such correlations are used to determine family legacies across generations, often with the interest, as we have shown, of determining whether or not the parental family's characteristics have created advantages or disadvantages for, or are inconsequential to, the lives of the children in terms of the very same characteristics. It is, in brief, a way of examining transmissions through family linkages or the emergence of congruent features between family-linked generations.

In contrast, efforts to explain the characteristics or experiences of a generation are not limited to the use of the same set of variables across generations. Pursuing one step further our example pertaining to education, we found variations in the educational attainments of the child generation in this study could be examined not just according to the parents' educational attainments, but also by means of other characteristics of the parent generation such as their values and the size of the household during the children's socialization. Efforts to explain the characteristics or experiences of a generation, however, need not be based upon the assumption that the sources of influence are always to be found in the intergenerational family context. Also relevant could be the societal expansion of educational opportunities, a source of influence outside of the family which affects the educational attainments of successive generations. Thus, the determination of intergenerational continuity could form part of a broader process of explanation, but the two types of effort are not equivalent.

In addition to the study of intergenerational differences and similarities, discontinuities and continuities, the examination of intergenerational processes involves the assessment of the degree to which the generations are integrated. In some families the generations are sharply separated from each other with little communication or help-giving between them; in other families, quite the opposite is the case, with parents and children deeply enmeshed in each others' lives. Intergenerational integration designates the degree of closeness between the generations in terms of behavioral acts such as visiting or the giving and receiving of help.

In sum, we undertook this study with the belief that, despite its limitation and the need for careful distinctions, the intergenerational family development approach would shed light upon a question which seldom has been the focus of research: *How do migration-induced events relate to intergenerational processes within the families*? To answer this question, our data will be used to identify intergenerational similarities and differences in the Puerto Rican families in the study, to explain characteristics forming part of the life experiences of the respective generations, to evaluate intergenerational continuities and discontinuities, and to assess intergenerational integration. Since little is known about intergenerational continuity or discontinuity among families who have moved from one sociocultural system to another, as have the Puerto Rican families in this study, we adopt the "selective continuity" view that transmissions or continuities between generations can be uneven, some characteristics being transmitted and others not. As we pursue this line of inquiry we shall be led to consider even broader issues relevant to the ways in which the intergenerationally linked migrant families are integrated.

The study was affected from its inception by the focus upon intergenerationally linked families. It required that the study group consist of families displaying such linkages. In addition, because of our interest in migration and in the structure of husband and wife relations, we selected Puerto Rican families who had intact marital unions at the time of data collection. After providing a brief sociobiographical profile of the migration of Puerto Ricans to the United States in Chapter II, we describe the selection of the study group, the field problems we encountered while collecting the data, how we coped with such problems, and how the team of interviewers adapted interviewing techniques in their approach to the families and to the generational differences in the families of the study group.

Generations are imbedded in the historical period of which they form a part. To understand them, history must be examined. In our study group, history begins in the years immediately preceding the Great Depression, in the farms, villages, and cities of Puerto Rico where the mothers and fathers of the parent generation were born and raised. Their life history spans the Great Depression and World War II, a period of convulsive social change in the island-home, and the large-scale postwar migration to New York City of which they formed a part. The child generation was born at about the time their parents emigrated; thus, the prevailing socialization experiences of the husbands and wives in this younger generation occurred in the highly complex urban setting of New York City. Chapter III sketches the historical changes in Puerto Rico and in New York City which were intertwined with the lives of the persons we studied: it seeks to determine how the characteristics of the two generations are similar to or different from appropriately selected comparison groups. The comparison groups will be identified at successive time periods to coincide with the specific time periods critically relevant to the lives of the persons studied. Such comparisons are relevant simultaneously to an issue of method and an issue of substance: with respect to method, the issue pertains to the representativeness of the study group; with respect to substance, the issue pertains to the degree to which the two generations fit the characteristics of larger populations which also were being caught in the changing society of Puerto Rico and in the migration process to New York City.

Although they have departed from a society with its familiar culture, values, and norms, migrants retain much of that culture, and their offspring acquire elements of the new and different culture. The interplay between the original culture and the host-society culture determines the ethnic identity of the new migrant and his/her offspring in the subsequent generation. Proceeding from the assumption that the strength of ethnic identity decreases with receptivity to influences stemming from the host society and according to the degree of exposure to such influences, a three-chapter sequence, Chapters IV, V, and VI, explores the relevance of intergenerational processes and other social forces in the lives of the Puerto Ricans in the study. In Chapter IV, ethnic identity is put in the intergenerational family context to examine differences between generations and the important issue of intergenerational transmissions in ethnic identity. The effort to understand ethnic identity leads to a consideration of broader, extrafamilial factors of relevance to the conditions which give rise to intergenerational continuity. Chapter IV shows clearly the utmost importance of the distinctions we have endeavored to make between the concepts of differences and similarities between generations, intergenerational continuity and discontinuity, and the efforts to explain elements forming part of the life experiences of generations. If we are to begin to understand the intricacies of familial intergenerational processes, these distinctions are necessary.

Utilizing such distinctions, while keeping at the forefront of attention the intergenerational issues which they represent, we examine in Chapter V the structure of husband and wife relations in both generations. Thus, from one chapter to the next, the focus changes from a set of properties of a person, his/her ethnic identity, to the properties of a dyadic relationship, that of husband and wife. However different the two properties are socio-culturally, with the intergenerational family development approach both can be the object of meaningful analysis. The marital relationship is examined according to the concept of role segregation, the degree to which husbands and wives separate themselves from each other, or share in the performance of household tasks, leisure-time activities, and decision-making. This is done by identifying the role culture plays in shaping generational differences in role segregation. Chapter V draws two contrasting perspectives on the theoretical relevance of culture from the literature on immigrant families in the United States and the macro literature on variations in role segregation among nations and then uses these perspectives to examine how the patterning of role segregation varies between the Puerto Rican husbands and wives of the parent and married-child generations. Data subsequently are brought to bear upon the intergenerational process of continuity and the conditions under which intergenerational continuity is created, this time, in the role of segregation between husbands and wives. In its entirety, Chapter V yields a multifaceted intergenerational perspective on the topic.

The focus of Chapter VI is socioeconomic mobility in the form of increased level of education and better occupations, a theme of central interest to the social sciences and one which characterizes the lives of the Puerto Rican immigrants and their offspring in this study. Intergenerational sequences in social mobility are examined historically, from their roots in Puerto Rico through their migration and settlement in New York City. Our examination uses the full armamentarium of intergenerational concepts and distinctions but ends with findings which are genuinely puzzling and incapable of comprehension within the customary sociological framework that dominates the literature on attainment of status. As the framework is qualified by the findings and expanded to include additional sets of variables, which are considered in the context of the migration experience from Puerto Rico to New York City, the puzzle begins to be solved. Without foreshadowing the findings of Chapter VI, it is appropriate to state the need for substantial modifications in customary explanations of social mobility processes if we are to understand such processes across ethnic groups and across family-interlinked generations.

Ethnic identity, husband and wife relations, and social mobility, the topics which correspond to Chapters IV, V, and VI, are, in each case, framed and developed according to the relevant research literature. It is particularly important to do this because researchers, in numbers, have been drawn to examine each topic, and the result has been the recognition that each topic is involved in broad and intricate sociocultural patterns and processes. Therefore, the presentation of each topic entails a critical but selective review of the pertinent literature. However, in the effort to examine each topic in the context of the relationship between migration-induced events and intergenerational family processes, what we attempt is different from what others have attempted. Time and again, we return to this issue. Of relevance also is the fact that the order in which the three chapters are presented coincides substantially with the chronological order in which the topics were analyzed. This means that in addition to bringing the conclusions of other research to bear upon each topic, we bring to bear also what we have learned from the analysis of a prior topic, in particular, its relationship to migration and intergenerational processes. In this respect, the three-chapter presentation is programmatic.

The programmatic sequence continues to Chapters VII and VIII. As the findings from the preceding chapters grew and evolved, it became a matter of compelling importance to us to examine the integration of the intergenerationally linked families. In less abstract terms, we wanted to see what the families looked like *in vivo*, as holistic functioning organizations composed of a membership of first- and second-generation Puerto Ricans attempting to make their way in the unfamiliar environment of New York City. To do this, we proceeded to examine the data in a variety of ways: statistical patterns representing intergenerational visits and reciprocal help-exchanges were analyzed, under the assumption that such patterns were directly relevant to the concept of intergenerational integration; the flow of help between the intergenerationally linked families was examined to see which nuclear units played the prevailing role of donor or beneficiary. Since the base data collected in the field included an inventory of help-giving and help-receiving exchanges occurring during the year preceding the interviews, it was possible to identify the institutional nexus of such exchanges, whether in the family or outside it. Such findings are relevant to the degree of dominance exercised by the family in the governance of reciprocal help-exchanges. In keeping with the study's programmatic efforts, the impact of migration-induced events upon intergenerational integration was evaluated.

By building upon such specific attempts, Chapters VII and VIII deal with the results of a more global assessment of the integration between generations at an overarching level of family life. Based upon the qualitative examination and classification of all 100 intergenerationally linked family units, the assessment distinguishes between prevailing and variant forms of integration. Such distinctions are important, because intergenerational integration takes on an identifiable shape or form when the entire family unit is looked upon as a case study. In the case studies presented, exemplifying prevailing and variant forms of integration, variables cease to be the focus of analysis, and persons with assigned fictitious proper names assume a role in a system of interrelationships comprising the family and how the family copes with the external demands imposed upon it. Chapter VIII terminates the presentation of the lives of the Puerto Rican immigrants and their married offspring. Chapter IX brings together the study's major findings to determine what has been learned from the research.

We embarked upon this study with the conviction that a field study of intergenerational processes in Puerto Rican migrant families would be an intellectually rewarding contribution. This book is a product of our commitment to this venture.

REFERENCES

1. Hill, R. 1970. *Family Development in Three Generations*. Cambridge: Schenkman Publishing Co.

2. Hill, R. and H. Stanton, cited in Hill, R. 1970. "The Three Generation Research Design: Method for Studying Family and Social Change," p. 541, in Reuben Hill and Rene Konig (eds.), *Families in East and West*. The Hague, Netherlands: Mouton and Co.
3. Tumin, M. M. and A. S. Feldman. 1961. *Social Class and Social Change in Puerto Rico*. Princeton: Princeton University Press.
4. Wolf, K. L. 1952. "Growing Up and Its Price in Three Puerto Rican Subcultures." *Psychiatry* 15: 401-433.
5. Landy, D. 1959. *Tropical Childhood: Cultural Transmission and Learning in a Rural Puerto Rican Village*. Chapel Hill: University of North Carolina Press.
6. Roberts, L. and L. R. Stefani. 1949. *Patterns of Living in Puerto Rican Families*. Rio Piedras, P.R.: Editorial Universitaria.
7. Hill, R. et al. 1959. *The Family and Population Control: A Puerto Rican Experiment in Social Change*. Chapel Hill: University of North Carolina Press.
8. Rogler, L. H. and A. B. Hollingshead. 1965. *Trapped: Families and Schizophrenia*. New York: John Wiley and Sons.
9. Hollingshead, A. B. and L. H. Rogler. 1963. "Attitudes Toward Slums and Public Housing in Puerto Rico," in L. J. Duhl et al., *The Urban Condition*. New York: Basic Books.
10. Mintz, S. W. 1955. "Cañamelar: The Subculture of a Rural Sugar Plantation Proletariat," in J. H. Steward et al., *The People of Puerto Rico: A Study in Social Anthropology*. Urbana: University of Illinois Press.
11. Brameld, T. 1959. *The Remaking of a Culture: Life and Education in Puerto Rico*. New York: Harper and Brothers.
12. Rogler and Hollingshead, see note 8.
13. Cochran, T. C. 1959. *The Puerto Rican Businessman: A Study in Cultural Change*. Philadelphia: University of Pennsylvania Press.
14. Troll, L. and V. Bengtson. 1979. "Generations in the Family," pp. 130-131 in W. R. Burr et al., (eds.), *Contemporary Theories About the Family*, Vol. 1. New York: The Free Press.
15. *Ibid*.
16. *Ibid*.
17. *Ibid*.

II

Field Research Procedures

The specific research problems described in the preceding chapter required that the field research utilize a complex intergenerational family model. It required also lengthy interviews with the Puerto Rican families in a setting, New York City, that is uncongenial to social research. In general, field problems in research arise from the interplay between the requirements of the research design and the human context under study. If the design's requirements are undemanding and the study's context congenial to the intrusions of field research, then few problems will arise, but, if the design is demanding and the context uncongenial, field problems will emerge frequently and with great intensity. While other combinations are possible, it is the latter combination which we experienced as we tried to select the study group and collect the data. This chapter discusses the issues we confronted in the selection of the study group, then turns to the problems we experienced and the solutions we attempted while trying to collect data for the study.

The intergenerationally linked families depicted in this book have been historically part of the mass transfer of Puerto Rican people and their culture to the mainland, in particular, to New York City. We needed to know: Who are they? When did they arrive? Where are they located in New York City's system of social stratification? To provide a background for the presentation of the study's field research procedures, we turn first to a brief sociodemographic sketch of the Puerto Rican migration and those who took part in it.

SOCIODEMOGRAPHIC PROFILE

The Puerto Rican population in the continental United States is a young and relatively recent immigrant population. In 1910, when the first census data on the Puerto Rican population were reported, there were only 1,513 persons of Puerto Rican origin reported living within the continental United States. By 1920 that figure had reached 11,811, dispersed throughout 44 states. By 1940 the census reported approximately 70,000. Ten years later the mainland Puerto Rican community, both island-born and those of Puerto Rican parentage, had more than quadrupled to over 300,000 persons. In the 1950s the number nearly tripled to 892,000 persons, and by 1970 persons of Puerto Rican birth or parentage living on the mainland numbered about 1,429,000. In 1980, the Puerto Rican community on the mainland leveled off at approximately 2,000,000 persons, 45 percent more than the population enumerated in 1970.

In the past 20 years some 651,000 people have left Puerto Rico for the mainland. "The magnitude of this net migration flow in comparison to the 1970 census of Puerto Rico of 2,712,033 is unmatched in the 20th century by any other national group."[1] The outflow has had a pronounced impact upon the economic and social structure of Puerto Rico. As a result of migration about one-third of all Puerto Ricans live on the mainland, and about one-fifth of the total reside in New York City. Almost all of the Puerto Rican migrants have chosen urban areas of settlement, and New York City has been the dominant traditional area of first settlement. New York's share of the migration has fluctuated through the decades largely in response to the capacity of the labor market to absorb new workers. Although the absolute size of New York City's Puerto Rican mainland population has been increasing, the city's relative share of the Puerto Rican population in the United States has decreased from 88 percent in 1950 to 59 percent in 1970. However, New York City still maintains the largest Puerto Rican community on the mainland.

This community tends to be quite young. In 1976 its median age was 20.4 years, in contrast to 29.2 years for the total U.S. population.[2] The youthfulness of this group is even more pronounced when those born on the mainland are considered separately. Second-generation Puerto Ricans comprised 42 percent of the mainland Puerto Rican population in 1970 and had a median age of 9.3 years. In New York City 73 percent of second-generation Puerto Ricans and 38 percent of all Puerto Ricans were under 15 years of age. This age structure results from the recency of their migration and the generational composition of the current population.

Educationally and occupationally Puerto Ricans compare unfavorably with the general population. In 1978, only 36 percent of the mainland Puerto Rican population were high school graduates, compared to 67 percent of the non-Hispanic population. In 1970 in New York City, the median education completed by island-born Puerto Ricans 25 years old and older was less than 9 years, compared to more than 12 years for the total population; 56 percent of all adult Puerto Ricans had only a grade school education or less, almost twice the percentage of the general population. However, for second-generation Puerto Ricans the median schooling increased to 11.5 years, close to that of the total population.

Throughout the history of migration to the mainland the labor-force participation of mainland Puerto Ricans has been concentrated in low-skill jobs since a disproportionate number of Puerto Ricans lack the educational background and English skills required for white-collar occupations. The employment problems such deficiencies create are further compounded by the discrimination Puerto Ricans experience. Among employed Puerto Ricans in 1977, 62 percent worked in the four lowest paid occupational groups and were underrepresented in white-collar categories.[3]

There is a close relationship among the socioeconomic indicators of education, unemployment, and income for Puerto Ricans. As a group, the Puerto Ricans in the mainland are the poorest Hispanics in the United States. Their median family income in 1977 was $7,972, almost $4,000 less than that of Mexican Americans, the next poorest Hispanic group, and about half the average income of American families.[4] The low income of the Puerto Rican population puts a large number of families at risk to experience considerable economic hardship. Thus, the 100 intergenerationally linked families in our study form part of a young, recent immigrant population experiencing acute disadvantages in education, occupation, and income.

SELECTION OF THE STUDY GROUP

Hill's intergenerational family development framework[5] focuses upon husband-wife pairs in successive generations within the family. The framework, however, does not necessarily restrict the parent-child linkages to husband-wife pairs. For example, a study of intergenerational processes could well focus upon one-parent families and their children. The proportion of one-parent families among Puerto Ricans, in fact, has been increasing, but the predominant family unit in which their children are raised is still the two-parent family. Thus, in view of time and funding constraints which limited the number of families we could study and because our research would be the first intergenerational study of Puerto Rican immigrants and their children, we followed Hill's strategy of focusing on husband-wife families. One advantage of requiring that both the parent and child generations consist of married couples is that it enables the intergenerational study of the structure of marital relationships. Another advantage is that differences associated with stages of the life cycle are minimized in comparison to those in most inter-generational studies in which adolescent high school or college students are the subjects. In our study both the children and the parents are independent adults who have established their own households.

Another important decision in selecting families relates to the ethnicity of the spouses. A major way in which immigrant groups become integrated into the new sociocultural environment is through intermarriage. Inter-marriage brings a man and woman from different cultures together into an intimate primary group relationship. While the determinants and conse-quences of intermarriage among Puerto Ricans is an important topic in its own right, we limited our intergenerational families to persons of Puerto Rican birth or parentage. By choosing a study group which is ethnically endogamous, we made certain that representation was given to the prevailing pattern of Puerto Rican marriages occurring in New York City, that of in-group marriages.[6]

Troll and Bengtson[7] used two key methodological criteria in their review of the intergenerational literature to select noteworthy studies. First, both the parent(s) and child must be interviewed; if one generation provides the information on the other, the opportunity arises for misperception and misreporting of problems. Second, to determine intergenerational continuity the parent's score on the variable selected must be related to that of his/her own child; as the preceding chapter indicated, comparisons which examine only intergenerational differences in group characteristics do not consider familial transmission or continuity. Both in the collection of information and in the analysis of the data, our research fulfills the two key criteria.

As has been noted, the intergenerational family model required that the 400 persons interviewed had to (a) be Puerto Rican by birth or parentage, (b) represent 200 husband-wife pairs, and (c) be grouped in husband-wife pairs linked to other husband-wife pairs in the study group either as a parent or child, thus representing 100 intergenerationally linked families. To convert these substantive requirements into steps in order to screen intergenerational families for the study group meant that the person selected or identified, through whatever means, had to be (1) Puerto Rican by birth or parentage, (2) legally or consensually married, (3) living with his/her spouse, and (4) will-ing to cooperate through a series of interviews. The spouse of the person selected had to be (5) Puerto Rican by birth or parentage and (6) willing to cooperate through a series of interviews. In turn, either the person initially selected or his/her spouse had to be (7) intergenerationally linked to a parent or adult offspring who (8) lived sufficiently near to be interviewed during the course of one day's work. The parent or adult offspring had to be (9) legally or consensually married and (10) living with his or her spouse who was of (11) Puerto Rican birth or parentage. Finally, the parent or adult offspring had to be (12) willing to cooperate through series of interviews, as would (13) his/her spouse. Each and every step was necessary to specify the study group we sought. One missing step was sufficient to disqualify or eliminate the family from the study group. It was difficult, indeed, to convert the requirements stemming from the intergenerational family model into a successful 13-step screening sequence.

At first, the possibility of conducting multistage probability sampling was considered. Sampling procedures would have to be instituted from the level of census tracts, on to neighborhood blocks, on to households, and then on to the person selected within the household. However, the selection of the person within the household would initiate the first step in the 13-step screening sequence. The failure to attain any one of the 13 steps would have meant, once again, that the entire case had to be discarded, and another person sampled to begin anew the screening sequence. The substantive requirements of the model, based upon the combination of criteria pertaining to ethnicity, marriage, and the intergenerational linkage would reduce to an unknown size the population appropriate to the study group, meaning that new cases would have had to be selected repeatedly through sampling. Beyond the substantive requirements, however, intrinsically difficult to fulfill was the requirement that four persons linked together by marital and intergenerational bonds would have to cooperate through a series of interviews. Additional field trips and contacts would have been required to determine whether or not such cooperation would be forthcoming. Calculations based upon the more or less usual response rate of sample studies in urban areas indicated a small probability of securing the simultaneous cooperation of four persons. The refusal of any one of the four persons to cooperate would mean the loss of the intergenerational case, thus multiplying many times over the sampling biases common to survey studies. Not surprisingly, the study's pretest experience indicated that a 13-step screening procedure set into the framework of a probability sample would have created serious logistical problems in the fieldwork, been prohibitively expensive, and still carried with it the risk of highly uncertain outcomes.

The procedure for the selection of the study group we finally settled upon was simpler and more flexible but is devoid of the theoretical advantages of a probability-based selection of samples. Using the 1970 census, we rank-ordered the census tracts in the borough of the Bronx from high to low according to the percentage of Puerto Ricans with a high school education.

Education was selected as the criterion for rank-ordering because it is associated with other socioeconomic characteristics. Then, to incorporate into
the study group a range of socioeconomic differences among the Puerto
Rican families, we focused our screening efforts on the census tracts at the
top and at the bottom of the rank-order in a two-pronged effort to secure the
families. Schools, Catholic and Pentecostal churches, spiritualist centers,
Puerto Rican compatriot organizations, and civic groups were visited, as were
households in door-to-door visits in selected neighborhood blocks. The
persons contacted through such visits provided the point of departure for
the 13-step screening procedures; in addition, they were asked if they knew
other Puerto Rican families who fulfilled the intergenerational model. If they
did, we visited and screened the families they identified. This procedure
incorporated biases into the study group, not the least being that, within the
context of the substantive requirements of the study group, the families
tended to know each other, were cooperative toward the research effort,
and very likely were disproportionately involved in the organizational life
of their neighborhoods and ethnic group. Other biases also are apparent. The
next chapter will examine the study group's representativeness in the context
of historically appropriate comparison groups in settings which range from
the birth of the parents in Puerto Rico to the present lives of the married
offspring in New York City.

Once a family fitting the intergenerational model was identified and
cooperation secured, four persons were interviewed: wife, husband, child,
and child's spouse. More than twice the amount of information was required
from women than from men: the average interviewing time for women was
5 hours and 45 minutes; for the men, 2½ hours. The study's data-collection
phase required the labors of slightly more than five full-time fieldworkers
over a 23-month period from July 1976 to May 1978. Thus, the requirements of the study were demanding in terms of both the complexity of the
criteria defining the study group and the length of interviews.

In addition to a demanding study design, we faced the problem of a setting
for the study that was uncongenial to research. In general, if rates of nonresponse are taken as the measure, the larger the urban area, the more difficult
the collection of data. Robins' study[8] of reluctant respondents in St. Louis
found refusal rates to be higher for residents of the city compared to those
living in areas outside of the city. Dunkelberg and Day[9] found that city size
was the most important variable in explaining patterns of nonresponse: the
larger the city, the higher the nonresponse rate. Kohn[10] reported that the
larger the community, the more difficult it is to obtain long interviews from
employed men. Finally, the Survey Research Center of the Institute for

Social Research at the University of Michigan reported that small towns and rural areas have consistently lower rates of nonresponse than more urbanized areas.[11] By requiring the application of a complex family model to one minority group, with the further requirement of lengthy interviews in the uncongenial research setting of New York City, we made our research task much more problematic than is customary in survey research. Some of the problems and the solutions we attempted are discussed below.

PROBLEMS OF DISTRUST

As early as the start of the study's one-year pretesting period, we became aware of the fact that, even after a family was identified as fulfilling the intergenerational family model, considerable effort was still necessary to secure the cooperation of the four persons in each intergenerationally linked family. The prevailing and most immediate obstacle was distrust. One fieldworker's initial experiences in interviewing a respondent, Ignacio Nuñez, were typical. The field worker wrote:

> Mr. Nuñez was a dry person who tried very much to keep his distance from strangers, including myself. He was very aware of what was written in the interview schedule and was trying to verify that the questions I read to him were in fact written in the schedule. He was reluctant to participate in the study. I had to make several visits to his home and to telephone him several times in order to change his attitude.

This respondent's distrust was overcome or at least mitigated and the interviews completed. Distrust generally was evident not just in the respondents' reaction to the fieldworkers but also as a common topic of conversation regarding the ways Puerto Ricans change as a result of living in New York City. The topic usually arose when nostalgic memories of the warmth and hospitality of the people in Puerto Rico were contrasted with the situation in New York City. The topic drew such responses as:

> The circumstances in New York are different from those in Puerto Rico. You can't trust people here.

> When they come here, Puerto Ricans begin not to trust others. I guess they are afraid of having others take advantage of them.

When people come to live in this city, they become more suspicious of other people.

Life is harder in this city. After they move here, people become more distrustful. If they trust too much, then others can take advantage of them.

Life in this country is different. Here one tries to help someone and later on that same person tries to take advantage of one.

Information is often suppressed as a generalized and functional distrustful reaction to the conditions of urban bureaucratic life. This distrust as a social pattern was displayed by the respondents. It focused upon Puerto Ricans and non-Puerto Ricans. During the data collection the respondents identified the interviewers as welfare, sanitation, vice-squad, Social Security, Medicare/Medicaid officials, or as tax inspectors. Some thought the interviewers were working for the police and landlords. Others even thought they might be muggers or thieves. One member of a small Protestant denomination saw them as "agents of the devil." It was not only the fieldworkers who elicited distrust but also the type of information they sought to collect. They asked about household composition, migratory and employment history, education, income, and age. In sociology such information carries the neutral designation of sociobiography, but to inner-city residents this information is not neutral. To divulge it could be prejudicial to the resident, even damaging, concerning regulations of apartment living, number of dependents reported for welfare allotments, board of health and fire department regulations, and food stamp and Medicaid/Medicare regulations. If divulging such obvious items of information could be prejudicial, why risk divulging other less public items of information? No assumption of guilt or breach of regulations need (or ought) to be made to understand that among inner-city residents, not just Puerto Ricans, there are deep sensitivities associated with the reporting of information.

Who were the persons in our study who displayed the most distrust? To answer this question, we used a Likert-type trust scale that contains seven items such as: children should learn that if they don't look out for themselves, people will take advantage of them; you can only trust people whom you know well; it is not good to let your friends know everything about you, for they might take advantage of you.[12] The manifest content of the scale's items indicates face validity; their meaning explicitly focuses upon trust. The scale's alpha reliability score is .751, an acceptable level. We also have a rough measure of the scale's criterion validity. At the end of the interviews with each person, the interviewer assessed the degree of cooperation of the interviewees. Since cooperation is more than a matter of trust, one would not expect a high correlation, but the correlation is .148, which is statistically significant ($p < .05$).

The answer to the question on respondents' display of distrust is that trust is related to generational status, the younger generation of married couples being more trustful than the older generation ($r = .372$, $p < .05$). Persons with higher levels of education were more trustful ($r = .391$, $p < .05$), as were those with a better knowledge of English ($r = .361$, $p < .05$). The younger generation had more education than the older generation ($r = .650$, $p < .05$) and a more advanced knowledge of English ($r = .547$, $p < .05$). We believe that the younger generation is more trustful than the older generation because they were exposed at an earlier age to the host society. Higher education and a better knowledge of English favor trust because they represent skills conducive to integration in the host society. Such skills are much more characteristic of the younger generation than the older generation.

At the time that the data were being collected, we did not, of course, know these findings. Retrospectively, however, they do coincide with the differences we experienced in contacting and interviewing the two generations and with the adaptations that had to be made to cope with such differences. Thus, distrust was a general problem affecting fieldwork, but the problem was more pronounced with the older generation. To allay the distrust and maximize the cooperation of the respondents, we made decisions regarding the selection of interviewers, the way in which the interviewers were to identify themselves in the field, the approaches to be used in response to specific interviewing problems, and methods of adaptation to generational differences among the respondents.

SELECTION OF INTERVIEWERS

We were aware of the problem of the distrust of marginal Hispanics, those who have moved away from the inner-city and are sometimes viewed as having joined the Anglo world of the middle-class outgroup and are divorced from Hispanic sentiments and experiences. The word *blanquitos* (a diminutive for "whites") was used scornfully to describe such persons. Thus, we were very careful in the selection of the field team. Those we selected for data collection were Hispanic, bilingual, and bicultural, but, because they were middle class in terms of background, educational level, dress, appearance, and bearing, their interest in the Hispanic community had to be honest and abiding. In addition, they had to be emotionally committed to the Hispanic community and to the research. We have learned that lack of interest creates difficulties in securing the cooperation of respondents, presents obstacles to the interviewing, and threatens the participation of the interviewees in the study. Indifference to the Hispanic community also makes it difficult for the interviewer to face the daily vicissitudes of fieldwork, as does the failure to believe in the value of the research. In the quick give-and-take of repeated interviews, the absence of such interest cannot be disguised or feigned. In order to allay respondent distrust, those prospective fieldworkers who showed indications of separating themselves emotionally and attitudinally from the Hispanic community were excluded, as were those who felt that the research was an irrelevant and exploitative academic exercise carried out at the expense of inner-city residents.

To many of the interviewees, the linkage between ethnicity and research in the form of a Hispanic interviewer, associated with a university widely recognized in New York City, was incongruous but gratifying. In addition to the status conferred by association with the university, the fact that Hispanic interviewers were attempting to understand the Puerto Rican *nuestra manera de ser* (our way of being) was a source of satisfaction. Also, there was ease of communication because the interviewers' bilingual skills provided the respondents with the opportunity to choose the language in which they felt comfortable.

INTERVIEWERS' SELF-IDENTIFICATION

The interviewers selected received a one-month sequence of group training sessions that included an examination of the study's procedures and objectives, the discussion of relevant literature, role-playing in simulated interviews with "respondents," and the observations of the interviewers more experienced in actual fieldwork. Decisions were then implemented about the way the interviewers were to identify themselves, explain the study, and give assurances of compliance with the protection of human subjects. The interviewer's institutional affiliation was made clear, along with other information relevant to the identification. If skepticism was expressed, the respondents were encouraged to check the veracity of our statements about identities and institutional affiliation. We offered to provide transportation for the respondents to visit our offices at the university or, if a visit was not convenient, to telephone our offices or homes, or, if they wished, the project director would visit them or write them a letter on official stationery. We brought one family to our offices for morning coffee, answered innumerable telephone calls at all hours of the day and night at work and at home, and wrote many letters affirming our identity and expressing our thanks for their cooperation. The invitation to check upon our authenticity as a means of allaying distrust had the manifest effect of corroborating what we said about our identity while conveying the latent meaning that we respected the respondent's right to test our veracity.

In explaining the research, the interviewers made it clear that we were not there to study the psychosocial problems of alcoholism, drug addiction, crime, delinquency, or educational "underachievement" (what has come to be termed "deficit model" research). While recognizing the value of such research in documenting the magnitude and source of these problems, our questions focused on how Puerto Ricans struggle to survive in an environment such as New York City's with many making notable advances in life-career attainments. As the respondents could see, our questions dealt with family structure, cultural values, coping procedures in response to problems, supportive networks, and educational and occupational attainment. When research focuses upon everyday family life, the respondents can see themselves in the central research questions. Living in a milieu that deprecates Puerto Ricans, they saw in the Hispanic identity of the researchers and in the subject matter of the research something worthy of ethnic pride with which they could identify.

After the introduction and explanation of the research and a statement of our willingness to work always at the convenience of the interviewee (whenever and wherever that might be), the interviewer went step by step through the stipulations concerning the protection of human subjects: informed consent, voluntary cooperation, confidentiality of the data, protection of the data under lock and key, use of the data only for purposes of research, the respondent's freedom to refuse to answer questions, and freedom also to withdraw from the research at any time. (Four families chose to withdraw from the research after the interviews had begun.) At about the time that the team was ready to begin interviews, a letter from one of the funding agencies pointedly raised questions about our seeking verbal consent instead of written consent from the respondents and requested "a methodological justification as to why you will not obtain written consent." In his reply to the letter, Rogler, one of the authors of this book, indicated the type of relationship to be established with the respondents:

Any and all questions raised by the subjects concerning the purpose of this research and its procedures will be answered with complete and absolute honesty.

Over the years, in the research I have conducted in Puerto Rico and on Puerto Ricans in the United States, I have sought the subjects' verbal consent and the protection of their rights very much according to the type of assurances stated above. The assurances conveyed to the subjects were presented in the context of the humanistic, warm relationship we developed with them, always with full regard for their integrity and the respect we owed them. They believed in us, and we believed in them – all within the interpersonal normative system embedded in Puerto Rican culture. We plan to conduct our fieldwork on Puerto Rican families in New York City by establishing such a relationship with the subjects.

It seems to me that if in this context the subject is presented with an officious document requesting his signature for *written* consent, an issue of trust is raised. It could prove offensive, perhaps even insulting, to the subject, implying as it does that neither his words nor those of the interviewer suffice in establishing mutual respect. Customarily, the medium of an agreement among Puerto Ricans is verbal.

The funding agency accepted the explanation. In retrospect, had we been forced to secure written consent, we believe the probabilities of conducting the study would have been minimal or nonexistent.

To be consistent with the type of relationship we wanted to establish with the respondents we did not want to buy or give the appearance of buying their trust through the payment of money, even though each nuclear family was paid $50.00 upon completion of the interviews. Such payments were given little or no emphasis in securing the respondents' cooperation. We did not want to base the relationship upon the pecuniary gain of the respondents. The payment was presented with the perfunctory explanation that money was available in the budget for such purposes.

APPROACHES TO SPECIFIC INTERVIEWING PROBLEMS

Through the 23 months of fieldwork, there were regularly scheduled staff meetings. The informal give-and-take among the team members while drafting field reports in the office provided an opportunity for sharing experiences in the field, defining problems associated with contacting and interviewing specific families, and developing procedures for coping with such problems. Group discussion focused upon specific instances of persons resisting cooperation and expressing distrust toward the fieldworkers.

The first step in such discussions required that the interviewer report the problem and render a clear behavioristic description of how the respondent evidenced resistance and the social context in which the resistance was being expressed. The second step involved interpreting the resistance by means of a tentative hypothesis regarding the source of resistance. Was it distrust of our identity? Was the respondent involved in some clandestine rule-breaking or illegal activity such as distilling *pitorro* rum, trafficking in drugs, or violating the rules of welfare payments, and fearful of being exposed? Was the respondent being pressured by someone else not to cooperate? This method enabled the team members to see if the hypothesis squared with the observations being reported and led to the third step, the development of ways to cope with the problem.

Broadly speaking, there were two, not mutually exclusive, ways of coping with problems of resistance. One was to address directly the source of resistance. For example, we would speak to the person whom we felt was advising the respondent not to cooperate in an effort to reaffirm our identity and demonstrate the legitimacy and value of our research. Or, we would make it a point to emphasize to uncooperative respondents that we were not agents of the welfare or criminal justice system and would encourage them to check upon the truth of our identity. Some respondents were persuaded, but the approach did carry the risk of attributing an incorrect source to the resistance and then committing the error of aiming our efforts at an invalid target, all to the confusion of the respondent. Fieldworkers, however, premised their approach to problems of respondent resistance according to the causes they believed to be operative. The other way of coping with resistance was indirect, for it did not make assumptions as to the source of resistance but attempted to increase the tone of pleasant interaction between the interviewer and interviewee while implicitly trying to get the resisting interviewee's cooperation. The procedure essentially is one of emphasizing the cultural amenities in social contacts, as will be presently discussed, while avoiding any semblance of overt pressure. The respondent knows that information is wanted and, once the bond of ethnicity and friendship is established, will likely volunteer cooperation without any further solicitation. This procedure attempted to enhance the respondent's enjoyment of contacts with the interviewer to counterbalance resistance, whatever its source. In this approach, the fieldworker's personal skills and cultural attributes became resources to be used in coping with the field problems.

Although the interviewers' bicultural background helped to gain and sustain the rapport required in the interviews with the parent generation, of the two generations the parent group were the more difficult to interview.

The staff members' bilingual skills provided flexibility in adapting to generational differences in the respondents' more comfortable language. In the parent generation, 91 percent chose Spanish mostly or entirely, while in the married-child generation 75 percent chose English mostly or entirely for the interviews. The generational difference in the use of language in the interview was related to more general patterns affecting the situation of the interview. As discussed earlier in this chapter, the younger generation had a better mastery of English and more education than the older generation. The older generation had less command over the functional skills that would have connected them more fully to the host society and were, in general, more distrustful than the younger generation. Thus, upon first contacting them, it was somewhat more difficult to secure their cooperation. In subsequent interviews, the cultural amenities prescribing the tone, distance, and quality of the relationship between the interviewer and respondent differed sharply according to generation.

First and foremost among the cultural amenities we obeyed while interviewing the parent generation was the form of address using the pronoun *usted* (or Señor or Señora, Don or Doña). *Usted* connotes respect, establishes an appropriate distance in the relationship, and is a formally correct way of addressing elders. Used with the parent generation, *usted* conveyed our view of the respondents as persons in their own right, honorable and worthy. The use of *usted*, however, can rapidly become insulting if the interviewers' behavior does not match the indicated respect. This meant that the respondents were not to be rushed or scheduled rapidly through the sequence of interviews: if a respondent was listening to a radio program or a favorite soap opera (*novela*) the interviewer waited until the program was over. In using Spanish during the interviews, an effort was made to avoid anglicisms that would sound alien and make Spanish-speaking respondents feel left out. Finally, and consistent with the cultural concept of respect, the interviewers graciously accepted the hospitality offerings of the respondents because not to have done so would have diminished the generous intent of the act.

Carrying out the culturally prescribed amenities came naturally to the bicultural interviewers, and it helped to establish an appropriate relationship between interviewer and interviewee. Also helpful in strengthening the underlying ethnic bond between the two was the spontaneous give-and-take of reminiscing nostalgically about the island-home (*añorar*). Puerto Rico's tropical weather, the food, the warmth of the people, and good times with friends and relatives at reunions, parties, and festivals are common topics of conversation, but nostalgia toward the past becomes intertwined with hostility toward the present. Such topics evoke the sharing of feelings associated with the loss of treasured objects while validating the common view among Puerto Ricans that, in New York, their traditional amenities have eroded.

Although the interviewers shared occasional nostalgic memories regarding Puerto Rico with the young couples in the married-child generation, the prevailing topics of informal talk in these instances referred to the life cycle of the respondents — how to raise children, husband-wife relations among the recently married, and women's drive toward liberation — or to the contemporary Hispanic culture of New York City — how and where to dance the *salsa*, the city's annual Puerto Rican parade, and the activities sponsored by ethnic organizations. Here there was no need for the formal *usted* or, for that matter, Señor or Señora, Don or Doña. With less of an age and educational disparity between interviewer and respondent in the married-child generation, the relationship was more fluid and informal, the form of address being *tú* (you), and less structured. The research was more understandable to this generation, and the interviews took less time. Although English was the language used most often in the interview, Spanish colloquialisms were permissible, with some use also of hybrid "Spanglish" words. With this generation, the ethnic bond sustaining rapport between interviewer and interviewee was developed out of the common experiences of Hispanics in New York City, as such experiences were viewed through similarities in age and education. The bicultural background of the interviewers was, thus, important in both the married-child generation and the parent generation.

Were we to describe the most prevalent modality in the respondents' reactions to us through the sequence of events, it would begin with distrust or resistance and end with some form of cooperation. The Borinquen family illustrates this modality. One interviewer reports her experiences with Elia Borinquen, a wife-mother in the parent generation:

The impression I had of Mrs. Borinquen when I first met her and the one I left with were quite different. When I first saw her, she was very curt with Dolores (another interviewer) and me, telling me quite frankly that she had no time to spend with us as she was too busy. . . . Mrs. Borinquen seemed cold and impersonal. She is a reserved and cautious woman who takes time to know a person and size him or her up.

During the second visit when I started the interviews, however, I was surprised: she was friendly and quite willing to cooperate. She became more relaxed, more personable, and volunteered information about her life. She called me *negrita* and the diminutive of other terms of endearment. At one point, she stopped the interview to show me pictures of her grandchildren. She adored them, affection being reflected in her face as she talked about them. She expressed concern that *niñas* like Dolores and myself would be interviewing at night in "bad" neighborhoods.

The interviewer succeeded in this case because she gained acceptance as part of the ingroup.

SUMMARY

The 100 intergenerationally linked families in this study form part of a young, recent immigrant population experiencing acute disadvantages in education, occupation, and income. To study them, a complex intergenerational family model, consonant with the study's research problem, was used in the uncongenial research setting of New York City. Thirteen screening steps were required to select each member of the 100 intergenerationally linked families. The screening was focused upon census tracts in the borough of the Bronx. The census tracts were at the top and at the bottom of a rank-order based upon the percentage of Puerto Ricans with a high school education. The study group does not derive from a probability-based sample. It reflects socioeconomic diversity among Puerto Ricans.

The major problem we experienced while collecting data was the pervasive distrust of the respondents. Other, too, have encountered the same problem. Josephson[13] calls attention to the fact that some residents of inner-city neighborhoods view research as useless and interpret it as "a form of exploitation by the investigators for their gain or for the gain of the institution and powers they serve." Similarly, Cromwell, Vaughn, and Mindel[14] point to the following sources of resistance: the animosity or discontent created by some findings that have depicted minorities and low-income people in ways unappealing to them; the threats to individual and group privacy; the failure of outside investigators to consult with individuals and groups within the community being studied; and the perception of research endeavors as "establishment oriented." Our experiences, thus, were not unique.

We did not look upon the distrust of our respondents as a psychiatric symptom of mental illness or as an enduring psychological trait. Rather, by viewing distrust as a functional sociopsychological response to the conditions of urban life among persons with a language and culture different from those of the host society, we could understand why the older generation with less education and a weaker command of English were more distrustful than the younger generation. To cope with the problem of distrust, we attempted to put the interviewer into the respondent's cultural world and, at the same time, to encourage the development of primary social bonds between the two. Specifically, distrust was mitigated by the presence of bilingual and bicultural interviewers who had an abiding interest in the Hispanic community, the inviting of the respondent to test the veracity of what we said if skepticism was expressed, efforts to make the interviews enjoyable to the respondent, the interviewers' adaptation to generational differences, and compliance with cultural amenities.

These, then, were the field research procedures utilized to select the study group and to cope with field problems while collecting the data. The next chapter looks into the historical background of the study group, tracing the lives of the parent generation and their married offspring from the time of their birth, through their migration from Puerto Rico to New York City, and on to the time when we interviewed them.

REFERENCES

1. Puerto Rico Planning Board. 1972. *Puerto Rican Migrants: A Socio-Economic Study*, p. 104.
2. U.S. Bureau of the Census. 1978. "Persons of Spanish Origin in the United States: March 1978." *Current Population Reports*, Series P-20, No. 328. Washington, D.C.: U.S. Government Printing Office.
3. Newman, M. J. 1978. "A Profile of Hispanics in the U.S. Work Force." *Monthly Labor Review* 101 (August): 3-14.
4. U.S. Bureau of the Census, see note 2.
5. Hill, R. 1970. *Family Development in Three Generations*. Cambridge: Schenkman Publishing Co.
6. Fitzpatrick, J. P. and D. T. Gurak. 1979. *Hispanic Intermarriage In New York City: 1975*. Monograph #2. New York: Hispanic Research Center, Fordham University.
7. Troll, L. and V. Bengtson. 1979. "Generations in the Family," in W. R. Burr et al., (eds.), *Contemporary Theories About the Family*, Vol. 1. New York: The Free Press.
8. Robins, L. N. 1963. "The Reluctant Respondent." *Public Opinion Quarterly* 27: 276-286.
9. Dunkelberg, W. C. and G. S. Day. 1973. "Nonresponse Bias and Callbacks in Sample Surveys." *Journal of Marketing Research* 10 (May): 160-168.
10. Kohn, J. L. 1977. *Class and Conformity*. Chicago: The University of Chicago Press.

11. Hawkins, D. F. 1977. *Nonresponse in Detroit Area Surveys: A Ten-Year Analysis*. North Carolina: Institute for Research in Social Science Publications.

12. Kahl, J. A. 1965. "Some Measurement of Achievement Orientation." *The American Journal of Sociology* 70(6): 669-681.
    Rogler, L. H. 1972. *Migrant in the City: The Life of a Puerto Rican Action Group*. New York: Basic Books, Inc.

13. Josephson, E. 1970. "Resistance to Community Surveys." *Social Problems* 18 (1): 117-129.

14. Cromwell, R. E., E. C. Vaughn, and C. H. Mindel. 1975. "Ethnic Minority Family Research in an Urban Setting: A Process of Exchange." *American Sociologist* 10 (August): 141-150.

III

From Puerto Rico to New York City

Almost all of the mothers and fathers in the parent generation were born in Puerto Rico during the late 1910s and during the decade of the 1920s. They came from a historically impoverished, colonial, agrarian society where educational opportunities were limited and illiteracy was high; where malnutrition was widespread and conditions of ill health prevailed. The society, however, was not static. From the time the parent generation was born, throughout their childhood and early adult years, and up until the time they began to migrate to New York City soon after World War II, Puerto Rican society experienced a transformation. The migration, following the experience of rapid social change on the island-home, projected the parent-generation mothers and fathers into the markedly different and also changing socio-cultural environment of New York City during the time their children were born, raised to assume adult roles, married, and established their own households. Thus, the principal theme running through the lives of the persons we studied is a changing environment: change in Puerto Rico, change in the move to New York City, and change in New York City.

This chapter focuses upon a series of historically interrelated questions relevant to how social change and migration entangled the lives of the persons in our study. In brief terms, in what way was Puerto Rican society changing from the time of the birth of the parent generation to the time of its migration? How did the parent generation fit into such changes? How did they fit into the post-World War II streams of migration from the island-home to New York City? What changes in New York City have converged upon its Puerto Rican population? Further, what about the persons in the married-child generation? How have they fared in New York City in comparison to their Puerto Rican compatriots of about the same age? To answer these questions we begin with a brief historical statement describing selected changes occurring in Puerto Rico from about the time the parent generation was born to the time of their migration. This period extends, in rough chronological terms, from about 1925 to about 1950, when close to one-half of the parent generation had migrated to New York City. The section which follows delineates the background characteristics of the parent generation in relationship to the social changes occurring in Puerto Rico during this period. We then turn to the characteristics of the parent generation in relation to those of other Puerto Ricans who migrated to New York City in the late '40s and the '50s. We then present changes occurring from about 1950 to 1976 in New York City which affected the city's Puerto Ricans. Subsequently, we describe how the parent generation have fared 27 years after their arrival in New York City. Finally, we discuss the married-child generation raised and educated predominately in New York City.

Wherever relevant, the discussion includes historically appropriate comparisons between each of the generations and properly selected Puerto Rican populations. Such comparisons enable us to relate the parent generation across historical periods to the process of social change in Puerto Rico and to the migratory movements from the island to New York City; also, similar comparisons enable us to understand how the child generation fits into its corresponding population in New York City. These comparisons, also, are of methodological value because they provide a historically dynamic view of the study group's representativeness, an issue which was raised in the preceding chapter in relation to successively delineated comparison groups. In the final section we interpret and summarize the findings.

SOCIAL CHANGE IN PUERTO RICO FROM THE BIRTH OF PARENT GENERATION TO THEIR MIGRATION

Between 1930 and 1960 the population of Puerto Rico grew from 1,543,913 to 2,349,544, because of the substantial difference between birth and death rates which were declining, the former slowly, the latter rapidly. For example, with a population of 100,000 as the base of the rate, the birth rate went from 40.2 in 1935 to 32.2 in 1960; during the same period the death rate went from 19.2 to 6.7. While population was rapidly increasing there was a migratory movement from rural to urban areas. In 1930, 72.3 percent of the population lived in areas with a population of less than 2,500; by 1960, 55.8 percent of the population lived in such areas. A decade later Puerto Rico had become a solidly urban society, and metropolitan San Juan, its primary city, contained about one-third of the island's population.

The first decades of the twentieth century saw the change from a semi-feudal *hacienda* economy to an economy dominated by capitalist plantation agriculture. The amount of land under cultivation increased, but a larger share of this land was devoted to cash crops, such as sugarcane, with a decrease in the area used for subsistence crops. In 1898, food crops accounted for 32 percent of the cultivated acreage, but by 1930 they represented only 14 percent. Puerto Rico was becoming increasingly dependent on the export of a few agricultural products, with sugar displacing coffee as the island's leading export. The rise of a capitalist-based sugarcane plantation system in the rural coastal areas changed traditional relationships between employer and employee from that of the more comprehensive, interpersonal *patrón-peón* relationship to one which was purely of economic character; the nature of the work itself, for the worker no longer sold his product but his labor power; and, existing social distinctions, because the cane worker lived almost exclusively within his own class, were reinforcing the development of a more or less clear-cut class culture.[1] The rural-based proletariat of cane workers were the precursors of the urban-based laborers mobilized for the subsequent industrialization of Puerto Rico. About 17 percent of the 200 fathers of the parent generation were sugarcane workers.

The decade of the '30s, when the parent generation was growing up, was a period of great uncertainty and economic crises. Thousands of coffee workers had become migrants to the cane fields and urban slums.[2] Landless workers, both urban and rural, grew in numbers, their lives subject to the vicissitudes of a changing economic system. According to a study by the Brookings Institution,[3] the Puerto Rican sugarcane worker "had to work 104 days to pay for his family's food in 1930, a task that had required only 70 days of work in 1897." At the end of the 1920s, the Puerto Rican sugarcane worker was spending 94 percent of his income for food.[4] Because of tariffs imposed in the U.S. on imported goods, islanders paid the same prices as mainland consumers for foodstuffs and other everyday products, at a time when their per capita income was less than one-tenth the mainland level.[5] Under the additional impact of the Great Depression, the annual per capita income of Puerto Ricans declined from $126 in 1930 to $120 in 1940.[6] Luis Muñoz Marin, subsequently the first elected governor of Puerto Rico, graphically described the four decades of Puerto Rican development after the military intervention by the United States in 1898 as follows: ". . . Puerto Rico [is] a land of beggars and millionaires, of flattering statistics and distressing realities. More and more it becomes a factory worked by peons, fought over by lawyers, bossed by absent industrialists, and clerked by politicians. It is now Uncle Sam's second largest sweatshop."[7]

The statistics, certainly, were not flattering. For the majority of the Puerto Rican population, World War II served to perpetuate the economic damage of the Great Depression. Migration to the mainland, the export of sugar, and the flow of food supplied to the island were all impeded by the German submarine blockade of the island and by the commitment of the United States maritime fleet to the war effort. Major changes, however, were occurring in the island's political climate. The Jones Act of 1917 conferred United States citizenship upon Puerto Ricans. The United States Government retained control of Puerto Rican education, the judicial, police, and prison systems, and the executive branch through the appointment of the governor. Contributing to the rise of a new political climate was Rexford Tugwell, appointed by President Roosevelt to the governorship of Puerto Rico three months before the attack on Pearl Harbor. An experienced planner, Tugwell collaborated with Muñoz Marin, leader of the Popular Democratic Party, who had been dominating the political scene since the late '30s, and other Puerto Rican leaders. They were the prime movers behind gaining Commonwealth status and the Operation Bootstrap industrialization program. During the years the parent generation were growing up on the island, Puerto Rico's political status was that of an "unincorporated territory" of the United States. However, by the time the parent generation had begun to migrate from the island, the Jones Act had been amended to increase political autonomy by providing for the election of the governor.

As the parent generation entered adulthood in the years immediately after World War II, the island's government made determined efforts to invite mainland investors, offering a cheap labor supply, comparatively underdeveloped labor unions, and liberal tax incentives. An important provision of legislative measures taken in 1947 was a program of exemption from insular taxes for any corporation that built a plant in a new industry, expanded in an approved existing industry, or constructed a new hotel. With the assistance of the insular government, the number of factories increased from 548 in 1957-1958 to 1,819 in 1970, when Puerto Rico became one of the world's most industrialized areas.[8] Industrialization progressed from labor-intensive to capital-intensive. By the mid-1950s high-technology, capital-intensive industry had established itself in Puerto Rico, with many operations requiring highly skilled specialists, thus marginating the less skilled, often native workers. Along with increasing investments from the mainland, Puerto Rico subsequently experienced during some years an increasing percentage of unemployed laborers.[9] It became a manufacturing center as it simultaneously became a consumer society, the sixth largest market in the world for United States manufactured goods. The island was growing into an urban society at such a fast rate that soon overflow of "sprawl" began to take place as suburbs (*urbanizaciones*) developed. In adaptation to these changes, much of the landscape was cemented over. When the parent generation were entering adulthood, such changes were highly visible.

During this period, progress toward educating the population was also made. By 1940 illiteracy had been brought down to 31.5 percent and then further reduced in 1960 to 12.4 percent. As Clarence Senior reports: "Enrollment in public schools rose from 304,000 in 1940 to 635,000 in 1961-1962; the number of teachers rose from 6,000 to 15,000; schoolrooms more than doubled in number; and expenditures for public education rose by 1,038 percent. Private schools also began to appear on a wide scale with the rise of a middle class. Higher education has seen a phenomenal expansion. The number of enrolled students at the University of Puerto Rico rose from 4,987 in 1939-1940 to 21,262 in 1961-1962."[10] By 1964, when 90 percent of the persons we studied in the parent generation had moved to New York City, Puerto Rico's Department of Education could report the following: "Between the years 1959 and 1964, school enrollment had increased at a rate greater than that of the school age population, so that 82 percent of the students of school age were in attendance, with some 600,406 attending public schools. The number of teachers had increased 20.4 percent to a total of 15,957, and basic salaries had risen 17 percent. Double sessions in public schools had also dropped from 42.1 percent to 26.9 percent, so that nearly 450,000 students attended full sessions. In addition, special programs such as industrial education, student aid to some 20,000, transportation to some 72,000, achievement-progress tests, televised instruction, adult education expansion, art and music expansion, classes for the slow learner and retarded children, kindergartens, noon meals for 309,583; increased library services, notably in rural areas; summer recreational activities for 10,000 children; a job training camp; a program to improve school-community relations; curriculum centers; special programs for the gifted; and a reorganization of school districts to achieve more effective supervision had been initiated."[11] Puerto Rico, thus, was making strides in the expansion of its educational system.

The health conditions of the population also improved markedly. At the time the parent generation were born and raised, only one-fourth of the population had ever worn shoes, resulting in hookworm infestations in 90 percent of the rural population.[12] In the decade of the '30s the death rate from gastrointestinal disease was 360 per 100,000 population, compared to 25 per 100,000 in the United States. The death rate from tuberculosis was 325 per 100,000, compared to 60 per 100,000 in the United States.[13] However, in the '40s the health budget of the government of Puerto Rico increased fivefold. By 1957 the death rate had dropped to 7.2 per 100,000 population.[14] Diseases such as malaria were eradicated altogether. Diarrhea and enteritis mortality rates decreased during the period from 1940 to 1961, from 405 deaths per 100,000 population to 36; tuberculosis from 260 to 26; pneumonia from 169 to 38; and nephritis from 108 to 6. The infant mortality rate was reduced by more than half, and the general death rate was reduced from 18.4 to 6.8 per 1,000 (even lower than the U.S. rate of 9.3 in 1961).[15] Along with the decrease in the mortality rates attributable to infectious and parasitical disease, the mortality rate of the degenerative diseases more commonly found in developed countries, such as heart disease and cancer, increased.

Thus, from the time of the birth of the parent generation to the time they became adults, Puerto Rican society experienced a convulsion of change: rapid population growth and a drive toward political autonomy; a shift from a rural-based economy dominated by sugarcane toward an urban-industrial society; and, increasing educational opportunities accompanied by an improvement in the health conditions and longevity of the population. The historical background during the first three decades of the parent generation's lives is that of Puerto Rico as a rapidly emerging modern society.

THE PARENT GENERATION'S RELATIONSHIP
TO SOCIAL CHANGE IN PUERTO RICO

There were 97 mothers and 98 fathers in the 100 parent-generation families who were born in Puerto Rico. Their birthplaces are located throughout the island in 55 of the 77 municipalities, ranging from the highly urbanized area of San Juan on the northern coast to the highly rural area of Utuado in the heart of the island, and from Fajardo on the east coast to Rincón on the west coast. Municipalities are subdivided into geographic units called *barrios*. Information on the size of the *barrio* from the Census of Puerto Rico allows us to compare the urban/rural distribution of the island population as a whole with the birthplace of the parent generation. The census that most closely approximates the period of the parents' birth is that of 1930. Thus, figures from the 1930 census were used to determine the size of the *barrios*.

In 1930, As shown in Table 3.1, 72.3 percent of the island population lived in rural *barrios* which are defined as having fewer than 2,500 people. By this definition, a majority of both mothers and fathers in the parent generation were born in rural areas, but more of them were born in urban areas than the island population. Since in 1930 the urban dwelling places of Puerto Rico included such small towns and villages as Llanos Tuna and

TABLE 3.1

Comparison of Island Population and Parent Generation, 1930: Birthplace and Place Raised

(in percent)

Barrio	Island Population	Parent Generation	
		Birthplace	Place Raised
Rural			
(less than 2,500)	72.3	54.1	36.6
Small towns and villages (2,500- 25,000)	14.4	32.3	35.0
Small cities (25,000-100,000)	5.9	7.1	13.7
Large cities (more than 100,000)	7.4	6.5	14.7

Source: U.S. Bureau of the Census, U.S. Census of Population: 1950. Volume II. Characteristics of the Population, Part 53 Puerto Rico. U.S. Government Printing Office. Washington, D.C., 1953, Table 2.

Canovanas as well as the three largest cities of San Juan, Ponce, and Maya-guez, the more urbanized birthplaces of the parent generation are primarily the result of their greater concentration in small towns and villages. The proportion of parents we studied who were born in the three largest cities was similar to that of the island population. The overwhelming majority of both the mothers (91 percent) and the fathers (92 percent) were born and raised on the island. Only a few were taken by their parents to New York City at a very young age and were raised on the mainland. We restrict our attention now to those born and raised in Puerto Rico.

The substantial majority of this group (71.5 percent of the mothers and 67.3 percent of the fathers) did not migrate during childhood but were brought up in the same *barrio* in which they were born. The others were taken by their parents at a young age to more urbanized areas in Puerto Rico, with approximately one-half migrating from rural areas to small towns, while the other half migrated from both the rural areas and small towns to the large cities, San Juan, Ponce, and Mayaguez. Although the trend of increasing urbanization is evident for the island population as a whole during this period, the migration pattern of the parent generation shows considerably greater mobility into the urban areas: they were raised in urban areas to an even greater extent than their birthplaces indicate. This urban migration of the parent generation continued into their young adult years. Prior to migrating to New York, a significantly large minority of mothers (29.7 percent) and fathers (27.2 percent) spent at least a year living in one of the large cities. The concentration of the parent generation in the largest cities is high even when compared to the island population 20 years later. According to the 1950 census, by which time slightly more than one-half of the parent generation had migrated to New York City, the percentage of the population living in San Juan, Ponce, and Mayaguez was only 17.3.

We next attempted to determine the socioeconomic status of the parent generation at the time they were raised. The two most common indicators of a family's socioeconomic status are the education and occupation of the father. Unfortunately, data on educational attainment are not available in the 1930 census; thus, our comparison of the family background of the parent generation with that of the island population is restricted to occupation.

As shown in Table 3.2, the occupational category providing the largest percentage of employment for both male islanders and the fathers of our parent generation was farming; however, less than one-half of the fathers of the parent generation were so employed in comparison to two-thirds of the

TABLE 3.2

Comparison of Male Island Population and Fathers of Parent Generation, 1930: Major Occupational Categories

(in percent)

Occupational Categories	Male Island Population[a]	Fathers of Parent Generation
Professional/managerial	6.5	12.6
Sales/clerical/craftsmen	14.4	26.2
Operatives/laborers/service	12.6	15.8
Farmers/farm laborers	66.5	45.4

[a]Based on the gainful occupation reported for males, aged 10 and older.

Source: U.S. Bureau of the Census, Fifteenth Census of the United States: 1930. Outlying Territories and Possessions. Washington, D.C.: Government Printing Office, 1932. Table 4 in occupational subsections for Puerto Rico.

male islanders. The more urban environment in which the parent generation was raised accords with the finding that their fathers were considerably less likely to be in farming than the male island population in 1930. In contrast to their underrepresentation in farming, the proportion of fathers employed in managerial/professional and sales/clerical/craftsmen occupational categories is almost double the proportion of the male island population. These large differences are related to the disproportionately higher number of fathers found in entrepreneurial positions, such as owners and managers of small businesses, and in skilled blue-collar trades such as carpenters and electricians.

In order to compare the socioeconomic status of the occupations of the fathers of the parent generation with that of the general island population, we needed to rank-order the major occupational categories. In the absence of definitive studies of the socioeconomic status of occupational categories in Puerto Rico either in 1930 or later, we premise our rank-order upon the conclusions of cross-national studies which generally have found a high degree of similarity between occupational rankings in different countries.[16] Moreover, we deal with only four gross categories of occupations to avoid the risk of assumptions underlying the rank-ordering of more refined classifications of occupations. The highest status occupational categories are generally considered to be professionals and managers; the next highest are sales, clerical, and craftsmen; followed by operatives, service workers, and non-farm laborers; and lastly farmers and farm laborers are generally considered to be of the lowest status. With this rank-ordering, the fathers' occupational data clearly indicate that the socioeconomic origins of the parent generation who subsequently migrated to the mainland were considerably higher than the socioeconomic origins of the Puerto Rican population in 1930.

The fathers of the parent generation played a critical role in defining the socioeconomic status of their families. In contrast to the comparatively high-status occupational achievements of the fathers, the employment pattern reported for the mothers of the parent generation was very similar to the employment pattern of all women on the island. While the proportion of women, aged 14 and older, with a gainful occupation was 0.26 for Puerto Rico in 1930, the proportion of mothers of the parent generation who were reported as usually working while their children were growing up was 0.23. Among both the island women and mothers of the parent generation who did work, a majority were concentrated in semiskilled operative occupations. The specific occupations reported most frequently for the mothers were in garment manufacturing – sewers, stitchers, and pressers. Thus, to the extent that the parent generation experienced socioeconomic advantages during their childhood in Puerto Rico; it was primarily through the fathers' achievements.

THE PARENT GENERATION AND
MIGRATION TO NEW YORK CITY

The majority of the parent generation, born and raised in Puerto Rico, migrated to New York City during the period from 1945 through 1954, when they were young adults in their mid-twenties. This period coincides with the census of 1950, the median year of migration for the parent generation. We begin our discussion of the migration transition by comparing the characteristics of parents when they left Puerto Rico with the general island population that they left behind in 1950, and with Puerto Ricans born on the island but living in New York City whom they joined in 1950.

We calculated the median age of the island and New York City populations by excluding very young children and focusing on persons aged 15 and older in order to maximize comparability with the parent generation at the time of their migration. As shown in Table 3.3, the parent generation were considerably younger than both the island population they left behind and the first-generation Puerto Ricans already living in New York City. The median age of the mothers was 25; that of the fathers a year and a half older. The median age of both the island population and first-generation Puerto Ricans in New York City was in the early 30s.

The majority in the parent generation (almost two-thirds) were married when they left the island; very few were divorced or widowed at the time of migration. The remaining fathers (28 percent) and mothers (33 percent) in the parent generation came to the mainland before marrying. Considering their younger median age, one might expect a higher proportion of the parent generation than of the island and New York City populations never to have married. However, we found the proportion of the parent generation never married lower than that of New York City first-generation Puerto Ricans, but higher than that of the island population. In fact, the parent generation were considerably more likely to be married than the island population. The fact that migration streams from Puerto Rico to New York City generally included a higher concentration of married persons also is evident in the comparison between first-generation Puerto Ricans living in New York City with the island population. In spite of their similar median age, New York

TABLE 3.3

Comparison of Island Population, First-Generation New York City Puerto Ricans, and Parent Generation, 1950: General Characteristics

General Characteristics	Island Population		1st-Generation NYC Puerto Ricans		Parent Generation	
	Males	Females	Males	Females	Males	Females
	Years	Years	Years	Years	Years	Years
Median age[a]	32.2	31.0	32.6	32.2	26.5	25.1
Median education[b]	4.1	3.3	7.1	6.4	8.0	6.5
	%	%	%	%	%	%
Marital status[c]						
Never married	40.8	29.8	28.5	21.2	32.6	27.5
Widowed/divorced	4.6	12.9	3.3	14.2	4.3	5.5
Married	54.6	57.3	68.2	64.2	63.1	67.0

[a]Based on all persons aged 15 and older for both island and New York City populations.

[b]Based on persons aged 25 and older for both island and New York City populations. This age limitation was imposed by the census publication.

[c]Based on persons aged 14 and older for both island and New York City populations.

Sources: U.S. Census of Population: 1950. Volume IV. Special Reports, Part 3, Chapter D, Puerto Ricans in the Continental United States. U.S. Government Printing Office, Washington, D.C., 1953, Tables 3 and 5; and U.S. Census of Population: 1950. Volume II. Characteristics of the Population, Part 53, Puerto Rico. U.S. Government Printing Office, Washington, D.C., 1953, Tables 13, 16, 18, 23, and 25.

Puerto Ricans born on the island were more likely to be married than the island population they left behind.

At the time they left Puerto Rico, the parent generation had a notably higher education than the island population. In fact, the median years of schooling completed by the fathers and mothers of the parent generation were almost double that of the island male and female populations in 1950. The high education of the parent generation, however, more closely resembled that of first-generation Puerto Ricans living in New York City in 1950, which suggests that higher education compared to that of the island population was characteristic of migrants from Puerto Rico to New York during this period.

Although the parent generation migrated to New York in their mid-20s, a substantial majority of the mothers and almost all of the fathers had worked prior to leaving the island. The percentage of mothers (45 percent) who had work experience on the island was more than double the percentage of female island population (21 percent) aged 14 and older who were in the labor force in 1950. Even when we compare the work experience of the parent-generation mothers with the work experience of their own mothers while they were growing up, we find that their participation in the labor force was more than double their mothers'. The greater work experience among the parent-generation mothers, however, was similar to the high labor force participation rate (41 percent) of first-generation Puerto Rican females living in New York City in 1950.

At the time they left Puerto Rico, as shown in Table 3.4, very few of the parent-generation fathers were working in the lowest paid category of rural occupations. While almost one-half of the island males were still employed as farmers or farm laborers, only one-fifth of the fathers were so employed. The majority of parent-generation fathers were working either in middle-status urban occupations or in the lower status urban jobs, most notably as laborers. While the proportion of parent-generation fathers employed in the two highest occupational categories of professionals and managers was less than that of the male island population, the overrepresentation of parent-generation fathers in the higher paid urban jobs in general and the substantial overrepresentation in lower white-collar and skilled blue-collar occupations, in particular, strongly suggest that the fathers already had achieved a moderate degree of occupational success before leaving Puerto Rico.

The first job of the parent-generation fathers upon migrating to New York City differed sharply from their last job in Puerto Rico. More than 77 percent of the parent-generation fathers were in the lower paid urban occupational categories, the majority in semiskilled operative and service jobs. (In general,

TABLE 3.4

Comparison of Island Population, First-Generation New York City Puerto Ricans, and Parent Generation, 1950: Major Occupational Categories, Males

(in percent)

Occupational Categories	Island Population[a]	1st-Generation NYC Puerto Ricans[a]	Parent Generation	
			Last Job in Puerto Rico	First Job in NYC
Professional/managerial	10.2	7.7	4.6	0.0
Sales/clerical/craftsmen	19.2	20.0	38.1	20.2
Operatives/laborers/service	22.6	72.3	37.9	77.6
Farmers/farm laborers	48.0	0.0	19.4	2.2

[a]Based on persons aged 14 and older for both island and New York City populations.

Sources: See Table 3.3.

Puerto Rican males born on the island already living in New York City in 1950 also were concentrated in operative and service jobs, although the proportion in operative jobs was slightly lower.) The absence of professional or managerial jobs among parent-generation fathers, in conjunction with the dramatic decline in their employment from 38 to 20 percent in the middle-status occupational category of sales/clerical/craftsmen jobs does more than suggest a decline in the father's occupational position upon first entering New York City's labor market. Although the first job of parent-generation fathers compared to those of first-generation Puerto Rican males in New York City suggests that some upward mobility into professional and managerial jobs was possible, the fact stands that the major job opportunities for male Puerto Rican migrants to New York City in 1950 were in the lower status operative and service jobs.

THREE DECADES OF CHANGE IN NEW YORK CITY

The demographic profile presented in Chapter II described New York City's Puerto Ricans as forming part of a young, recent immigrant population experiencing acute disadvantages in education, occupation, and income. The disadvantages continued, from one decade to the next, from 1950 to the late 1970s, the period of time during which the parents and married children we studied lived in New York City, but intricate patterns of change during this period were entangling the city and its Puerto Rican population. Thus, having experienced changes on the island prior to their migration, then a change from one sociocultural system to another, the Puerto Ricans in the study and their numerous immigrant compatriots came to experience significant changes in New York City, all in the context of their generally disadvantaged economic and educational status.

In the city, the Puerto Rican population grew rapidly: comprising in 1950 less than a quarter of a million persons (3 percent), in 1980 they had increased to 860,000 persons (12 percent). To these numbers should be added the growing presence of Dominicans, Colombians, Cubans, and other Central and South American immigrants. By 1970, non-Puerto Rican "Spanish" in the city comprised about 30 percent of the city's Hispanic population.[17] Since the city's total population decreased by 10 percent during the decade of the '70s, the scope of the city's Hispanic cultural environment was increasing both in relative and absolute terms. At the same time, the increasing size of the non-Puerto Rican Hispanic nationalities added diversity to the Hispanic cultural environment. Settlement patterns of the groups differed, with concentrations of Dominicans in the upper West Side and Washington Heights areas in Manhattan and in Queens; of South Americans in north-central Queens; Cuban communities in Queens, and Central Americans in Brooklyn, though more evenly dispersed throughout the city than the Dominicans and South Americans. The Cubans and Central Americans were disproportionately concentrated in Manhattan, and Puerto Ricans in the Bronx, Brooklyn, and Manhattan. In the context of Hispanic national diversity and differences in settlement patterns the Puerto Ricans remained distinct in two respects: first, they continued to be socioeconomically the most disadvantaged Hispanic nationality in the city[18]; second, their rates of intermarriage with other nationalities, Hispanic and non-Hispanic, were lower than those of the more recent immigrant Hispanic groups, and the second generation exhibited no tendency toward outgroup-nationality marriages.[19] The low socioeconomic status of Puerto Ricans, in conjunction with their strong patterns of ingroup marriages, evidenced assimilative problems and the impact of isolating social structural forces.

The Puerto Ricans' residential patterns during the almost three decades under consideration, however, were not stable. Manhattan, having experienced a rapid increase of Puerto Rican residents during the high immigration years following World War II, subsequently began to lose Puerto Ricans to the other boroughs, in particular to the Bronx and Brooklyn. Thus, from 1960 to 1970, Manhattan registered an almost 18 percent decline (40,300) in its Puerto Rican population while the Bronx, where 85 percent of the parent- and married-child generation families lived, was experiencing a 70 percent *increase* (129,000) and Brooklyn, a 51 percent increase (91,700). Queens and Richmond also registered substantial increases in the percentage of Puerto Ricans during this period, but since the initial baseline number of Puerto Ricans living in these boroughs was substantially small, the change had a negligible effect upon the overall structure of Puerto Rican residential patterns in the city. In 1970, 39 percent of the city's Puerto Rican population (316,772) lived in the Bronx; 33.5 percent (271,769) lived in Brooklyn; and 22.8 percent (185,323) lived in Manhattan.[20] From the time of their migration to the time we came to know them in the study, the intergenerationally linked parents and married children experienced a pronounced residential redistribution of Puerto Ricans in the city.

The pattern of residential dispersion toward the Bronx and Brooklyn in the delimited locale of New York City coincided with the residential redistribution of Puerto Ricans on the mainland. In fact, of all newcomers to the United States, few have been so concentrated in New York City as persons of Puerto Rican origin. Between 1930 and 1940 the island-born population in New York City increased more than eightfold, and the city's share of natives of Puerto Rico living in the United States increased from 62 to 88 percent. In 1950, 81.6 percent of all persons of Puerto Rican birth and parentage living in the mainland were enumerated in New York City. This proportion declined to 59 percent in 1979, and by 1980 less than half of all persons of Puerto Rican descent in the United States (43 percent) were living in New York City.

While the residential dispersion of Puerto Ricans on the mainland was increasingly away from New York City, net migration between the island and the mainland fluctuated widely during the time period under consideration. The decade of the '50s registered the highest net transfer of Puerto Ricans to the mainland, with an average annual net transfer of about 46,000 persons, the peak year of 1953 bringing the net balance to the mainland of more than 73,000 Puerto Ricans. However, during the '60s, net migration from the island declined sharply in an uneven trend extending into the '70s. Finally, the '70s brought the first sizeable net reverse migration to Puerto Rico, with the year 1970 experiencing the net movement of more than 44,000 persons in the opposite direction to Puerto Rico.[21] Because Puerto Ricans are American citizens, there are no legal or political restrictions on migration; this allows many other variables to shape the size of the double migration stream: economic incentives; economic differentials between the island and the mainland; transferability of unemployment insurance and social security credits; and the cost of air transportation. Whatever may have been the combination of such variables and their influence in the '70s, the reverse stream of migration toward the island began to stabilize the size of New York City's Puerto Rican population.

Before this stabilization, a proliferation of small businesses accompanied the increasing number of Puerto Ricans in the city and the expansion of their neighborhoods. Service establishments, such as beauty parlors, laundries, and barber shops, and small retailers, such as jewelry shops, record stores, drugstores, and the ubiquitous family-owned grocery stores, *bodegas* (which served also as neighborhood meeting places), mushroomed throughout the Puerto Rican neighborhoods. Small restaurants serving the customary ethnic dishes became part of the neighborhood scene. Such businesses, however, remained marginal to the city's economic structure and precariously balanced in terms of earnings, always vulnerable to slight variations in the economic cycle. Even with more or less normal times, the businesses seemingly underwent rapid shifts in ownership. Consistent with their marginal economic status, the Puerto Ricans during this period remained politically weak in relation to their numbers, with proportionately few appearing as registered voters, and only a very small handful elected to the state government; one Puerto Rican was elected to the Federal House of Representatives in those years.

Yet, two events converging in the '60s had a resounding impact upon the organizational structures enmeshing the Puerto Ricans: the nationwide rise of minority-group activism initiated by the black civil rights movement, and the enactment as well as the aftermath of President Lyndon Johnson's Great Society programs. The events were mutually reinforcing, premised upon the assumption of a federal responsibility to address the inequities afflicting disadvantaged groups. The consequence was the rise of a vast and almost bewildering array of organizations extending throughout the federal, state, and municipal administrations to the neighborhood level of Puerto Rican life. The purpose was to improve the economic, social, political, and cultural life of disadvantaged minority groups, although the much publicized promise of eradicating poverty in the United States through federally supported anti-poverty programs quickly proved to be as premature as it was erroneous. Nonetheless, New York City's Puerto Ricans came to form part of a vast landscape of organizations composed of community projects, housing developments, and tenant associations; health service organizations; nursery and foster-care programs; job training and placement programs, and leadership training; consumer education and cultural enrichment projects; bilingual educational programs; open admission programs in the city's universities; and research and educational programs focused upon ethnic minorities.

The rise of this vast structure of organizations was an important part of the experiences of the mothers, fathers and married children in our study. It also affected the lives of their numerous compatriots in the city, while nurturing a growing sense of Puerto Rican self-consciousness and ethnic awareness. Symbolically, such feelings were expressed in a variety of institutional settings and activities: the city's Puerto Rican Day parade, the museums and food fairs, the art galleries, the theatrical productions, the rallies for Puerto Rico's independence from the United States, and the university-based programs focusing upon the island's literature, folklore, and history. During the almost three decades under discussion, the Puerto Ricans moved to affirm symbolically, through a variety of public expressions, their ethnic roots as part of a more general, nationwide celebration of ethnicity. (The following chapter will show how such symbolic expressions of ethnicity were linked to the ethnic identity of the persons in the study.)

In the context of such changes, the most enduring and perhaps most important fact of Puerto Rican life in the city was the continuing disadvantaged socioeconomic status of Puerto Ricans. Their low-income status is

attributable to a variety of factors. As newcomers, Puerto Ricans are handicapped by their lack of familiarity with the city's institutions, customs, and
employment practices and by their lack of transferable skills, educational
qualifications, and fluency in English. An aging but still youthful population,
they experienced serious employment difficulties: in 1970 their median age
was 20.5 years; in 1980, 23.7 years. However, their median age in 1980 still
contrasts markedly with the median age (32.6 years) of the total New York
City population, a difference of 8.9 years. By no means the least important
factor is the discriminatory practices to which they are subjected, as stated by
the U.S. Department of Labor in 1975: "Puerto Ricans have lower incomes
than other New Yorkers even when age, education, and vocational training
are taken into account."[22]

Economic changes occurring in New York City during this period ad-
versely affected the Puerto Ricans' welfare. Most notable was the long-run
decline in manufacturing, in which the number of jobs declined by one-third
between 1950 and 1970. There was also declining employment in food
products, metal products, and apparel manufacturing. For example, apparel
manufacturing in New York City, one of the largest employers of minorities,
lost 127,000 jobs, or 40 percent of the total employment from 1960 to 1970,
thus increasing the unemployment of Puerto Rican women who did mostly
needlework. The decline in manufacturing jobs continued into the '70s. Since
Puerto Ricans were concentrated in manufacturing jobs (40 percent of Puerto
Rican workers had factory jobs in 1970, as opposed to 20 percent of all New
York workers), the rapid decline in the number of such jobs disproportionately
affected their livelihood. Data from the 1970 census indicated that, as a group,
Puerto Ricans had lower labor force participation rates and higher unemployment rates than all New Yorkers taken together. One result of this was that,
compared to other groups in New York and in the United States, Puerto Ricans
were falling behind in terms of income. Thus, between 1959 and 1969, the
real income of Puerto Rican families increased 13 percent, while that of
blacks increased 26 percent and that of the total city population increased 23
percent. In 1969, 28 percent of Puerto Rican families and 13 percent of the
majority population families were below the poverty level. By 1976, the Puerto
Rican poverty-level rate had risen to 32 percent while the majority population
rate had declined to 9 percent.[23] Much of this pattern can be attributed to the
rapid increase during the '70s of female-headed households, which are low-income households; in the city's Puerto Rican population there was a 57 percent
increase in female-headed households. By 1980, 44 percent of the city's Puerto
Rican households were headed by females, compared to 26 percent of the
households in the rest of the city. In the borough of the Bronx where the

Hispanic population is predominantly Puerto Rican, the difference in the 1980 annual income was striking: the income of female-headed Hispanic households was $6,581; of intact Hispanic households, $15,872.

Another process creating economic differentials in the Puerto Rican population was the rise of a second generation. By 1970, 41 percent of the Puerto Rican population belonged to the second generation. Significantly, as early as 1950, considerable differences were noted in the occupational distribution of first- and second-generation Puerto Ricans: the second generation was more like the total New York City population in occupational distribution than the first generation.[24] Kantrowitz,[25] using 1960 census data from New York City, found that the second generation was generally upwardly mobile between 1950 and 1960; data relevant to labor force participation, occupational distribution, and educational attainment indicated that the children of Puerto Rican migrants, much like the second generation of other migrants before them, were improving their socioeconomic position and becoming more like the total population of the host society. In age-specific rates, mainland-born Puerto Ricans, in comparison to those born on the island, had less unemployment, higher education, more white-collar occupations, and higher incomes; expectedly, they were also more fluent in English than their island-born compatriots.[26]

ALMOST THREE DECADES LATER: THE PARENT GENERATION IN NEW YORK CITY

The parent generation experienced the changes occurring in New York City and were part of the changing character of the city's Puerto Rican population from the time they migrated from Puerto Rico to the time the study's data were collected. To see how this generation fits the pattern of changes of the city's Puerto Rican population, it is necessary to match it against an appropriately designated comparison group of all the other Puerto Ricans who arrived in New York City at about the same time as the parent generation and who were roughly of the same age. We refer to such a group as the "migration cohort" of the parent generation. By taking into account the time period of the migration and the age of the migrants in specifying the migration cohort, we are provided with a logically adequate and general basis for assessing the experiences of the parent generation. Specifically, the migration cohort of the parent generation includes all island-born Puerto Ricans who migrated to the United States during the '50s or earlier, a period which approximates the time when the parent generation arrived; and, it includes persons who were at least 15 years of age in 1950 or, the equivalent, 41 years of age in 1976 when the study's data were collected. The migration cohort, therefore, parallels the parent generation both in the range of years over which the migration occurred and in the range of their ages. This comprises our best effort to reconstitute a migration cohort comparable to the study's parent generation.

The comparisons between the migration cohort and the parent generation immediately produced two surprising findings. First, the parent generation at the time the interviews were conducted were slightly older than their 1950 migration cohort, which is a reversal of the 1950 pattern when the most notable difference between the parents and the island-born Puerto Ricans was the younger age of the parents. Second, at the time of the interviews, the parent generation were substantially more highly educated than the migration cohort even though their educational differences in 1950 were only slight and, at that time, attributable to the younger age of the parent generation. The parent generation's higher education is not due to the mothers' and fathers' acquiring more education after their migration to New York City; the median years of education at the time of migration (1950) was the same as at the time of the interviews (1976), 8 years for fathers and 6.5 for mothers. Over this 26-year period, however, the migration cohort's median education declined from 7.1 to 6.3 years for males and from 6.4 to 6.0 years for females. This decline accounts for the parent generation's higher education at the time of the interviews, but still it remains puzzling, accustomed as we are to the pattern of increasing, not declining, educational levels in populations at large. To understand the unexpected findings on age and education we return to the material presented in the previous section which dealt with the return migration to Puerto Rico and the dispersion of Puerto Ricans on the mainland away from New York City.

Data on return migrants to Puerto Rico show that their median age is three years more than that of the island-born migrants remaining on the mainland. In fact, a small but significant number return to Puerto Rico to retire. Return migrants also are more likely to have come from higher educational and occupational levels of the Puerto Rican mainland population. In addition, the dispersion of Puerto Ricans on the mainland was selective. For example, Puerto Ricans who had initially settled in New York in 1955 and 1965 and who had migrated to another state by 1960 and 1970, respectively, were considerably more likely to be high school graduates than the Puerto Ricans who did not leave New York during these two five-year periods.[27] Out-migration from New York to the island and to other states operated selectively to take away older, better-educated Puerto Ricans while leaving behind in New York those who were younger and less educated. The findings, once again, highlight the parent generation's residential stability in having lived in New York City for almost three decades; they were neither a part of the return migration to the island nor of the dispersion of Puerto Ricans to states other than New York. Thus, residential stability is an important element in the life experiences of the parent generation which is not typical of its migration cohort.

One criterion utilized in the selection of the study group required that the parent generation (and child generation) be married at the time of the interviews. This criterion, however, did not require that the persons in the parent generation remain married to their first spouses. While a small minority were in their second and third marriages, the substantial majority of the parent-generation fathers (74 percent) and mothers (84 percent) were still married to their first spouses. The level of marital stability of the fathers is similar to that of the males in their migration cohort who were ever married. However, the marital stability of the mothers stands in sharp contrast to the females in the migration cohort who were ever married; in the migration cohort only 46 percent of the females ever married remain married to their first spouses. The high rates of marital disruptions among the females in the migration cohort is consistent with the pattern already documented in the preceding section, the rapid increase in the percent of Puerto Rican households headed by females.[28] It is clear that the greater marital stability of the parent-generation mothers had important effects upon the familial environment in which the child generation was raised: their experience of strong primary group bonding is not at all typical of their migration cohort.

After almost three decades of living in New York, two-thirds of the parent-generation fathers, as shown in Table 3.5, are concentrated in the lowest status urban category, involving semi-skilled and unskilled jobs. Although employment in these lower status jobs is high, this concentration represents a decline from 78 percent employment in these jobs when they first came to New York. Another indication of improvement in occupation is found in the highest status urban occupational category of professionals/ managers. Whereas none of the parent-generation fathers was employed in professional/managerial jobs when they first came to New York, almost 15 percent had attained such jobs 27 years later when they were interviewed. Employment in the middle-status urban occupational category of sales/ clerical/craftsmen remained stable at 20 percent. While these comparisons of the father's last or current job in New York with his first job upon arrival reflect considerable stability after 27 years, they do, nevertheless, suggest improvement in the father's occupational status. The initial downward

TABLE 3.5

Comparison of Migration Cohort and Parent Generation, 1976: Major Occupational Categories, Males

(in percent)

Occupational Categories	1950 Migration Cohort	Parent Generation Last or Current Job
Professional/managerial	10.4	14.6
Sales/clerical/craftsmen	41.5	20.2
Operatives/laborers/service	48.1	65.2

Source: U.S. Bureau of Census, Survey of Income and Education, 1976.

mobility which the fathers experienced upon leaving Puerto Rico was followed by a pattern of slight upward mobility while living in New York City. The accomplishments of the parent-generation fathers, however, are modest when compared to their migration cohort. Although our fathers were older and had higher educational achievements than their cohort counterparts who had remained in New York City, the parent-generation fathers were considerably more likely to be in the lower status urban jobs (65 versus 48 percent) and one-half as likely to be in the middle-status urban occupational category (20 versus 41 percent). Only in terms of the professional/managerial category do the fathers have a slight advantage of 5 percentage points. The occupational achievements of the 1950 migration cohort between 1950 and 1976 suggest that greater occupational mobility out of the lower status urban jobs and into the middle-status jobs should have been possible, especially in view of the higher education of our parent-generation fathers.

At the time the parent generation migrated to New York City, they resembled other island-born Puerto Rico migrants in terms of marital status, education, and labor force participation. The only notable exception was their younger age. Twenty-seven years later several features distinguish the life experiences of the parent generation from their 1950 migration cohort. The persons in the migration cohort have not been as residentially stable as the parents. Many of the older and better educated migrants have left New York to go to other parts of the United States and to return to Puerto Rico. The findings accentuate the residential stability of the parent generation. The comparisons also demonstrate the stronger marital stability of the parent-generation mothers and the modest occupational achievement of the parent-generation fathers.

TWENTY-SEVEN YEARS LATER: THE CHILD GENERATION IN NEW YORK CITY

The majority of the child generation were born in the period of economic prosperity and growth following World War II and also at the time of the large-scale migration of the parent generation to New York City. Not surprisingly, the birthplace of the child generation reflects the migration of the parents. Almost one-half were born in Manhattan or the Bronx four or five years after their parents arrived, while the other half were born in Puerto Rico prior to their parents' migration to the United States. The substantial majority of the child generation born in Puerto Rico, however, were brought as small children by their parents to New York City. Thus, while the places of birth of the child generation are evenly split between New York City and Puerto Rico, almost all of the child generation were raised in New York City. In the discussion which follows we focus upon the 89 children raised in New York City.

Our primary aim is to compare the child generation with other Puerto Ricans living in New York City who have similar migration experiences. Thus, a child-migration cohort was selected to include both young adult U.S.-born Puerto Ricans and island-born Puerto Ricans who migrated to the United States during the '50s or earlier, and who at the time of their migration were of grammar school age or younger. In addition to birth and migration experience, the child cohort was selected from those born approximately in the same historical period. Since almost all the child-generation adults in our study were born during the '40s and '50s, the cohort's birth years were restricted to those decades.

Although both groups are in their late 20s, as shown in Table 3.6, almost 40 percent of the migration cohort have never been married, in contrast to the child-generation persons who had to be married to be included in the study. This disparity in current marital status between the child generation and their migration cohort is much greater than the disparity in current marital status between the parent generation and first-generation Puerto Ricans either at the time of migration or at the time of interview. Already there is an indication that the experiences of the child generation are less typical of their migration cohort than the experiences of the parent generation with their migration cohort.

TABLE 3.6

Comparison of Migration Cohort and Child Generation, 1976: General Characteristics

	Migration Cohort		*Child Generation*	
General Characteristics	*Males*	*Females*	*Males*	*Females*
	Years	*Years*	*Years*	*Years*
Median age	27.4	28.6	28.2	28.8
Median education	11.3	10.9	12.4	12.4
	%	*%*	*%*	*%*
Marital status				
Never married	44.3	42.7	0.0	0.0
Widowed/divorced	11.1	20.2	0.0	0.0
Married	44.6	37.1	100.0	100.0

Source: U.S. Bureau of Census, Survey of Income and Education, 1976.

Educational attainments also differentiate the child generation from their migration cohort. The median educational attainment of the child generation is more than one year higher than their cohort group. The difference of one year, however, hides sharp disparities both in the percentage that completed high school education and the percentage that have gone on to college. Only 6.8 percent of the child generation raised in New York did not graduate from high school, compared to over 40 percent of the migration cohort. In contrast, the 46 percent of the child generation who have gone on to college is more than double the rate of their Puerto Rican cohort.

The pattern is even more strongly reinforced by the child generation's comparatively high socioeconomic achievements as evident in the high occupational attainment of the sons, shown in Table 3.7. A sizeable minority of the sons, 40 percent, are employed in each of the two highest status occupational categories of professionals and managers. This level of occupational achievement is triple that of their birth/migration cohort. In addition, employment in the lowest status urban jobs is noticeably less for the child generation than for their migration cohort. Both in terms of education and economic characteristics, the child generation's achievements are considerably higher than those of Puerto Ricans with similar birth/migration histories. The comparatively high socioeconomic achievements of the persons in the

TABLE 3.7
Comparison of Migration Cohort and Child Generation, 1976: Major Occupational Categories, Males

(in percent)

Occupational Categories	Migration Cohort	Child Generation
Professional/managerial	13.2	39.6
Sales/clerical/craftsmen	56.2	39.4
Operatives/laborers/service	30.6	21.0

Source: U.S. Bureau of Census, Survey of Income and Education, 1976.

child generation cannot be attributed simply to their being married: while the socioeconomic differences are slightly less when only married persons in the migration cohort are used in comparisons, the overall pattern, nevertheless, strongly persists.

The overall profile of the persons in the child generation indicates that their experiences are more atypical in relation to their migration cohort than were the experiences of their parents. At the time of migration, the parent-generation mothers and fathers were very similar in education, marital status, and labor force involvement to other Puerto Rican migrants. While these similarities dissipated somewhat during the next three decades, partially as a result of substantial return migration to Puerto Rico and movement to other places on the mainland, the overall profile of the parent generation reflects greater similarities to their migration cohort than does the overall profile of the child generation to their birth/migration cohort.

INTERPRETATION AND SUMMARY

We have sketched the sweeping historical changes which were moving Puerto Rico toward an urban, industrial society from the time the mothers and fathers of the parent generation were born to the time they migrated; we have highlighted their sociodemographic characteristics through a series of historically based comparisons with other Puerto Ricans. What is the connection between social change and the earlier lives of the parent-generation mothers and fathers in Puerto Rico? The changes affecting the island entangled the lives of the mothers and fathers who already were predisposed in the direction

the change was taking. Both born and raised in municipalities located throughout the island, they came disproportionately from the small towns and
villages. A sizeable minority went on to migrate to more urban settings thereby forming part of the mass rural-to-urban migration. Thus, in their earlier
socialization they were exposed to urban forces more than was the general
population of Puerto Rico. They came from parents of somewhat higher
socioeconomic status than the general population, a substantial minority
from the ranks of skilled laborers, small entrepreneurs, and managers.

When the mothers and fathers of the parent generation migrated from
Puerto Rico, they were younger, more likely to be married, and more highly
educated than the island population. The fathers were more highly concentrated in the middle-class occupations than was the male population of the
island. The mothers had acquired more work experience than the population
of females on the island. Such background factors and events tracing to their
earlier lives with their parents made them receptive to the stimuli produced
by social change in Puerto Rico, and put them in the vanguard of such
change.

Their search for further opportunities focused upon employment and
better wages which prompted the migration, as indicated by their accounts of
what brought them to New York City:

> The work here was better. They paid more than in Puerto Rico. Also,
> the working conditions were better than in Puerto Rico . . . those who
> lived in rural areas found that in New York they had better opportuni-
> ties than in Puerto Rico.

> Job opportunities here were better than in Puerto Rico. In order to
> find a job in Puerto Rico, you had to know someone in government.
> Here if you really looked for a job you had a good opportunity to
> find one.

> I came because there were more jobs here and the salaries were better
> than in Puerto Rico.

> I had several reasons for leaving Puerto Rico, but the most important
> one was economic. In Puerto Rico there was a lot of misery and hunger.
> My father had a stroke and was in bed for four years before he died. I
> remember seeing my father screaming out of hunger and there was
> nothing to give him but black coffee.

Accompanied by two friends, I walked all the way from Ponce to San Juan looking for work. When we arrived in San Juan we went to the docks but there was no work available. After returning to Ponce, I decided to come to New York.

Such accounts, told to us over and over again, coincide with the conclusions of analytically oriented research demonstrating the economic impetus underlying the migration. The time of the parent generation's migration soon after World War II and into the decade of the '50s coincides with the mass migration of Puerto Ricans to New York City. Annual variations in the net migration from Puerto Rico from 1947 to 1967 can be explained substantially by employment-related factors. Thus, Maldonado[29] demonstrated that changes in relative industrial wages and relative unemployment rates between Puerto Rico, on the one hand, and the states with the most Puerto Ricans, New York, Connecticut, New Jersey, and Illinois, during this 20-year period are the primary explanatory variables of migration flows from the island to the mainland. Jointly, the two variables explain 81 percent of the migration. The ratio of welfare payments in Puerto Rico to those in the states above plays no role in explaining the migration. The parent generation joined the migration stream of their compatriots in search of employment and higher wages, and, since both undertook the search for the same reasons, it is understandable why there are many critically relevant similarities between them: in comparison to the island population, both migrant groups include a higher proportion of married persons, persons with higher educational attainments, a greater involvement of women in the labor force, and a high concentration of males employed in operative and service jobs. (The parent generation, however, was somewhat younger than the general migration stream of persons from Puerto Rico to New York City.) Upwardly mobile, they were all stirred by the vision of a better life away from the poverty and hunger endemic to old Puerto Rico, but the emerging modern Puerto Rico, having instilled such a vision, could neither contain nor satisfy their rising aspirations.

In the 27 years they have lived in New York City, the persons in the parent generation have experienced a rapid increase in the size of the city's Puerto Rican population, followed by a declining rate of increase in this population to the point of almost stable size; increasing numbers of non-Puerto Rican Hispanics, with a dramatically increasing presence of Hispanic culture in the city; more than the other Hispanic groups, a continuing tendency to marry within the Puerto Rican ingroup in both the first and second generation; the strong erosion of the manufacturing sector in which their jobs were and still are concentrated; and, the growth of a vast organizational network, ranging from service programs to grassroot ethnic groups, arising from programs of the Great Society and the black civil rights movements of the 1960's. Through all these changes, the women in the parent generation have remained maritally stable in the face of a pattern of rapidly increasing female-headed households among Puerto Ricans. Along with their husbands they thought their earlier vision of a better life, nurtured in the island-home and causing them to migrate, would be realized, if at all, in New York City. They were in the vanguard of the modernizing changes affecting Puerto Rico, but, once they migrated, they remained residentially stable. Many of their compatriots, better educated and better employed than the New York City Puerto Ricans they left behind, moved on to return to the island or away from New York in the mainland dispersion of Puerto Ricans. During the 27-year period, three migration streams from Puerto Rico to New York City, the return to Puerto Rico, and the dispersion of Puerto Ricans in the mainland, were selectively redeploying Puerto Ricans who already had socioeconomic advantages relative to the compatriots they left behind at the place of origin, whether Puerto Rico or New York City. Through all of this, the parent generation remained in New York City.

The hopes and aspirations which led the persons in the parent generation to migrate to New York City are much more fully realized in their offspring, the members of the married-child generation. The higher educational and occupational achievements of the child generation are related to broader historical trends associated with industrialization, urbanization, and modernization which have shaped educational and occupational opportunities both in Puerto Rico and the United States. In our study, the majority of persons in the parent generation were raised and educated in Puerto Rico, the majority of those in the child generation in New York City. The study's data indicate, however, that the socioeconomic achievements of the child generation are greater than one would expect, if such attainments were to conform only to historical trends. There are several reasons for this. The educational and occupational attainments of the parent generation at the time of migration were higher than those of the island's population but similar to those of other Puerto Ricans coming to New York City. While the fathers did experience an improvement in occupations in New York City, the improvement was modest in comparison to their migration cohort. In sharp contrast, the child generation raised in New York City have achieved substantially more education and higher-level occupations than their comparable migration cohort. The parent generation's modest level of achievement does not explain the children's extraordinary success.

When viewed methodologically, such comparisons shed light upon the study group's representativeness, provided we keep in mind that the parent and child generations differ from other Puerto Ricans wherever they may reside, in terms of their greater residential and marital stability. The facts relevant to the issue of representativeness in their appropriate historical and population context indicate the following: in comparison to the island's population, at the time of early upbringing and at the time of migration, the parent generation were atypical with respect to characteristics signifying upward mobility. Such characteristics, however, made them typical of first-generation Puerto Rican migrants in New York City. The married-child generation's exceptionally high socioeconomic attainments, however, stand in atypical contrast to those of their own appropriate comparison groups.

REFERENCES

1. Quintero Rivera, A. G. 1974. "The Development of Social Classes and Political Conflicts in Puerto Rico," in A. Lopez and J. Petras (eds.), *Puerto Rico and Puerto Ricans.* Cambridge: Schenkman Publishing Co.
2. Christopulos, D. 1974. "Puerto Rico in the Twentieth Century: A Historical Survey," in A. Lopez and J. Petras (eds.), *Puerto Rico and Puerto Ricans.* Cambridge: Schenkman Publishing Co.
3. Clark, V. et al. 1930. *Porto Rico and Its Problems.* Washington, D.C.: Brookings Institution.
4. Christopulos, see note 2, p. 130.
5. Christopulos, see note 2, p. 132.
6. Morley, M. 1974. "Dependence and Development in Puerto Rico," in A. Lopez and J. Petras (eds.), *Puerto Rico and Puerto Ricans.* Cambridge: Schenkman Publishing Co.
7. Muñoz Marin, L. 1929. "The Sad Case of Porto Rico." *The American Mercury,* Vol. XVI, No. 62, February, pp. 138-139.
8. Wells, H. 1969. *The Modernization of Puerto Rico: A Political Study of Changing Values and Institutions.* Cambridge: Harvard University Press.
9. Bonilla, F. and R. Campos. 1981. "A Wealth of Poor: Puerto Ricans in the New Economic Order." *Daedalus, Journal of the Academy of Arts and Sciences,* Spring.
10. Senior, C. 1961. *The Puerto Ricans: Strangers, Then Neighbors.* Chicago: Quadrangle Books.
11. Puerto Rico, Department of Education. 1964. *Progress in Education: Facts and Figures,* pp. 2-4.
12. Christopulos, see note 2.

13. Steiner, S. 1974. *The Islands: The Worlds of the Puerto Ricans.* New York: Harper Colophon Books, p. 120.

14. Le Veness, F. P. 1968. *The Commonwealth of Puerto Rico: Democracy Thrives in the Caribbean.* Doctoral dissertation, St. John's University New York. Ann Arbor, MI: University Microfilms #68-11257.

15. Senior, see note 10.

16. Treiman, D. J. 1977. *Occupational Prestige in Comparative Perspective.* New York: Academic Press.

17. U.S. Department of Labor, Bureau of Labor Statistics. 1975. *A Socio-Economic Profile of Puerto Rican New Yorkers,* Regional Report 46 July. New York: U.S. Department of Labor, Middle Atlantic Regional Office.

18. Gurak, D. T. and L. H. Rogler. 1980. "Hispanic Diversity in New York City." Hispanic Research Center *Research Bulletin,* Fordham University, Vol. 3, No. 3, July, pp. 1-5.

19. Fitzpatrick, J. P. and D. T. Gurak. 1979. *Hispanic Intermarriage in New York City: 1975* (Monograph No. 2). New York: Hispanic Research Center, Fordham University.

20. U.S. Bureau of the Census. 1973. *U.S. Census of Population: 1970; Subject Reports; Final Report PC(2)-1E,* (Tables 34 and 129 for New York State). Washington, D.C.: U.S. Government Printing Office.

21. U.S. Department of Labor, Bureau of Labor Statistics, see note 17.

22. *Ibid.*

23. Gurak and Rogler, see note 18.

24. Jaffe, A. J. (ed.). 1954. *Puerto Rican Population of New York City.* New York: Bureau of Applied Social Research, Columbia University, January.

25. Kantrowitz, N. 1968. "Social Mobility of Puerto Ricans: Education, Occupation and Income Changes: New York, 1950-1960." *International Migration Review,* Vol. 2, Fall, pp. 53-70.

26. U.S. Department of Labor, Bureau of Labor Statistics, see note 17.

27. Hernández Alvarez, J. 1967. *Return Migration to Puerto Rico* (Population Monograph Series, No. 1). Berkeley: Institute of International Studies, University of California at Berkeley.
    U.S. Department of Labor, Bureau of Labor Statistics, see note 17.
    Cooney, R. S. and A. E. Colon Warren. 1979. "Declining Female Participation among Puerto Rican New Yorkers: A Comparison with Native White Non-Spanish New Yorkers." *Ethnicity,* Vol. 6, September, pp. 281-297.

28. Angel, R. and M. Tienda. 1982. "Determinants of Extended Household Structure: Cultural Pattern or Economic Need?" *American Journal of Sociology,* Vol. 87, No. 6, pp. 1360-1383.

Cooney, R. S. and A. E. Colon. 1980. "Work and Family: The Recent Struggle of Puerto Rican Females," in C. E. Rodriguez, V. Sanchez Korrol and J. O. Alers (eds.), *The Puerto Rican Struggle: Essays on Survival in the U.S.* New York: Puerto Rican Migration Research Consortium.

U.S. Bureau of the Census. 1980. "Persons of Spanish Origin in the United States: March 1979." *Current Population Reports*, Series P-20, No. 354. Washington, D.C.: U.S. Government Printing Office.

29. Maldonado, Rita M. 1976. "Why Puerto Ricans Migrated to the United States in 1947-73." *Monthly Labor Review* 99(9) (September): 7-18.

PART 2

INTERGENERATIONAL DIFFERENCES AND DISCONTINUITIES

Introduction

Although the parent-generation mothers and fathers were in the vanguard of the modernizing social changes in Puerto Rico, they chose to move to New York City in search of opportunities to fulfill their lives and aspirations. In moving they were incessantly exposed to a culture different from their own, yet during almost three decades of living in New York City and experiencing the city's changes they retained much of their Puerto Rican culture. The intergenerational legacy was Puerto Rican culture, but the children in the married-child generation were socialized from early childhood into the culture of the host society. Both generations, therefore, were the repositories of the culture of their society of origin and the recipients of the host society's culture. The interplay between the two cultures, as embodied in the persons of both generations, produced variability in the ethnic identity of the parents and their adult offspring. Thus, the examination of ethnic identity in Chapter IV derives clearly and directly from the historical and demographical account presented in the preceding chapter, for ethnic identity is an important emergent product of the migration experience from Puerto Rico to New York City.

In Chapter III we noted that the intact marriages which characterized the two generations make them atypical in relation to their corresponding cohort group and an exception to the rising pattern of single-parent Puerto Rican households in New York City. These marital unions provided support to each person's well-being, buttressing the members of these unions against the formidable changes in the environment we have already described. Nevertheless, despite the stability of these marriages, the role relationships between husbands and wives varied greatly. From one intact union to the next, differences were found in the degree to which husbands and wives shared in the performance of tasks, the making of decisions, and in their leisure-time activities. The components of these role relationships, of interest in and of themselves, are shaped by the persistent effect of external influences. The experience of moving from one culture to another provided the context for the examination of these components in Chapter V, as they appear in the lives of the persons in both generations.

Perhaps the most striking finding in Chapter III is the extraordinary success of the child generation: on every measure of socioeconomic attainment they exceeded by far their cohort group. Their success, however, was not accidental. It forms part, once again, of a history of intergenerational changes starting with their predecessors in yesterday's Puerto Rico and moving through the experience of migration from one culture to another. Chapter VI examines this success in social mobility by applying and then altering customary models of status attainment and by highlighting intergenerational historical changes culminating in the lives of the married-child generation. The examination of these analytical problems — ethnic identity, husband and wife relations, and social mobility — all rooted in Chapter III's account, attempts to illuminate the basic questions and distinctions posed by the discussion in Chapter I of intergenerational processes within families.

IV

Ethnic Identity

In Chapter III we traced the lives of the persons in our study from their roots in Puerto Rico to their arrival in New York City. We now want to learn what they retained of their Puerto Rican cultural origins while living in New York and up to the time they became part of our study. This question raises the concept of ethnic identity which is central to the literature on ethnicity. However, the literature reveals inconsistencies in its treatment of the concept of ethnic identity. For example, ethnic identity has been defined as subjective identification, a single dimension in a broader concept of assimilation[1]; and as a concept with many facets, including language, behavior, values, knowledge of ethnic group history, and subjective identification.[2] Despite such inconsistencies, there is more than just a glimmer of order at the operational level in the conversion of the abstract concept of ethnic identity into scales or measures with their corresponding items. Sets of items tend to converge upon mastery of, use of, and preference for the ethnic language or the language of the host society; use of and preference for ethnic foods, music traditions, and literature; knowledge of cultural heritage; pride in the elements of ethnicity; subjective identification of self in terms of ethnic group descent or attributes of the ethnic group; belief in the values of the ethnic group; and behavioral conformance to cultural norms of the ethnic group. Our work assumes the multifaceted character of the concept by defining it according to the following domains: *language ability and use of either Spanish or English*; *values pertaining to familism and fatalism*; *orientation toward modernity*; and, *self-identification in relation to Puerto Rican or American culture or experiences*.

Little research has focused upon intergenerational change in ethnic identity within the family. We mentioned before that generational comparisons usually are made between unrelated individuals differentiated by place of birth: ethnic group members born in a foreign country (first generation) and those born in the United States of foreign or mixed parentage (second generation). Underlying this procedure is an assumption often made that the differences observed between generations reflect changes occurring within immigrant families. Our data on intergenerationally linked Puerto Rican families permit a direct examination of this assumption. Therefore, the first part of this chapter examines the differences and similarities between the parent and child generations in the area of ethnic identity. The second part uncovers factors which affect ethnic identity in each generation.

The study's design also permits the examination of the degree of intergenerational continuity in each area of ethnic identity. In keeping with the distinctions already made, intergenerational continuity signifies the correlations between parents and their married children with respect to the characteristic being examined in this chapter, the specific area of ethnic identity. As noted in Chapter I, intergenerational studies of parents and children living in the same sociocultural system have generally found a pattern of selective continuity, that is, continuity with respect to some things but not others. Thus, the third part of this chapter examines intergenerational continuity and goes a step further by bringing data to bear upon the underlying conditions which promote selective continuity.

ETHNIC IDENTITY OF THE PARENT AND CHILD GENERATIONS

The move from Puerto Rico to New York City entailed a change in the prevailing language of the culture of the immigrants. Each person studied was asked to evaluate his/her knowledge of English according to the ability to speak, write, read, and understand others speaking it. The same questions were asked about Spanish. The respondents were asked which language they used most often in speaking to their spouses, children, and friends. Since the parent generation was raised predominantly in Puerto Rico and the child generation in New York City, it is not surprising, as shown in Table 4.1, that the child generation, as a group, reported greater language ability in English, less language ability in Spanish, and less usage of Spanish in speaking with their spouses. Each and every comparison between the married children and their mothers and between the married children and their fathers yields statistically significant differences. Thus, there are marked intergenerational differences in the *language domain* of ethnic *identity*.

Such differences, however, do not mean that the parent generation spoke poor or bad English. Both the mothers and fathers reported that their overall knowledge of English in speaking, writing, reading, and oral comprehension was about average. The parents' greatest difficulties with the English language

TABLE 4.1

Average Scores of Ethnic Identity Variables for Parent and Child Generations

Ethnic Identity Variables by Major Domains	Mothers	Mean Scores Adult Children	Fathers
Language Ability & Usage			
Knowledge of English[a]	2.88*	4.06	3.05*
Knowledge of Spanish[a]	4.06*	3.51	3.92*
Language spoken[b]	2.72*	1.72	2.62*
General Values			
Familism[c]	2.33*	1.81	2.43*
Fatalism[c]	2.38*	1.90	2.37*
Individual Modernity[d]	.56*	.67	.58*
Self-Identity			
Subjective affiliation[e]	.66*	.45	.51
Subjective closeness[f]	.59	.57	.50
Attitudinal preferences[g]	2.58*	2.24	2.60*

*Significant difference between parent and child using paired t-tests, $p < .05$.

[a] Category values: 1 = none, 2 = bad, 3 = average, 4 = good, 5 = excellent

[b] Category values: 1 = exclusively English, 2 = both Spanish and English, 3 = exclusively Spanish

[c] Category values: 1 = strongly disagree, 2 = disagree a little, 3 = agree a little, 4 = strongly agree

[d] Category values: 0 = traditional, 1 = modern

[e] Category values: 0 = part-Puerto Rican and part-American, 1 = exclusively Puerto Rican

[f] Category values: 0 = feel as close to Americans as to Puerto Ricans, 1 = consider Puerto Ricans my real people

[g] Category values: 1 = responses favoring United States, 2 = no favoritism, 3 = responses favoring Puerto Rico

were in the areas of reading and writing: almost 20 percent of the parents reported that they were not able to write English at all; 10 percent reported no reading ability in English. In contrast, none of the children reported an inability to write or read in English; their overall knowledge of English was good.

The sharpest difference between the parent and child generations' knowledge of English was in writing. A similar pattern was observed in reverse for Spanish. The child generation had not lost the Spanish language but had the greatest difficulties in writing and reading Spanish: almost 10 percent reported an inability to write in Spanish; 13 percent reported they could not read Spanish or read it poorly. Their communication skills in either speaking or understanding spoken Spanish were good or excellent. Overall, the knowledge of Spanish of the child generation tended to be slightly better than average, while the knowledge of Spanish of the parent generation was good in all respects.

In spite of their fluency in oral Spanish, almost one-half of the child generation reported relying on English exclusively in communicating with their spouses and children at home. The other half used both languages equally, with very few limiting themselves to Spanish at home. In contrast, the parent generation relied almost exclusively on Spanish at home even when their adult children came to visit them. In sum, while there are clear differences between the parent and child generations in their knowledge and use of Spanish and English, the differences should be seen as matters of degree. The linguistic patterns of the child generation indicated an involvement in both cultures.

Familism is a traditional modality in Puerto Rican culture, and cultural values give shape and direction to human conduct. Thus, accompanying the importance of the family in the institutional structure of Puerto Rican society is a value system in support of the family. The value system of familism, in its broadest terms, emphasizes the almost sacred bonds between relatives, the compelling obligations toward relatives, the duty to help and to express concern for them. The importance of this value system has been repeatedly documented by studies conducted on the island[3]; its continuing significance among Puerto Ricans on the mainland also has been noted.[4]

The persons in our study were classified according to the degree to which they adhered to the value of familism. They were asked whether they strongly agreed, agreed a little, disagreed a little, or strongly disagreed with the following statements: if one has the opportunity of helping a person get a job, it is always better to choose a relative than a friend; when one has a real problem, only a relative helps one; when looking for a job a person ought to find a position located near his parents, even if that means losing a good opportunity elsewhere; nothing in life is worth the sacrifice of moving away from one's parents; in marriage, the foremost love is owed to one's parents instead of to one's spouse. As shown in Table 4.1, marked differences were the pattern in the comparisons between the mothers and their children and the fathers and their children concerning familism.

The two familism items scoring the greatest disparity between the parent and child generations were: if one has the opportunity of helping a person get a job, it is always better to choose a relative rather than a friend; and, the foremost love is owed to one's parents instead of to one's spouse. While 40 percent of the mothers and fathers strongly agreed with both of the above statements only 10 percent of the child generation did so. In fact, almost three-quarters of the child generation either disagreed a little or strongly disagreed. Two familism-related statements which the parent generation did not endorse as strongly were the items that directly related to migration: when looking for a job a person ought to find a position in a place located near his parents, even if that means losing a good opportunity elsewhere; and, nothing in life is worth the sacrifice of moving away from your parents. Almost one-half of the parent generation strongly disagreed with these statements; the child generation was again even less familistic, almost 70 percent disagreeing with these statements.

Fatalism as a value represents another traditional modality of Puerto Rican culture, in particular the culture of older, preindustrial Puerto Rico. Fatalism is the belief that events are preordained by an overarching metaphysical process, that destiny is responsible for success or failure in life, and that the actions of human beings are largely ineffective in influencing their future lives. The roots of fatalism in yesterday's Puerto Rico have been attributed to the rigidity of the stratificational system in constraining social mobility,[5] the otherworldliness of the Catholic Church's attribution of difficulties to God's will,[6] and the lingering colonial status of Puerto Rico which fosters in Puerto Ricans the passivity of a colonized people.[7] All persons in the study were classified according to four responses, ranging from strongly agree to strongly disagree, to the following statements: children should be taught not to expect too much out of life so they won't be disappointed; nowadays the wise parent will teach the child to live for today and not to worry about tomorrow; it is important not to plan life but to accept what comes; true happiness in life consists of adapting oneself to what one has and taking advantage of whatever comes; children should learn that planning only makes a person unhappy since your plans hardly ever work out anyway; children should be taught that when a man is born success is already in the cards so he might as well accept what comes.

A similar pattern of differences between the parent and child generations was evident in their responses, as shown in Table 4.1, to statements relating to the value of familism. For illustrative purposes we select two statements which reflect the greatest difference between the parents and their children. More than 75 percent of the child generation but only one-third of the mothers and fathers expressed a strong disagreement with the statement: children should be taught that when a man is born success is already in the cards so he might as well accept what comes. On the other hand, almost 60 percent of both the mothers and fathers and fewer than 20 percent of the child generation strongly agreed that children should be taught not to expect too much out of life so they would not be disappointed. National statistical norms for either the United States or Puerto Rico on these statements are not available so it is difficult to evaluate the extent to which the child generation's responses were bicultural. The children, however, appeared to be significantly less committed than the parents to values associated with traditional Puerto Rican culture.

Individual modernity is a concept used by Smith and Inkeles[8] in their cross-cultural studies in six developing countries. In their usage it refers ". . . to a set of attitudes, values, and ways of feeling and acting, presumably of the sort either generated by or required for effective participation in modern society" (p. 353). A modern society is characterized by ". . . a complex of traits including urbanization, high levels of education, industrialization, extensive mechanization, high rates of social mobility, and the like" (p. 353). Through elaborate psychometric procedures, Smith and Inkeles developed a simplified scale for the measurement of individual modernity. Sample items in the scale include references to such attitudes as the schooling the respondent thinks persons such as he/she should have, factors which qualify a person for high office, feelings toward birth control, and to such behaviors as frequency of participation in associations and clubs and frequency of getting news and information from newspapers.

We administered the individual modernity scale with minor adaptations to the persons in our study. Table 4.1 shows that the married children significantly exceeded their mothers and fathers in individual modernity. Again, there is a pattern of significant intergenerational differences: the greatest differences between the two generations are in the areas of birth control, openness to other cultural ways of thinking, and religion. Almost all of the child generation were in favor of limiting the number of children in a family so that better care could be taken of each child. Although a slight majority of the parent generation was also in favor of voluntarily limiting the number of children in a family, they did not approve of birth control as often as their children. More than 60 percent of the child generation felt that if they met someone of another culture they would be able to understand that person's way of thinking. In the parent generation, 60 percent felt they would *not* be able to understand a person from another culture. The question on religion was usual in demonstrating differences between generations, but it was unusual in demonstrating *dissimilarity* between the mothers and fathers in the parent generation. In other words, feelings about religion not only differentiated parents from their children but also mothers from fathers. Almost two-thirds of the mothers believed that a man cannot be truly good without religion; only one-half of the fathers and one-third of the children agreed. The different pattern in this case probably reflects the traditional habits of Puerto Rican women, in general, being more involved in religion than the men.

Although there are significant differences in the overall individual modernity orientation between generations, one observation should be made: the parent generation's average individual modernity score is located at about the midpoint of the possible range of scores of this scale. The child generation's score is two-thirds of the way in the direction of modernity. This means that the parent generation could have scored as substantially less modern in orientation than they did. That they did not, in fact, is consistent with their earlier history in Puerto Rico as presented in Chapter III, and the direction of change which they have taken as a result of living in New York City for almost three decades.

The migration from Puerto Rico to New York projected the parents and their children into a situation of two encroaching cultures. We have already examined changes that specifically focus on three domains of the culture: language behavior, values, and orientations toward modernity. The next domain, *self-identity*, refers to the way persons attribute aspects of the two cultures to themselves and to the social environment. Self-identity includes subjective affiliation with Puerto Rican culture, with American culture or with both according to the values of the cultures; feelings of closeness toward Puerto Ricans and Americans; preferences for living in Puerto Rico or on the mainland, for the English or Spanish language, for their children's retention of Puerto Rican ways and traditions, and for their children's marrying non-Puerto Ricans. The findings for self-identity, as shown in Table 4.1, are not as uniform as in the other domains of ethnic identity, but the pattern still remains. The parent generation's self-identity was more rooted in things Puerto Rican than was the child generation's.

To assess subjective affiliation with one or the other culture, we asked each respondent whether in their values they considered themselves purely Puerto Rican, part-Puerto Rican and part-North American, or purely North

American. Two-thirds of the mothers, 51 percent of the fathers, and 45 percent of the children answered they were purely Puerto Rican; the others reported they were part-Puerto Rican and part-North American. *Not one mother, father, or child responded that he/she felt purely North American in values!*

To assess their subjective closeness to one or the other culture, they were asked about their feeling of closeness to Puerto Ricans and Americans: 59 percent of the mothers felt very close to Puerto Ricans and considered them their real people, as compared to 50 percent of the fathers and 57 percent of the children. The child generation's response to this item is surprising on two counts: more than their fathers, the child generation felt Puerto Ricans are their own real people; and, their feelings of subjective closeness to the Puerto Rican community were much stronger than their perceived value similarities with Puerto Ricans. The remaining mothers, fathers, and children reported they felt as close to Puerto Ricans as to Americans. *Not one member of the child generation reported feeling closer to Americans than to Puerto Ricans nor does anyone else in their generation consider Americans to be his or her own real people.* The findings on subjective affiliation and closeness show clearly that the child generation's movement is toward a bicultural orientation and not toward the abandonment of a Puerto Rican identity. Again, in keeping with the transitional character of the parent generation in the changes experienced in Puerto Rico and New York City, it is notable that a substantial minority of this generation perceived their values to be part-Puerto Rican and part-North American and their feelings were equally close to Puerto Ricans and Americans.

The last set of items in the domain of self-identity tap the attitudinal preferences for Puerto Rico and/or the mainland in terms of where they prefer to live, which language they prefer to use, whether or not they prefer their children to keep Puerto Rican ways and traditions, and whether they prefer their children marry a Puerto Rican or non-Puerto Rican. Only on this aspect of self-identity did we observe significant differences between the child generation and both the mothers and fathers. The greatest preference for Puerto Rico was expressed in the item on children's keeping Puerto Ricans ways: almost all the parent generation and more than 80 percent of the child generation wanted their children to keep Puerto Rican traditions. The remaining 20 percent in the child generation expressed mixed feelings rather than preferring that their children not keep Puerto Rican traditions. Among the parent generation, the least preference for Puerto Rico was shown in the item on their children's marriages. A majority of both mothers and fathers said that it made no difference whether their children marry a Puerto

Rican or a non-Puerto Rican. More than two-thirds of the child generation also endorsed this neutral alternative. None of the child generation, however, reported that marriage to a non-Puerto Rican was preferable or even more desirable. The greatest difference between the parent and child generations in attitude preferences was in language and place of residence. Parents preferred to use Spanish and to live in Puerto Rico; the greatest number of children preferred to use both Spanish and English and the majority preferred to live in New York. While the parent generation in their responses showed greater preference than their children for Puerto Rico, the child generation still retained a strong preference for their ethnic cultural traditions.

In contrast to the significant intergenerational differences in the mastery and usage of the respective languages, the endorsement of the values of familism and fatalism, orientation toward modernity, and relative preference for Puerto Rican or American culture or objects, the child generation was similar to the parent generation in perceiving itself as Puerto Rican with respect to values and feelings associated with the homeland. The similarities indicate that the child generation's strongest link to their Puerto Rican heritage was found in their symbolic self-perceptions. Its members were losing mastery of Spanish and removing themselves from familism and fatalism, but they were clearly retaining their self-perception as Puerto Rican at a level similar to that of their parents. In addition, the strength of their Puerto Rican self-identification was not related to their knowledge of Spanish or adherence to familism and fatalism. Caught in the flux of changing languages and values, the child generation maintained its strongest ties to the ethnic culture in the form of its self-concept as Puerto Ricans: 45 percent of the persons in the child generation considered themselves to be exclusively Puerto Rican, the remainder, as part-Puerto Rican and part-American. Not one considered himself/herself exclusively American. Of the domains examined which comprise ethnic identity — language, values, orientation toward modernity, and self-identity — it is in the self-identity domain where the greatest intergenerational similarities were found, and it is the expression of self-identity which most strongly bound the child generation to their ethnic heritage.

FACTORS AFFECTING ETHNIC IDENTITY

Earlier in the chapter the point was made that ethnic identity as a concept is ambiguous in the literature, with some formulations conceiving of it as a single domain, others as having several domains. Our treatment of it distinctly favors the latter formulation. Now we find that, in contrast to the ambiguities in the formulation of this concept, there is notable convergence in the independent variables used to explain variations in ethnic identity in specified cultural groups. *Generation*, specified according to the birthplace criterion is a variable used repetitively, along with other variables such as *age*, *sex*, and *education*; *age at arrival, length of residence on the mainland, and ethnic composition of the neighborhood* are used less frequently.[9] The choice of such variables is not altogether arbitrary. Underlying their use is a theoretical postulate which states that the strength of ethnic identity decreases with receptivity to influences by the outgroup host society and according to the degree of exposure to such influences.

How does the choice of independent variables in our research relate to this postulate? Variables relevant to the concept of receptivity and their hypothesized relationship to ethnic identity are: (1) Age at arrival on the mainland. Arrival at a younger age constricts past social experiences on the island and, thus, the sense of ethnic identity is less firmly established. (2) Years of education. An increase in education tends to weaken ethnic identity because it expands cognitive life through the teaching of alternative values and life styles either in different historical periods or in different cultural settings. More educated people, whether their education was received on the island or on the mainland, are less bound by tradition and more open to change and new ideas.

In turn, variables relevant to the concept of exposure and their hypothesized relationship to ethnic identity are: (1) Number of years of residence on the mainland. This is a direct measure of exposure to the host society; the greater the exposure, the weaker the ethnic identity. (2) Ethnic composition of the neighborhood. The degree to which the neighborhood is composed of Puerto Ricans signifies the relative exposure to the Puerto Rican ingroup as opposed to the outgroup in the host society. Again, the postulate states that exposure to the host society weakens ethnic identity. (3) Sex. Men may have weaker ethnic identities than women because their employment in jobs away from home increases the likelihood they will come into contact with non-Puerto Ricans.

The choice of variables in this research, therefore, is not exceptional. What is exceptional, however, is that we attempt to explain ethnic identity as an integral part of intergenerationally linked individuals — parents and their children. Thus, our research enjoys a double advantage: by focusing upon the family it places the study group in an institutional context faithful to central traditions based in the island-home of Puerto Rico,[10] while it increases precision in the specification of generations. For example, in our discussion of the life experiences of the parent generation in Chapter III, we focused our attention on the substantial majority of the parent generation who were born, raised, and educated in Puerto Rico and who migrated to New York as young adults. A minority of the parent generation (17) however, did not fit this pattern. They were either born in New York or brought to New York by their parents at a very young age (median age at arrival, 4 years). This minority (9 mothers and 8 fathers) was raised and educated predominantly in New York City. Since the numbers are small, they must be interpreted cautiously. The substantial majority of the child generation was raised in New York City and was the focus of our interest in Chapter III. A minority (11 of the child generation) did not fit this pattern. They were born, raised, and educated in Puerto Rico, coming to the mainland as young adults during the mid-1960's (median age at arrival, 18 years). This number was small also and must be cautiously interpreted. Nevertheless, these data on the child and parent generations do provide an unprecedented opportunity for investigating how differences in ethnic identity of the two generations were influenced by early socialization experiences.

Although our explanatory variables derive from a literature focused upon individuals and not upon intergenerational processes, the pattern of inter-generational differences is largely what would be expected. The child generation, raised predominantly in New York, were exposed at a much younger age to American society than were the island-raised parent generation. The child generation achieved a much higher level of schooling than did the parent generation. Not surprisingly, the parent generation lived in neighborhoods with a larger proportion of Puerto Ricans than did the child generation. Thus, in comparison to the men and women of the parent generaion, the men and women of the child generation were younger upon arrival in New York, more highly educated, lived in neighborhoods with proportionately fewer Puerto Ricans, and had a more attenuated ethnic identity as Puerto Ricans, although that identity was distinctly bicultural. With the exception of length or dura-tion of residence in New York, which fails to distinguish between the genera-tions, the pattern of intergenerational differences was as expected. We shall return presently to the examination of ethnic identity from an intergenera-tional perspective, but now we turn to a consideration of how these variables affect the ethnic identity of the parents and their children.

The major variables affecting the ethnic identity of the two generations are *age at arrival* and *education*. Once we take into account education and/or age at arrival, the other variables − duration of residence on the mainland, Puerto Rican composition of the neighborhood, and, for the child generation, sex − did not have a significant independent effect on ethnic identity. Table 4.2 shows separately for mothers, fathers, and children the interrelationships

TABLE 4.2
Partial Regression Coefficients of Ethnic Identity Variables for Parent and Child Generations

Independent Variables	Knowledge of English	Knowledge of Spanish	Language Spoken	Familism	Fatalism	Modernity	Subjective Affiliation	Subjective Closeness	Attitudinal Preference
Mothers									
Age at arrival[a,b]									
New York raised	.56*	-.21	-.53*	-.02	-.09	.05	-.11	-.19	-.34*
Arrive 20-30	-.20	.09	.15	-.29	-.12	.08	.14	.03	.02
Arrive 31+	-.55*	.15	.18	.13	.12	.04	.17	.01	.13
Education (interval)	.15*	.08*	-.04*	-.10*	-.06*	.01*	.01	-.02	.01
Adjusted R^2	.63*	.31*	.38*	.25*	.20*	.12*	.01	.02	.06*
Fathers									
Age at arrival[a,b]									
New York raised	.30*	-.61*	-.38*	-.04	-.05	.01	-.39*	-.04	-.41*
Arrive 20-30	-.30*	-.02	.18	-.05	-.06	.01	.13	.02	.02
Arrive 31+	-.65*	-.09	.26*	.40*	-.08	-.07	.23	-.09	.10
Education (interval)	.16*	.09*	-.04*	-.08*	-.06*	.01*	-.01	.01	-.01
Adjusted R^2	.59*	.24*	.27*	.25	.11*	.10*	.02	.01	.14*

Children

Age at arrival[b,c]

Born P.R., Arrive ≤ 5	−.01	.21	.03	.05	.17	.01	.19	.12	.11
Born P.R., Arrive 6-14	−.25	.20	.05	.09	.19	.04	.39*	.14	.36*
P.R. raised	−.67*	.94*	.93*	−.02	.18	.01	.58*	.39*	.39*
Education (interval)	.12*	.08*		−.09*	−.11*	.03*			
Education (categorical)[b,d]									
Less than 12			.20*				.17*	.06	.02
Adjusted R^2	.29*	.13*	.19*	.16*	.18*	.13*	.11*	.04	.08*

*p < .05

[a] Reference group category for mothers and fathers age at arrival is 15-19 years.

[b] Coefficients for remaining categories are expressed as deviations from the reference group, holding other variables constant.

[c] Reference group for child's age at arrival is born in the U.S.

[d] Reference group for child's education in categorical form is 12+ years.

of age at arrival and education with each of the nine measures of ethnic identity. While the importance of education and age at arrival varies among the measures of ethnic identity, there is a pattern: for language ability and usage measures, both education and age at arrival were important; for values and modernity, only education was significant; and for self-identification, only age at arrival was significant.

Turning first to language ability and usage, we find that parent-generation mothers with more years of schooling reported greater knowledge of English, greater knowledge of Spanish, and less use of Spanish at home than did the parent-generation mothers who completed fewer years of schooling. This pattern was characteristic also for the parent-generation fathers. The child generation showed a similar pattern for knowledge of English and knowledge of Spanish. For language spoken with family and friends, children with less than a high school education spoke Spanish more frequently than children who completed high school. Education beyond high school, however, did not lead to greater reliance on English. Those with a college education were just as likely to use Spanish in the home as were children with only a high school diploma. *Regardless of level of education, age at arrival was related to language ability and usage*, with those who arrived at an older age reporting less ability and use of English than those who arrived at an earlier age. For example, parent-generation mothers and fathers raised in New York reported greater knowledge of English, less knowledge of Spanish, and use of Spanish less often than parent-generation mothers and fathers who came as young adults (ages 15-19). Parent-generation mothers and fathers who arrived when they were in their thirties or older reported less knowledge of English and greater reliance on Spanish than those parents who migrated in their late teens. Because the majority of the child generation was either born on the mainland or brought at a young age, it is possible to distinguish birthplace from early arrival ages. We find that the child-generation's knowledge of English, knowledge of Spanish, and language spoken with family and friends was similar for children born in New York and those born in Puerto Rico who migrated at a young age. No matter what the level of education, children raised in Puerto Rico reported less knowledge of English, greater knowledge of Spanish, and greater reliance on Spanish in the home than children raised in New York. *It is the sociocultural context of the early socialization experience, not simply place of birth, that shaped language patterns*. Concerning cultural values and modernity orientation, we find education is important, but not age at arrival. Among parent-generation mothers, *those with more years of education were less familistic, less fatalistic, and more modern than those with fewer years of education.* The pattern is similar for the parent-generation fathers and the child generations.

For the final set of measures dealing with self-identity, the findings are mixed. We were unsuccessful in identifying correlates of the mothers' subjective affiliation and the mothers' and fathers' subjective closeness to Puerto Rican culture. When significant variables were uncovered, the pattern was for age at arrival to be important, but not education. The parent-generation mothers and fathers raised in New York showed weaker preferences for Puerto Rican culture than the parent-generation mothers and fathers who arrived as adults, no matter what their age at arrival as adults. The child generation raised in Puerto Rico not only had greater preferences for Puerto Rican culture, but also were more likely than were the children, either born in New York or born in Puerto Rico and arriving prior to grammar school age, to view themselves as exclusively Puerto Rican or feel that Puerto Ricans were their real people. The sociocultural context of early socialization was important in shaping ethnic self-identification while formal schooling, whether acquired in Puerto Rico or New York, shaped cultural values and orientation toward modernity. The sociocultural context of socialization and level of formal schooling were both important in influencing which language the persons felt able to use and in fact did use.

In contrast to conclusions based upon bivariate relationships which predominate in the literature, our conclusions regarding the variables affecting ethnic identity of the parent and child generations are based upon a technique of analysis which assesses the independent contribution of each variable on ethnic identity after controlling for the other variables. This procedure produced two major findings: *both education and age at arrival had significant independent effects upon the ethnic identity of mothers, fathers, and children*; and, *once these variables were controlled, the other independent variables included in the analysis no longer were significantly related to ethnic identity*.

INTERGENERATIONAL CONTINUITY

The intergenerational research design of our study not only provides information on the cultural changes of both parents and their children, but also allows us to examine the extent to which the ethnic identity characteristics of immigrant parents are correlated to the same characteristics of their children. As we noted in Chapter I, intergenerational studies of parents and children within a single sociocultural system have generally found a pattern of selective continuity: some things are transmitted, others not. We now ask the question: Is there intergenerational continuity between the parents and their children in their ethnic identity? To address this question, we examined in Table 4.3 the 18 correlations relating the individual score of the mother to the individual score of her child and the score of the father to his child for each variable of ethnic identity. Only two correlations were statistically significant: the mother's knowledge of English was related to that of her child and the father's attitudinal preferences were related to those of his child. In the context of the array of correlations presented in Table 4.3, importance ought not to be attached to the occurrence of an occasional statistically significant relationship. Thus, the overall pattern of findings on the ethnic identity variables indicates an absence of continuities between the parents and their children. *The pattern of selective continuity documented in the intergenerational literature is not evident within immigrant Puerto Rican families.* The divergence of our findings cannot be accounted

TABLE 4.3

Correlations of Ethnic Identity Variables for Intergenerationally Linked Parent and Child

Ethnic Identity Variables by Major Domains	*Correlations*	
	Adult Child with Mother	*Adult Child with Father*
Language Ability & Usage		
Knowledge of English	.28*	.16
Knowledge of Spanish	.01	.11
Language spoken	.16	.13
General Values		
Familism	.15	.14
Fatalism	.11	.04
Individual Modernity	.04	.14
Self-Identity		
Subjective affiliation	.09	−.04
Subjective closeness	.09	.02
Attitudinal preferences	.14	.27*

*Statistically significant, $p < .05$.

for simply by historical or life-cycle differences between the generations. In the studies reviewed by Troll and Bengtson[11] and in our own study, parents and children were raised in different historical periods and were studied at different stages of the life cycle. While differences in historical period and life-cycle stage may affect the process of intergenerational continuity from the parent to the child, it is notable that the finding of selective continuity in the earlier studies occurred in spite of such confounding influences. The major factor differentiating our study group from the earlier studies is that the parents were raised in a different sociocultural environment than their children. *Our findings suggest that a migration-induced change in sociocultural environment affects the intergenerational process of familial transmission.* These findings are not in accord with Troll and Bengtson's proposition that "there is substantial but selective continuity within the family" (p. 136). The failure of our data to support this proposition, however, does not and should not lead to abandoning the selective continuity approach endorsed earlier.

While the unexpected pattern of discontinuities highlights the importance of considering the sociocultural context in which parents and their children were raised, it also presents a challenging puzzle. We must go beyond describing the puzzle to increase our understanding of the dynamics of familial continuity within immigrant families. We began by asking under what conditions we would expect intergenerational continuity in ethnic identity among immigrant families to be increased or decreased. First, we took stock. What did we learn from the analysis of factors affecting the ethnic identity of the generations that would help us understand the dynamics of familial transmission?

The most important variables related to the ethnic identity of the mothers, fathers, and their children were their age at arrival and their education. Age at arrival in New York City affected the current cultural or ethnic characteristics of the individual in the intergenerational families. This finding accentuates the critical role of having been raised in one sociocultural environment as opposed to another. Not only did the child generation raised in Puerto Rico differ in their ethnic identity from the child generation raised in New York City, but also mothers and fathers raised in Puerto Rico differed in their ethnic identity from mothers and fathers raised in New York City. The dynamics of cultural adaptation at the level of the individual were consistent with the suggestion that a migration-induced change in sociocultural environment affects the intergenerational process of familial transmission. The ability of parents to influence their children may well be rooted in the sharing of socialization experiences in a common culture. Being raised in a common culture facilitates the effectiveness of communication between parents and children, even when both confront a changing society. Despite rapid social change in American society, economically advantaged parents tend to pass on such advantages to their children, and parents who are liberal tend to have children who are liberal,[12] but when children are raised in a sociocultural context different from that of their parents, the impact of social change is magnified as it interacts with the generations' different earlier cultural experiences. At a very young age the child comes into contact with groups and institutions outside the family which challenge the immigrant parents' orientation. The challenge is not subtle when the parents lack the necessary language skills to understand the terms imposed by the host society. In this setting, parental influence is disrupted.

In addition to age at arrival, the education of the mothers, fathers, and children is importantly related to their current ethnic identity. This finding signals the influence of socioeconomic status. Within American and Puerto Rican society, important variations in attitudes and behaviors are associated with position in the stratification system. Ethnic identity is shaped not just by the cultural environments in which the persons are raised but also by their socioeconomic position in society: the majority of parents in our study had only grammar school education, while their children were high school graduates, with a sizeable minority having received some college education. We suggest that the effectiveness of communication between parents and children was disrupted also by the force of intergenerational socioeconomic mobility. The expectation, therefore, is that intergenerational transmission in ethnic identity is greater if parent and child were raised in similar sociocultural settings than if parent and child were raised in different cultural settings; in addition, intergenerational transmission increased if the parent and child were more similar in educational attainment than if parent and child were of vastly different educational levels.

Each person in the study was classified according to his/her place of early socialization: those born in New York or having arrived before the age of 15 were classified as having been raised in New York; those arriving at the age of 15 or older, as raised in Puerto Rico. Then three types of intergenerational families were identified as relevant to the socialization in the same-culture or a different-culture hypothesis. There were two groups of families in which the parents and children had the same culture in early socialization; in one group of 11 families both generations spent their formative years in Puerto Rico, while in the second group of 13 families the child and at least one parent were raised in New York; in the third group, the different-culture families (76 families), both parents were raised in one sociocultural setting and the child was raised in a different sociocultural setting.

To examine the socioeconomic hypothesis, fathers, mothers, and children who were graduated from high school were categorized as high education, while those who did not finish high school were categorized as low education. The majority of parent-child linkages (69 for mother-child; 66 for father-child) are those in which the parent and child had disparate educational attainment: the parent had low education and the child had high education. In the remaining parent-child linkages the parent and child had a similar education: in 11 parent-child linkages both parents and the child had low education, while in 20 mother-child and 23 father-child linkages the parent and child both had high education. While the small size of the sample limits the ability to refine further the independent variables of age at arrival in New York or level of education and it limits too the ability to examine simultaneously the socialization and socioeconomic hypotheses, the data do provide a unique opportunity to investigate the conditions affecting intergenerational transmission in ethnic identity among immigrant Puerto Rican families.

The analysis of conditions affecting intergenerational transmission parallels the earlier findings on the factors affecting ethnic identity: socialization and socioeconomic conditions are used to examine the language variables, the socioeconomic condition only is used to examine values, and the socialization conditions only to examine self-identity. To simplify the presentation of a complex set of findings we have chosen to focus on one measure from each ethnic identity domain. Table 4.4 presents the correlations between parent and child under varying sociocultural and socioeconomic conditions for language spoken, familism, and attitudinal preferences for Puerto Rican or American culture or objects.

Continuity in ethnic identity, we have hypothesized, will be greater when parent and child had their early socialization experiences in a common culture or were in a similar social class position. Both hypotheses are consistent with the findings relating to the language spoken. When the parents were raised in Puerto Rico and their child raised in New York, there was a rupturing of intergenerational continuity in the language spoken. The language the parents used in speaking to their spouses, children, and friends was not related to the language used by their children with the same set of persons in their own families. When both parents and children were raised in Puerto Rico and when both parents and children were raised in New York, the more often the parents used Spanish with spouses, children, and friends,

TABLE 4.4

Correlations of Ethnic Identity Variables for Intergenerationally Linked Parent and Child Re-Examined Under Varying Conditions

	Correlations	
Ethnic Identity Variable by Relevant Condition	*Adult Child with Mother*	*Adult Child with Father*
Language Spoken by Socialization Context		
Parent P.R. raised	−.09	−.12
Child N.Y. raised		
Parent P.R. raised	.28	.34
Child P.R. raised		
Parent N.Y. raised	.27	.29
Child N.Y. raised		
Language Spoken by Socioeconomic Level		
Parent low education	.13	.03
Child high education		
Parent low education	.29	.35
Child low education		
Parent high education	.23	.25
Child high education		
Familism by Socioeconomic Level		
Parent low education	.07	.10
Child high education		
Parent low education	−.04	.05
Child low education		
Parent high education	.21	−.01
Child high education		
Attitudinal Preferences by Socialization Context		
Parent P.R. raised	.05	.13
Child N.Y. raised		
Parent P.R. raised	.04	.64
Child P.R. raised		
Parent N.Y. raised	.45	.37
Child N.Y. raised		

the more often their children used Spanish with their spouses, children, and friends. Although the correlations are small when the socialization context was the same, they do differ significantly from the correlations when the parents and children were raised in different cultural settings. The evidence is consistent also with the socioeconomic hypothesis. Familial continuity was greater when parent and child both had similar educational levels, whether high or low, than when the parent and child had different educational levels. The preponderance of evidence from the other two language measures, not shown in Table 4.4, also supports both the socialization context and socioeconomic hypotheses as conditions affecting familial transmission of knowledge of English and knowledge of Spanish.

Since the value domain of ethnic identity is related primarily to education, we turn our attention now to the socioeconomic hypothesis. In contrast to the supportive findings in the language domain, the data on familism provide no support for the socioeconomic hypothesis. While a seemingly high correlation does appear in the mother-child linkage when both had high education, no pattern emerges when these correlations are examined in conjunction with the other general value measure, fatalism, or with individual modernity orientation. The correlations fluctuate randomly and insignificantly under varying socioeconomic conditions.

For the final set of ethnic identity dimensions, self-identity, once again the relevance of the socialization hypothesis is examined. In three of the four comparisons, the correlation between the parent's and child's preferences for Puerto Rico was greater for parents and children raised in a similar sociocultural environment than for parents raised in Puerto Rico and children raised in New York. Not only are the three correlations for parents and children raised in similar settings in the predicted direction, but they also differ significantly from the correlations in the situation of parents and children raised in different sociocultural contexts. Data from the other two self-identity measures, subjective affiliation and subjective closeness, are generally consistent with this supportive pattern of findings.

In summary, to examine the puzzling findings demonstrating the absence of intergenerational family transmission, we began by formulating two hypotheses pertaining to conditions under which intergenerational transmission in ethnic identity could increase: *familial transmission in immigrant families is affected by the cultural context of early socialization experiences and by socioeconomic positions in society*. These hypotheses derive from social science research focusing upon cultural changes among immigrants and from our own analysis of factors, at the individual level, affecting the ethnic identity of the mothers, fathers, and children. Accordingly, the correlations between the parent and child levels of ethnic identity were examined under varying socialization contexts and under varying socioeconomic conditions. The predominant pattern of findings from both the language and self-identity domains of ethnic identity is consistent with the hypotheses. With the exception of the value domain of ethnic identity, intergenerational continuity of ethnic identity was greater when both parents and children were raised in Puerto Rico or when both parents and children were raised in New York than when parents were raised in Puerto Rico and their children raised in New York; also, the intergenerational transmission of ethnic identity was greater for parents and children both of low education or both of high education than for parents of low education and children of high education. While these findings must be cautiously evaluated, they do provide a clue to the puzzle posed in Table 4.3: familial continuity was largely absent because a substantial majority of our intergenerational families represented parents and children raised in different sociocultural settings and of different socioeconomic status. Thus, underlying conditions selectively affect what is transmitted between generations within families.

SUMMARY AND CONCLUSIONS

Our effort to capture the rich diversity of the concept of ethnic identity dealt with the respondents' language ability and use of both English and Spanish, traditional Puerto Rican values of familism and fatalism, orientation toward modernity, and self-identification with Puerto Rican and mainland cultural experiences. Then with ethnic identity as its focus, we posed questions pertaining to the differences between generations, factors affecting ethnic identity in each generation, and the intergenerational continuity of ethnic identity. Chapter I showed that such questions, whether or not they focus upon ethnic identity, are of general and fundamental relevance to intergenerational research.

The findings pertinent to intergenerational differences indicate clearly the substantial differences between the generations in the direction expected, but with one exception: the shaping of the child generation's ethnic identity away from their Puerto Rican roots and toward the North American mainland culture. The child generation distanced themselves from the parent generation, adapting their ethnic identity in ways congruent with the host society. The exception to this process, however, is exceptionally important: both generations were similar in perceiving themselves as Puerto Ricans in values and feelings associated with the homeland. This exception, considered in relation to the prevailing pattern of intergenerational differences in ethnic identity, makes it clear that the child generation's strongest link to their ethnic roots was their self-concept, their subjective ethnic identification. Parent and married-child generations were alike, symbolically, in their ethnic self-concept, the latter generation turning toward biculturalism without stripping themselves of all residues of Puerto Rican heritage.

Proceeding from the idea that ethnic identity is influenced by receptivity to external influences of the host environment and by length of exposure to the new society, we considered an array of independent variables. The main findings indicate that both education and age at arrival in New York City had significant independent effects upon the ethnic identity of mothers, fathers, and children. Once these variables were controlled, the many other independent variables considered in the analysis proved to be no longer significantly related to ethnic identity; this highlights the need to go beyond bivariate analysis in such research.

We need to make one observation relating to the influences shaping ethnic identity: The fundamental importance of the age at arrival variable implicates issues of substance and method. The younger the person was at arrival, the more receptive he/she was to influences of the host society. One mechanism underlying the consistent finding of significant differences in ethnic identity between generations, when generations are defined by birthplace of the respondent and his/her ancestors, is generational differences in age at arrival. Moreover, age at arrival is also a significant variable affecting ethnic identity within generations differentiated by the birthplace criterion. Thus, ethnic identity cannot be equated simply with birthplace of respondent and his/her ancestors; rather it varies according to the age when the migrant was first exposed to the new set of influences in the host environment.

Although education is related to ethnic identity, the closest the high school graduates in the study came to self-identity as American was by identifying themselves as part-Puerto Rican and part-American. We believe the vitality of biculturalism explains this finding. During approximately the last 15 years there has been a renewed awareness of and appreciation for the contribution of immigrant groups to a pluralistic American society. This development began with the issue of civil rights in the political and economic arenas and now extends into the arena of mass culture where the publicity surrounding "roots"* reaffirmed interest and pride in cultural traditions. In

---

*This is in reference to Alex Haley's *Roots*, a book serialized by the American Broadcasting Company. ABC estimates that 130,000,000 persons (60,000,000 homes) saw the televised program on at least one evening when

the ethnic neighborhoods of cities with large concentrations of immigrant populations, such as New York, the mass culture's celebration of ethnicity legitimizes traditional ethnic-day events from parades and the paying of homage to historical personages in the ingroup, to "soul" food festivities, art displays, concerts, and athletic events. Such events are a part of the political structure of the locale and represent the collective products of a multitude of ethnically based organizations operating in the broader context of changes in New York City, as described in Chapter III. Thus, the celebration of ethnicity is an organizational phenomenon.

Graduation from high school projects the person into the celebration of ethnicity through the medium of organizations. Such exposure tends to stabilize the strength of ethnic self-identity. Here we apply to our study the prevailing finding that socioeconomic status is directly related to the number of voluntary organizations to which a person belongs.[14] The suggestion is that persons with more education participate more in their own ethnically based organizations or in organizations which have direct relevance to their ethnicity; whether the organization is an action group pursuing goals external to itself or an expressive group focusing upon sociability among the members, the celebration of ethnicity is inextricably tied to group participation.[15] The search for factors influencing ethnic identity in both generations led us to alter the original overly simple assumption that the host society's environment uniformly represents a nonethnic force. If Puerto Rico is being Americanized, then New York City is being Hispanicized.

The absence of significant correlations between the parent and married-child generations in the various domains of ethnic identity was a puzzle. To shed light upon the puzzle we began by focusing upon the two factors independently influencing ethnic identity, age at arrival in New York City and education, and considered them according to their broader sociocultural meaning. Thus, age at arrival signifies the cultural context in which the respondents experienced early socialization: if they were younger at age on arrival in New York City, the context was New York City; if older, the context was Puerto Rico. We reasoned further that if parent and child shared their context of early socialization, then intergenerational continuity would occur; there would be less continuity if there was no sharing in the context of early socialization. The underlying idea was that communication between parents and children tends to be disrupted when there are cultural differences in their early socialization experience.

---

it was first aired; at least 85 percent of the United States population viewed some part of the series.

A similar line of reasoning was used in formulating the relevance of education to intergenerational continuity, with the awareness that age at arrival directs attention to past events in early socialization, and education reflects the respondent's current socioeconomic position. We reasoned that similarity in socioeconomic status between parents and children would be conducive to intergenerational continuity; differences in socioeconomic status would diminish continuity. Once again, the underlying idea was that communication between parents and children would be disrupted when there were sharp differences in their socioeconomic status. Accordingly, the correlations between the levels of parents and children of ethnic identity were examined under varying contexts of early socialization and under varying socioeconomic conditions.

Intergenerational continuity in the language domain appears when both parents and their children experienced their early socialization in the same places, and when their educational levels are similar. It diminishes when they do not share a place of early socialization and when they are dissimilar in their education. In contrast, neither place of early socialization nor education affects the intergenerational continuity of cultural values or of modernity. Intergenerational continuity reappears in the self-identity domain when there is intergenerational sharing in the place of early socialization. The continuity of such preferences, however, is not affected by intergenerational similarities or differences in educational levels. This means that the pervasive absence of intergenerational continuity characteristic of the study group as a whole is caused by the fact that in a substantial majority of the families, parents and children were raised in different sociocultural settings and are now of different socioeconomic status. It also means that when either of the two conditions are met, similar cultural settings of socialization and similar socioeconomic status, there is more than the suggestion of a process of selective continuity, that is, continuity with respect to some things but not others. The selective continuity approach we embraced in the first chapter as the best method to lead us to appropriate empirical conclusions begins to show promise in this chapter. In subsequent chapters which examine other facets of the lives of the persons we have studied, attention once again will focus upon the same two underlying conditions likely to promote intergenerational continuity.

REFERENCES

1. Gordon, M. M. 1964. *Assimilation in American Life: The Role of Race, Religion, and National Origins*. New York: Oxford University Press.

Greeley, A. M. 1974. "An Alternative Perspective for Studying American Ethnicity," in *Ethnicity in the United States*. New York: John Wiley and Sons, pp. 291-317.

Berry, J. W. 1980. "Acculturation as Varieties of Adaption," in *Acculturation: Theory, Models and Some New Findings*, A. Padilla (ed.), Boulder, CO: Westview Press.

Padilla, A. M. 1980. "The Role of Cultural Awareness and Ethnic Loyalty in Acculturation," in *Acculturation: Theory, Models and Some New Findings*, A. Padilla (ed.), Boulder, CO: Westview Press.

2. DeVos, G. 1975. "Ethnic Pluralism: Conflict and Accommodation," in *Ethnic Identity: Cultural Continuities and Change*, G. DeVos and L. Romanucci-Ross (eds.). California: Mayfield Publishing Co.

Clark, M.; S. Kaufman, and R. C. Pierce. 1976. "Explorations of Acculturation: Toward a Model of Ethnic Identity." *Human Organization* 35: 231-238.

Singh, V. P. 1977. "Some Theoretical and Methodological Problems in the Study of Ethnic Identity: A Cross-Cultural Perspective." *Annals of the New York Academy of Sciences*, 285: 32-45.

3. Rogler, L. H. and A. B. Hollingshead. 1965. *Trapped: Families and Schizophrenia*. New York: John Wiley and Sons.

Tumin, M. M. and A. Feldman. 1961. *Social Class and Social Change in Puerto Rico*. Princeton, NJ: Princeton University Press.

Cochran, T. C. 1959. *The Puerto Rican Businessman: A Study in Cultural Change*. Philadelphia: University of Pennsylvania Press.

Steward, J. H. et al. 1956. *The People of Puerto Rico: A Study in Social Anthropology*. Urbana, IL: University of Illinois Press.

Lewis, O. 1968. *A Study of Slum Culture: Backgrounds for La Vida*. New York: Random House.

4. Fitzpatrick, J. 1971. *Puerto Rican Americans: The Meaning of Migration to the Mainland*. Englewood Cliffs, NJ: Prentice-Hall.

Torres-Matrullo, C. M. 1980. "Acculturation, Sex-Role Values and Mental Health Among Mainland Puerto Ricans," in A. Padilla (ed.), *Acculturation: Theory, Models and Some New Findings*. Boulder, CO: Westview Press.

Padilla, E. 1958. *Up From Puerto Rico*. New York: Columbia University Press.

5. Rogler, C. 1940. *Comerío: A Study of a Puerto Rican Town*. Lawrence, KS: University of Kansas Press.

6. Manners, R. A. 1956. "Tabará: Subcultures of a Tobacco and Mixed Crops Municipality." In J. H. Steward (ed.), *The People of Puerto Rico: A Study in Social Anthropology*. Urbana, IL: University of Illinois Press.

7. Maldonado-Denis, M. 1969. "Puerto Ricans: Protest or Submission," *Annals of the American Academy of Political and Social Sciences*, 382.

8. Smith, D. H., and A. Inkeles. 1966. "The OM Scale: A Comparative Socio-Psychological Measure of Individual Modernity." *Sociometry* 29 (December): 353-377.

9. Clark, M.; S. Kaufman, and R. C. Pierce, see note 2.

Singh, V. P., see note 2.

Keefe, S. E. 1980. "Acculturation and the Extended Family among Urban Mexican-Americans." In A. M. Padilla (ed.), *Acculturation: Theory, Models and Some New Findings*. Boulder, CO: Westview Press.

Olmedo, E. L. 1980. "Quantitative Models of Acculturation: An Overview." In A. M. Padilla (ed.), *Acculturation: Theory, Models and Some New Findings*. Boulder, CO: Westview Press.

Padilla, A. M. 1980. "The Role of Cultural Awareness and Ethnic Loyalty in Acculturation." In A. M. Padilla (ed.), *Acculturation: Theory, Models and Some New Findings*. Boulder, CO: Westview Press.

Szapocznik, J. and W. Kurtines. 1980. "Acculturation, Biculturalism, and Adjustment among Urban Americans." In A. M. Padilla (ed.). *Acculturation: Theory, Models and Some New Findings*. Boulder, CO: Westview Press.

Szapocznik, J. et al. 1979. "Theory and Measurement of Acculturation." *Interamerican Journal of Psychology* 12: 113-130.

Torres-Matrullo, C. 1980. "Acculturation, Sex-Role Values and Mental Health among Mainland Puerto Ricans." In A. M. Padilla (ed.), *Acculturation: Theory, Models and Some New Findings*. Boulder, CO: Westview Press.

Rogler, L. H. 1978. Help Patterns, the Family, and Mental Health: Puerto Ricans in the United States. *International Migration Review* 12(2): 248-259.

11. Troll, L. and V. Bengtson. 1979. "Generations in the Family," in W. R. Burr et al., (eds.) *Contemporary Theories About the Family*, Vol. 1. New York: The Free Press.

12. *Ibid*. p. 139.

13. *Ibid*.

14. Wright, C. R. and H. H. Hyman. 1958. "Voluntary Association Memberships of American Adults: Evidence from National Sample Surveys." *American Sociological Review* 23: 284-294.

15. Rogler, L. H. 1972. *Migrant in the City: The Life of a Puerto Rican Action Group*. New York: Basic Books, Inc.

V

Spouse Relationships

In the course of daily life, families perform tasks, make decisions, and enjoy leisure activities. Sociocultural groups, however, differ in the degree to which husbands and wives participate together. In the traditions of Puerto Rican culture, gender has always been attached to specific tasks: there was *trabajo de hombre* (men's work) and *trabajo de mujer* (women's work); men were the cutters of sugarcane, the cultivators of land, and the muleteers; women were the caretakers of the home and the children. Throughout the island, the sharpness of the gender distinction in work varied by economic regions, by the occupation of the head of the household, by the economic importance of the wife, and by the educational level of the spouses, but the gender distinction itself was part of a general cultural pattern of sex-role segregation between men and women. On the mainland, in contrast, students of Puerto Rican life have noted that exposure to new influences in the host society has changed the role relationships between husbands and wives.[1] The direction of change is assumed to be away from the sharp segregation of conjugal roles toward a more egalitarian marital union in which spouses share tasks, decision-making, and leisure activities. The direction of the change may be as it is assumed to be, but to our knowledge no published study has demonstrated the direction of the change through systematically collected data.

This study collected data on spouse relationships in the performance of household tasks, in the making of decisions, and in participation in leisure activities. Interview items reflecting such dimensions were taken from Hill's intergenerational research[2] and modified and supplemented for our own purposes. These data permit us to examine directly the assumption that intergenerational change moves toward more egalitarian spouse relationships. Thus, we begin by presenting a detailed account of similarities and differences in relationships between the parent and child generations. Subsequently, we turn our attention to identifying factors affecting spouse relationships within each generation. This task is inherently more complex than that in the last chapter which examined ethnic identity. Ethnic identity focuses upon the specific attitudes and behavior of a single person or individual; spouse relationships focus upon the structure of two-person interactions. Marital relationships reflect the interpersonal dynamics of the partners, the organized conjoining of their intricate behaviors.

The design of our study permits also the examination of the degree of intergenerational continuity for three dimensions of spouse relationships: performing household chores, making decisions, and participating in leisure activities. As noted in Chapter I, intergenerational studies of parents and children living in the same sociocultural system have generally found a pattern of selective continuity — continuity with respect to some things but not to others. Chapter IV reported pervasive discontinuity with respect to ethnic identity. Here we broaden our search for characteristics involved in selective continuity by examining spouse relationships and continue our effort to identify underlying conditions which promote selective continuity.

SPOUSE RELATIONSHIPS IN THE PARENT
AND CHILD GENERATIONS

The measures of relationships between husbands and wives used in this study are based on the wives' reports, that is, the mothers in the parent generation and the daughters (or daughters-in-law) in the child generation were asked whether the wife alone, the husband alone, or the husband and wife together usually did the household tasks, usually made the final decisions, and usually participated in various leisure activities. Each wife's report reflects her perception of the spousal relationship within the family and, as such, is a meaningful perspective on marital relationships. This strategy of interviewing the wife is consistent with the majority of research studies in this area. We are aware, however, that the husbands' reports as well as the reports of neutral observers are alternative perspectives.[3]

The measures of spouse relationships include a multiplicity of items. In addition to the total score for each measure, Table 5.1 presents a sampling of items from each of the three indexes for both the parent and the child generations. The items provide specific illustrations of which family functions are shared and where the greatest changes in sharing behaviors between the parent and child generations have occurred. Beginning with the overall scores for both generations, we note that the child generation, predominantly raised in New York, displayed more egalitarian marital unions than the parent generation, predominantly raised in Puerto Rico. In the sharing of both

TABLE 5.1

Comparison of Parent and Child Generations: Married Couples Sharing Household Tasks, Decision-Making, and Leisure Activities

(in percent)

Three Dimensions of Spouse Relationships	Parent Generation	Child Generation
Household Tasks Overall	22*	34
Washing clothes	8	12
Fixing breakfast	9	15
Bathing children	12	19
Repairing furniture	17	26
Cleaning car	14	30
Purchasing expensive items	50	76
Decisions Overall	51	58
Which house/apt. to take	71	83
Where to go for picnics/outings	65	81
What improvements to make around the house	53	55
How much life insurance to take	44	42
Whether wife should work	26	35
Whether husband should change his job	23	35
Leisure Activities Overall	71*	81
Visiting relatives	79	90
Going to beach/picnics	66	89
Going to the movies	65	85
Visiting friends	67	81
Watching television	61	72
Going for strolls	49	56
Attending sporting events	29	48
Attending community meetings	35	36

*Significant differences between parent and child using paired t-tests, $p < .05$. Significance only examined for overall indices.

household tasks and leisure activities, the intergenerational differences are statistically significant. Thus, the assumption made by students of Puerto Rican life in the United States that intergenerational change moves toward more egalitarian husband-wife relationships is supported by our data. Even at the level of specific items there is confirmation for this assumption.

Table 5.1 shows that among the three family functions the greatest sex-role segregation occurred in the performance of household tasks: less than one-quarter of such responsibilities was shared by husbands and wives in the parent generation, compared to one-third in the child generation. In both the parent and child generations, husbands and wives participated together in approximately three-fourths of leisure activities and in slightly more than one-half of decision-making. Thus, if the model of role segregation is taken as the traditional Puerto Rican pattern, there was a stronger adherence to such a pattern in the performance of household tasks than in leisure activities and in decision-making.

The six household tasks presented in Table 5.1 were selected from an inventory of 23 tasks for which data were collected. As a matter of common knowledge of the culture, three of the tasks can be considered the wife's responsibility (doing laundry, preparing breakfast, and bathing children) and three the responsibility of the husband (repairing furniture, cleaning the car, and making major purchases). The distinction between the tasks of men and women is culturally appropriate and also useful in understanding patterns of sex-role segregation and intergenerational change in such patterns.

Two major findings relate to the extent of sharing and the degree to which the task is dominated by one or the other spouse. First, the least amount of sharing appeared among the female tasks, not only in terms of the three tasks in Table 5.1 but also among other traditionally defined female tasks not reported in the table (ironing, doing dishes, cooking, cleaning). Whether the focus is upon the male household tasks, reported in Table 5.1, or upon other tasks, not reported in the table (repairing the car, making major home improvements, disciplining the children), male household tasks were more likely to be shared than female household tasks.

A second perspective is gained when we focus upon the spouse who usually performed the household tasks when they were not shared. In approximately 85 percent of the married couples, female tasks were performed by the wife, in 10 percent they were shared, and in 5 percent the tasks were usually done by the husband. With respect to male tasks in which husbands dominate, in only approximately 60 percent of the couples were such tasks performed by the husband, while in 20 percent they were shared, and in 20 percent they were usually carried out by the wife. Two items were omitted before making this specific comparison – disciplining the children and making expensive purchases – since a high level of sharing is evident in these two male tasks. It is clear that wives were more likely to take on responsibility for performing traditional male tasks than the husbands were to take responsibility for traditional female tasks.

As noted earlier, the child generation was more egalitarian in the performance of household tasks than was the parent generation. This pattern is evident also when we examine specific household tasks. While the pattern of increasing egalitarianism in the child generation was evident among both traditionally defined male and female household tasks, Table 5.1 indicates that the greatest changes in sharing behavior were evident among the traditional male tasks. This finding is consistent with the finding already presented that there was greater flexibility among male tasks than female tasks both in terms of sharing and in terms of wives more than husbands assuming responsibility for non-traditional tasks.

When applied to decision-making, the prevailing view of the island-based model of husband-wife role segregation stresses the superior authority of the man as a by-product of the Spanish colonial culture that influenced family life in Puerto Rico: the husband makes decisions without consulting the wife; the wife is subordinate to the authority of the husband.[4] This view of decision-making means that there is not only very little sharing but also male domination. On both counts the data from our study contrast sharply with the island-based model. Table 5.1 presents the six items that were used in constructing the index of husband-wife sharing in decision-making. A majority of the husbands and wives in our families shared the making of three decisions. For two of these decisions, regarding where to live and the location for picnics or outings, almost three-quarters of the married couples made the decision jointly, whereas only slightly more than half of the couples decided jointly on improvements around the house. Not only does the high level of egalitarianism contradict the role-segregation model, but even when these three decisions were not shared, the husband did not dominate the decision-making. In fact, when decisions were not made jointly, the wife was twice as likely as the husband to make these decisions.

The remaining three decisions, but especially the two decisions pertaining to employment, reflect considerably less sharing. Only about 30 percent of the married couples decided jointly if the wife should work or if the husband should change his job. While these decisions do not reflect a high percentage of sharing, neither do they reflect the superior authority of the male. In fact, there is only one area in which the majority of the husbands usually made the decision: in two-thirds of the married couples the husband usually decided whether or not to change jobs, in 29 percent the decision was shared, and in 5 percent the wife usually decided. Although the decision about the wife's employment reflects a similar low level of sharing, the husband did not dominate. In 50 percent of the couples, this decision was usually made by the wife, in 30 percent the decision was shared, while in 20 percent the husband usually made the decision. While the husband had a more important role in the wife's employment decision than the wife had in his employment decision, the overall pattern of findings is not consistent with a role-segregation model grounded in the superior authority of the male.

For five of the six decisions, the child generation showed greater joint decision-making than the parent generation. The greatest changes between the child and parent generations relate to two shared decisions (choice of residence and location for picnics or outings) and to the single decision in which husbands dominated (whether or not to change his job). This change toward greater egalitarianism in the child generation was not solely at the husband's expense. In comparison to the husbands in the parent generation, the husbands in the child generation played a less important role in the decision of where to live and on the husband's employment and were more likely to share such decisions with their wives. However, the wives in the child generation played a less important role than the wives in the parent generation in the decision of location of picnics or outings, by now sharing this decision with their husbands. Thus, both men and women in the child generation were changing toward a more egalitarian relationship in decision-making than their parents.

The greatest discrepancy between the model of role segregation and the relationship between husbands and wives occurred in participation in leisure activities. The full inventory of eight items included in the leisure activities index is shown in Table 5.1. The highest level of joint participation was found in visits to relatives. In 85 percent of the married couples, the spouses visited relatives together. Although husbands and wives were slightly less likely to participate together in such activities as going to the beach, picnics, movies, and visiting friends, we still find that these were joint activities in three-quarters of the couples. Sharing was evident also in watching television (66 percent) and going strolling (53 percent). Overall, we found that a majority of the couples shared six of the eight activities which ranged from visiting relatives to activities inside and outside the home. The two exceptions were attendance at sporting events and community meetings. Although a sizeable minority of the couples shared these activities, over 60 percent did not.

An important characteristic that distinguishes these latter activities is that they come closest to being sex-typed. While a few wives did report going to sporting events alone, in almost 50 percent of the couples, going to sporting events was an activity in which only males participated. Although the level of sex-typing is lower for community meetings, the pattern is reversed. In almost 42 percent of the couples, attending community meetings was an activity which engaged only the wives. When there was no sharing with respect to the other six activities, the husbands and the wives participated in them at more similar levels.

The greater sharing of the child-generation couples, compared to those in the parent generation, is evident in seven of the eight specific activities. The one exception was the sex-typed activity of attending community meetings where no intergenerational change has occurred, but for the other sex-typed activity (attendance at sporting events) intergenerational change was dramatic: 29 percent of the parent generation, compared to 48 percent of the child generation, attended sporting events together. The decline in sex-role segregation in the child generation indicates the wife's sharing with the husband his interest in sporting events. This change of 19 percentage points is surpassed, but only slightly, by the changes of 23 percentage points between the generations in going to the beach or picnics together and in 20 percentage points in going to the movies together. Changes in these activities which are not sex-typed or one-sided reflect the fact that the spouses have shifted from engaging in these activities alone to engaging in them together.

In summary, the level of joint spouse activity in the two generations who have lived on the mainland for almost three decades differed markedly from the island-based cultural modality of sharp role segregation. This was particularly notable in leisure activities in which three-quarters of the activities involved joint participation of husband and wife and in decision-making in which slightly more than one-half of the decisions were shared. The greatest change away from the island pattern and toward a more egalitarian cultural norm was evident in the child generation. The pattern of more sharing in the child generation than in the parent generation reflects changes in the behavior of both wives and husbands. Both partners have become more involved in sharing leisure activities and decision-making. The major exception to this pattern occurred in the traditionally female household tasks which were still done predominantly by the wives. The greater sharing in household tasks in the child generation reflected the wives' greater involvement with their husbands in those household tasks traditionally done by the male.

FACTORS AFFECTING SPOUSE RELATIONSHIPS

As noted in Chapter III, an important focus of interest in studies of immigrant groups has been on changing cultural characteristics as immigrants become integrated into American society. Very little research, however, has examined the relevance of the immigrants' cultural characteristics to the relationship between husbands and wives. In this section, we turn our attention to the role that culture plays in shaping marital relationships in household tasks, decision-making, and leisure activities. We shall examine here two major perspectives on the role of culture. One perspective, most clearly developed in the literature on immigrant families, views culture as having a direct effect on spouse relationships. A second perspective, most clearly developed in the cross-national literature on decision-making, views culture as having an indirect effect on spouse relationships.

Fitzpatrick's writing[5] on immigrant Puerto Rican families is consistent with the first perspective that cultural characteristics directly affect spouse relationships. The argument is that the integration of immigrants into American society includes exposure to the egalitarian norms of American culture. Egalitarian norms clash with the traditional norms of role segregation and male superiority associated with the influence of Spanish culture in Puerto Rico. The impact of exposure to the egalitarian norms of the host society prevails over tradition as cultural norms change toward egalitarianism. Thus, integration into American society is associated with greater sharing between husbands and wives among immigrant families. Earlier chapters examined a variety of cultural characteristics relevant to the above argument, including language knowledge and usage, familism and fatalistic values, modernity orientation, and self-identification. Our examination of differences in ethnic identity between the parent and child generations and the analysis of factors affecting ethnic identity indicates that the greater the integration into American society (as reflected by higher socioeconomic achievement and earlier exposure to the sociocultural environment of New York), the greater the acceptance of American characteristics in language, values, and self-identification. Changes in such characteristics, particularly in values, are consistent with the explanation based upon the relevance of exposure to the egalitarian norms of American society. The argument for the direct importance of culture, however, goes beyond such findings and entails an examination of a possible direct relationship between cultural expressions of ethnic identity and the strength of the sharing patterns between spouses.

In terms of our study group, the question becomes: were parent- or child-generation married couples who expressed a weak identification with Puerto

Rican culture more likely to share household tasks, decision-making, and leisure activities than those couples who expressed a strong identification with Puerto Rican culture? No studies, to our knowledge, have examined this question for immigrant Puerto Ricans, but there are recent studies of two other Hispanic groups in the United States: Hawkes and Taylor[6] interviewed 76 Mexican-American farm laborers on spouse relationships in two areas that parallel our study, decision-making and household tasks. Information was collected also on two cultural characteristics, citizenship status and language spoken in the home. While the authors hypothesized that more egalitarian relationships would be found among citizens as compared to noncitizens and among bilingual speakers as compared to monolingual Spanish speakers, the data revealed no significant relationship between either one of these cultural characteristics and egalitarian spouse relationships. Richmond's findings[7] on Cubans were consistent with Hawkes and Taylor's findings on Mexican Americans. Richmond interviewed 120 Cuban wives and 30 Cuban husbands to collect information on spouse relationships in the areas of decision-making and performance of household tasks and also of their knowledge of English. There was no significant relationship between the spouses' knowledge of English and either measure of husband-wife relationships.

While neither study indicated a direct relationship between immigrant cultural characteristics and spouse relationships, it should be noted that the range of cultural characteristics examined was limited to language and citizenship measures. These studies are limited in their evaluation of this perspective since the argument that cultural integration into American society directly affects spouse relationships is highlighted by the importance of the value component of the culture. A more comprehensive evaluation of the direct importance of cultural characteristics should recognize the multifaceted character of culture and should include measures of values. Thus, our examination of cultural expressions of ethnic identity in Chapter IV relied upon language measures and subjective identification with the Puerto Rican way of life and included values embedded in Puerto Rican culture. In view of the scarcity of research linking different dimensions of ethnic identity to spouse relationships, we now return to the question raised earlier: Were couples expressing less ethnic identification with Puerto Rican culture more likely to share household tasks, decision-making and leisure activities than those couples expressing greater Puerto Rican ethnic identification?

Table 5.2 presents the relationship of the cultural characteristics of the wife and the husband on the one hand, with each of the three measures of spouse relationships, on the other hand. Only four of the 54 correlations for each of the generations are statistically significant. Not only could this small

TABLE 5.2
Zero Order Correlations of Sharing Household Tasks, Decision-Making, and Leisure Activities with Ethnic Identity Characteristics for Parent and Child Generations

Ethnic Identity Characteristics	Sharing Household Tasks		Sharing Decision-Making		Sharing Leisure Activities	
	Parent Generation	Child Generation	Parent Generation	Child Generation	Parent Generation	Child Generation
Wife						
Knowledge of English	.23*	.16	.14	.26*	.15	.11
Knowledge of Spanish	.15	.04	.11	.13	.01	−.03
Language spoken	−.11	−.09	−.01	.01	−.06	−.10
Familism	−.09	−.11	−.08	−.23*	−.21*	−.14
Fatalism	−.09	−.08	−.11	−.10	−.10	−.14
Modernity orientation	.12	.06	.06	.09	.04	.09
Subjective affiliation	−.09	−.08	.14	−.12	−.04	−.13
Subjective closeness	−.12	−.15	.02	.07	−.14	−.01
Attitudinal preferences	−.03	−.05	.06	.03	.02	−.06
Husband						
Knowledge of English	−.01	.09	.13	.09	.04	.08
Knowledge of Spanish	.12	−.09	.12	.16	−.05	.03
Language spoken	−.01	−.15	−.01	−.15	−.04	−.05
Familism	−.03	−.20*	−.01	−.13	−.13	−.12
Fatalism	−.09	−.11	−.04	−.13	−.02	−.22*
Modernity orientation	.21	.06	.13	.01	.01	.12
Subjective affiliation	−.04	−.14	.27*	−.11	.05	.02
Subjective closeness	.08	.04	.11	−.01	.06	−.06
Attitudinal preferences	.04	−.01	.07	.07	.03	−.06

*p < .05

number of significant correlations occur by chance, but also there is no pattern to the findings bearing upon either sex of spouse or type of spouse relationship. The only glimmer of a possible correlational pattern occurs when the correlations are considered within the major domains of ethnic identity — language, values/modernity orientation, and self-identification. For the parent generation, two of the four significant correlations relate to values: the greater the familism of parent-generation wives, the less the sharing of leisure activities; the greater the modernity orientation of parent-generation husbands, the greater the sharing of household tasks. For the child generation, three of the four significant correlations also pertain to values: the greater the familism of child-generation wives, the less the sharing of decision-making; the greater the familism of child-generation husbands, the less the sharing of household tasks; the greater the fatalism of child-generation wives, the less the sharing of leisure activities. When considered in conjunction with the nonsignificance of the other correlations relevant to values in the parent and child generations the findings do not strongly support the proposition that there is a *direct* relationship between cultural values and spouse relationships. Moreover, the significance of the correlations tends to vary randomly with the sex of the spouse and by type of spouse relationship. At the most, the findings highlight the greater salience of the value dimension of culture to spouse relationships than that of the language or self-identification dimensions of culture.

The second major perspective on the role of culture in shaping spouse relationships derives from cross-national research on decision-making. To understand the *indirect* role that culture is hypothesized to play, it is necessary to introduce resource theory. During the 1960s, research on decision-making among marital couples was guided predominantly by resource theory. As formulated by Blood and Wolfe[8] in their widely recognized study *Husbands and Wives*, resource theory hypothesizes that a spouse's power to make decisions within the family is influenced by his/her status in the larger community. Thus, the greater the socioeconomic status of the husband, as measured by educational and occupational levels, the greater the husband's power, and the greater the socioeconomic status of the wife, as measured by her education or employment levels, the greater her power to influence decision-making in the family. Resource theory received considerable support from a series of cross-national decision-making studies in Europe and the United States.[9] The majority of the studies show that the greater the socioeconomic status of the husband, the greater his decision-making power in the family. There are, however, notable contradictory findings. In particular, studies in Greece and Yugoslavia suggested that the greater the husband's socioeconomic resources, the less his power in decision-making within the family. In attempting to solve this paradox, Rodman[10] argued that socioeconomic resources must be evaluated within a cultural context. Cultural norms influence the meaning and definition of socioeconomic resources which, in turn, affect the relationship of socioeconomic resources to spouse relationships in the family. While Rodman's argument highlights the importance of culture, he does not argue that cultural norms directly affect decision-making in the family, as does the first perspective just presented. Rodman argues that cultural norms indirectly affect spouse relationships by providing a context which defines the meaning of socioeconomic characteristics.

To simplify the presentation of his theory of resources in cultural context, Rodman[11] devised a typology of four societies that roughly parallel levels of national economic development. At one extreme, representing low levels of economic development, are patriarchal societies such as India's where prescribed status governs an individual's position in the community. The patriarchal norms are strong and shared by all classes. The inflexibility of such norms make the husband's socioeconomic characteristics irrelevant to decision-making patterns among spouses. As nations begin to industrialize, a modified patriarchal society such as Greece's develops. The basis of individual worth is still prescribed, but the traditional norms emphasizing the superior authority of the man within the family slowly begin to change. Egalitarian norms emphasizing partnership and sharing between spouses emerge in the upper classes. Thus, a man's socioeconomic attributes, reflecting as they do varying degrees of exposure to and socialization into more modern egalitarian attitudes and values, are inversely related to his decision-making power in the family. At a still higher stage of economic development are transitional egalitarian societies such as that of the United States where the patriarchal tradition has undergone substantial change. Egalitarian norms replace patriarchal norms at all levels of society. In this context of pervasive social change, spouse relationships are more flexible and negotiable. Within industrialized societies, an individual's worth is no longer based upon prescribed status but upon socioeconomic achievements. Such achievements then become the basis for negotiation within the family. Thus, a man's socioeconomic status acts as a resource variable in the power relationship between husband and wife: the higher the socioeconomic status, the greater his power in making decisions. At the highest levels of economic development, representing the opposite extreme of patriarchal societies, are egalitarian societies such as Sweden's where egalitarian norms are strong and shared by all classes.

Because egalitarian norms are pervasive, a man's socioeconomic achievements are once again irrelevant to patterns of decision-making within the family.

According to Rodman's typology, the relevance of the husband's socio-economic characteristics to decision-making within the family depends on cultural norms which change as the country becomes industrialized. In both patriarchal and egalitarian societies, where there is little normative flexibility, the socioeconomic attributes of the husband are irrelevant to decision-making. In modified patriarchal societies where the husband's socio-economic attributes represent socialization into more modern attitudes and values, the husband's socioeconomic status is inversely related to his decision-making power. In transitional egalitarian societies where socioeconomic attributes determine the worth and power of the individual in the larger community, the husband's socioeconomic status represents a resource increasing his power in decision-making within the family. Thus, the apparent contradictions of cross-national findings can be resolved if socioeconomic characteristics are evaluated in the cultural context of national development.

Rodman's discussion linking resources and culture is focused primarily on the husband because inconsistent cross-national findings are evident when they are based upon the husband's socioeconomic resources. Cross-national studies examining the resources of the wife have been more consistent. Research on the wife's resources has concentrated predominantly on her employment. The results suggest that women who work, whether in more economically developed nations like the United States and Germany or in less economically developed nations like Yugoslavia or Puerto Rico, have more power in decision-making within the family than women who do not work.[12] The relationship between the wife's education and decision-making, however, has received less attention. Cromwell et al.[13] report for both Mexico and the United States that the higher the wife's education, the less the husband's power. Similar results are reported for Puerto Rico by Weller.[14] Whether the wife's socioeconomic attributes, that is, her employment status or education, are interpreted as representing a socialization experience increasing her exposure to egalitarian norms or as resources increasing her power in decision-making, the results are the same. In both modified patriarchal and transitional egalitarian societies, we expect that the higher the socioeconomic status of the wife, the less the husband's power in decision-making within the family.

Although Rodman's theory of resources in cultural context was designed to resolve contradictory findings in cross-national research, the theory may be relevant to understanding the decision-making patterns of immigrant groups within the United States. Immigration from Latin America is a case in point. The cultural norms of familial relationships within Latin American countries are more traditional than in the United States. Although some modification of traditional male dominance has occurred in Latin America because of urbanization and industrialization, Latin America's society is still one in which historical and religious norms support male domination in the family.[15] Rodman[16] does not explicitly classify any of the Latin American countries. Yet, if Rodman's classification of the United States as a transitional egalitarian society is correct, then the less economically developed Latin American countries would most likely be classified as modified patriarchal societies. In fact, Cromwell et al.[17] in their cross-national study of Mexico and the United States classify Mexico as modified patriarchal while agreeing with Rodman's classification of the United States as transitional egalitarian. Although Puerto Rico is legally a commonwealth of the United States, the level of economic development and cultural norms in Puerto Rico more closely approaches those of Latin American nations than those of the United States. Moreover, Rogler's examination[18] of the literature on research conducted in Puerto Rico would support the classification of Puerto Rico as a modified patriarchal society.

The integration of Puerto Rican immigrants in American society, therefore, can be viewed as a fundamental change in cultural environments from one which favors patriarchal norms to one which favors egalitarian norms. According to Rodman's theory, this type of change alters the qualitative meaning of socioeconomic attributes from that of an indicator reflecting socialization to modern values to an indicator reflecting power resources. Such a change results in there being no simple direct relationship between either socioeconomic attributes or cultural characteristics and the relative power of spouses in the making of decisions. To investigate the utility of Rodman's theory of resources in cultural context in this study, two assumptions about the intergenerational families are made: the sociocultural norms of the parent generation, born and raised in Puerto Rico, are assumed to be more similar to those of the modified patriarchy existing in Puerto Rico; the sociocultural norms of the child generation, born and raised on the mainland, are assumed to be more similar to those of the transitional egalitarianism existing in the United States. These assumptions are consistent with data presented earlier in Chapter IV showing a clear pattern of intergenerational differences in the direction of Americanization of ethnic identity.

Rodman's theory of resources in cultural context leads to the expectation that differences in the ethnic identity of the two generations affect the relationship between socioeconomic attributes and decision-making. In the modified patriarchical context of the parent generation, Rodman's theory would predict that the higher the husband's socioeconomic status, the greater his exposure to modern egalitarian values and, hence, the greater the tendency to share decision-making; while in the transitional egalitarian context of the child generation, the higher the husbands' socioeconomic status, the greater his power resources and hence the less the tendency to share decision-making. Thus, the relationship between the husband's socioeconomic characteristics and egalitarianism in decision-making will be positive for the parent generation and negative for the child generation. On the other hand, the wife's socioeconomic attributes should indicate similar relationships for both generations. Whether the wife's employment or education is interpreted as greater exposure to modern egalitarian values or as increasing her power resources, the results are the same: the greater the wife's socioeconomic status, the more egalitarian the decision-making.

In addition to decision-making, we will examine the sharing of household tasks and leisure activities from the same theoretical perspective. This procedure is justified because, even though Rodman's theory was developed to explain contradictory findings in cross-national research on decision-making, there is nothing inherent in the theory of resources in cultural context which logically restricts its applicability to the decision-making aspect of spouse relationships. If the distinction between modified patriarchy and transitional egalitarian societies represents an important and pressing difference in cultural environments, then other aspects of the spouse relationship should also be affected in ways which parallel the effects upon decision-making. The use of the theory in an intergenerational context expands its utility; the inclusion of additional aspects of spouse relationships comprehensively increases the scope of its focus.

Since the educational and occupational statuses of the spouses are the socioeconomic variables most commonly used in this type of research, they are the ones used in this analysis. Table 5.3 presents separately by generation the effects of the four socioeconomic variables upon the three measures of spouse relationships. The only socioeconomic characteristic that is significant for all three measures of spouse relationships and for both parent and child generations is the education of the wife. Consistent with expectations stemming from Rodman's theory, the higher the educational achievement of the wife, the greater the spouse sharing of household tasks, decision-making, and leisure activities. Once the interrelationships of the wife's employment status with the other socioeconomic characteristics within the family were controlled, her employment status had no direct influence on spouse relationships. In contrast to the greater importance of the wife's education as opposed

TABLE 5.3
Partial Regression Coefficients of Spouse Relationship Variables for Parent and Child Generations[a]

Socioeconomic Independent Variables	Sharing Household Tasks		Sharing Decision-Making		Sharing Leisure Activities	
	Parent Generation	Child Generation	Parent Generation	Child Generation	Parent Generation	Child Generation
Husband education	.001	.005	.004	−.007	−.003	−.000
Husband occupational status	−.000	.000	.010*	−.007*	.000	.000
Wife education	.013*	.021*	.013*	.031*	.012^m	.013*
Wife employment	.014	−.052	.012	.038	−.071	−.063
Adjusted R^2	.075^m	.16*	.17*	.20*	.02	.05

[a]Because of the theoretical importance of family life-cycle characteristics, the family characteristics included as control variables in the above analysis were: duration of present marriage, number of children present in the household, wife's age at first marriage, and marital disruption.

m = Marginal significance at $< .10$

* = $p < .05$

to her employment status, when the husband's socioeconomic characteristics emerged as significant it was the husband's occupational status rather than his education that was relevant. The husband's occupational status was a significant factor affecting decision-making in both the parent and child generations. These significant findings are also consistent with Rodman's theory. The findings on the husband's occupational status did not extend to the other two measures of spouse relationships. Overall, however, the findings demonstrate that Rodman's theory of resources in cultural context had predictive power extending beyond the original cross-national studies. Through Rodman's theory, we can better understand how culture affects the dynamics of spouse relationships within immigrant families.

In summary, we began our examination of factors affecting spouse relationships among immigrant Puerto Rican families with the question of the role culture plays in shaping marital relationships in immigrant famiilies. The first perspective views culture as having a direct effect on spouse relationships. Research taking this perspective is scarce, narrow in its sparse use of culture-relevant variables, and does not support the perspective. While our examination of ethnic identity included a substantially more comprehensive array of culture-relevant variables, the findings are consistent with those of other research, for they provide little or no support for the proposition affirming the direct effect of culture upon spouse relationships. The second perspective views culture as having an indirect, but no less important, effect on spouse relationships. Cultural norms influence the meaning of the spouses' socioeconomic attributes in such a way as to affect the relationship between such attributes and the husband-wife relationships. The strongest support for this perspective is to be found in the spouses' sharing of decision-making, but the findings on the importance of the wife's education in influencing the sharing of household tasks and leisure activities also are consistent with it. Thus, the weight of evidence affirms the important but complex connection between culture and marital relationships in immigrant families.

INTERGENERATIONAL CONTINUITY

The intergenerational research design of our study not only provides information on changes in marital relationships between immigrant parents and their children, but also allows us to examine the extent to which the marital relationships of immigrant parents were related to the marital relationships of their children. In Table 5.4, we present the correlations relating spouse sharing in the parent household to spouse sharing in their child's household.

TABLE 5.4
Correlations of Spouse Relationship Variables for Intergenerationally Linked Parent and Child Under Varying Conditions

		Correlations	
Relevant Conditions	*Sharing Household Tasks*	*Sharing Decision-Making*	*Sharing Leisure Activities*
Ignoring Relevant Conditions	.06	−.05	.06
Socialization Context			
Parent P.R. raised	.02	−.08	.01
Child N.Y. raised			
Parent P.R. raised	.22	.47	.19
Child P.R. raised			
Parent N.Y. raised	.18	.52	.25
Child N.Y. raised			
Socioeconomic Level			
Parent wife low education	.01	−.09	.02
Child wife high education			
Parent wife low education	.41	.15	.39
Child wife low education			
Parent wife high education	.38	.11	.17
Child wife high education			

Following the strategy developed in Chapter IV, we first present these correlations ignoring conditions which may affect the continuity process. None of the three correlations is significant. Consistent with our findings of pervasive discontinuity in ethnic identity in Chapter IV, we find discontinuity in another sphere of life experiences – spouse relationships. Neither in ethnic identity characteristics nor in spouse relationship did we find evidence of "selective continuity." These findings are part of the puzzle of pervasive intergenerational discontinuity we began to address in Chapter IV in the analysis of conditions affecting the familial transmission of ethnic identity. Here we continue to direct attention to this puzzle by seeking to identify conditions which affect intergenerational continuity in husband-wife relationships.

Clues to the discovery of such conditions have been provided by the findings already presented which indicate that being raised in a modified patriarchal society, such as Puerto Rico's, as compared to a transitional egalitarian society such as that of the United States affects the meaning of the socioeconomic attributes the spouses bring to their relationship. Thus, the cultural context of early socialization may once again play an important role: Could it be that intergenerational continuity in the sharing of household tasks, decision-making, and leisure activities is stronger when the parent and child are raised in a similar sociocultural setting than when the parent and child are raised in a different sociocultural setting? Before turning to this question we shall develop an argument linking educational attainment to intergenerational continuity in spouse relationships.

Earlier, we found that the wife's socioeconomic characteristics played a more important role in defining the marital relationship than the husband's socioeconomic characteristics: better-educated wives of both the parent and child generations were more successful in establishing sharing egalitarian relationships with their husbands in the performance of household tasks, in the making of decisions, and in the pursuit of leisure activities than less-educated wives. In contrast, the socioeconomic characteristics of the husband were relevant only in the area of decision-making. The meaning of the wife's education may reflect greater exposure to egalitarian norms in the modified patriarchal society in which the majority of the parent-generation mothers were raised and greater power resources in the transitional egalitarian society in which the majority of the child-generation wives were raised. Both cultural meanings, however, favor more egalitarian marital relationships when the wives had more education. The cultural norms may vary, but the underlying egalitarianism in families of the more educated wives may provide a common foundation which shapes intergenerational continuity. The specific argument we propose is that intergenerational continuity in the sharing of household tasks, decision-making, and leisure activities is stronger when the wives in the two generations have similar, rather than different, educational attainments.

The argument does not negate the important role culture plays in defining the meaning of socioeconomic characteristics. What it does instead is to call attention, once again, to the fact that in both cultural contexts the husband's education does not affect the relationship between husbands and wives, but the wife's education does. With respect to decision-making, the higher occupational status of husbands in the parent generation was associated with greater sharing while the higher occupational status of husbands in the child generation was associated with less sharing. This reversal, which occurred only in decision-making, suggests that the context of socialization, the cultural origins of the persons, acquires special importance in areas strongly imprinted with the tradition of male dominance. By tradition, decision-making is more allied to male dominance than to the performance of household tasks or participation in leisure activities, which are more allied to role segregation. Thus, both the context of socialization and the educational attainment of the wife should be relevant to intergenerational continuity in spouse relationships.

In Table 5.4 the correlations between spouse sharing in the parent generation with the spouse sharing in the child generation are presented under the two conditions of varying socialization contexts and varying wife's education. (Chapter IV explains how these categories were developed.) When parents were raised in Puerto Rico and their child was raised in New York, the pattern of pervasive discontinuity is once again evident: the level of sharing in spouse relationships among the parents was unrelated to the level of sharing in the spouse relationships among their married children. In contrast, for parents and child raised in Puerto Rico and for parents and child raised in New York, the more egalitarian the spouse relationship among the parents, the more egalitarian the spouse relationship among the children. Although only two of the six correlations under conditions of similar socialization contexts differ significantly from correlations under conditions of different socialization contexts, the pattern of all six correlations is in the expected direction. The evidence for the importance of the wife's education was also consistent with the argument presented. The structure of spouse relationships in the parent generation is more strongly related to spouse relationships in the child generation when the wives in both generations had similar educational levels, whether high or low, than when the parent-generation wife had low education and the child-generation wife had high education. The pattern which is established by six comparisons of correlations between similar and different levels of education among wives is in the expected direction, with three significantly different.

In summary, to re-examine the finding of intergenerational discontinuity in spouse relationships we turned to the social science literature focusing upon the role of culture in shaping marital relationships; we then analyzed the study's data to uncover the factors which affect the relationship between husband and wife in each generation. Two factors emerged as important: the cultural context of early socialization experiences, and the wife's education. The parent generation's marital relationships were more closely associated with the child generation's marital relationships when the parents and their children were raised in similar sociocultural contexts than when raised in different settings. Furthermore, this association also became stronger when the wives had similar, rather than different, educational attainment. The findings shed light upon the great complexity of intergenerational processes. Once again, two conditions based in the migration experience of the Puerto Rican families, the cultural change in socialization context and the educational mobility of the wives, were important factors influencing intergenerational continuity.

SUMMARY AND CONCLUSIONS

This chapter examined three important functions performed by husbands and wives: household tasks, decision-making, and leisure activities. In both generations there is more sharing in decision-making and in leisure activities than in the performance of household tasks. In turn, there is increased sharing from the parent to the child generation in all three activities. This latter finding confirms, for the first time, an assumption frequently presented in the relevant literature, namely, that egalitarianism in conjugal relationships among Puerto Rican immigrants increases from one generation to the next within family lineages. However, one related observation needs to be made: the meaning of increased egalitarianism in household tasks must be seen in the specific way in which such tasks are redistributed from one generation to the next. The greatest intergenerational increase in sharing is in the performance of household tasks, but the underlying process involves the wife's performing more traditional male tasks, not the husband's doing traditional female work.

What role does culture play in shaping the sharing of functions between husbands and wives? To answer this question, we first took the perspective that cultural factors *directly* shape the sharing of functions between husbands and wives. Research focusing upon immigrant families which takes this perspective is scarcely to be found; and, when found, the usual procedure is to consider a small number of variables. In contrast, we greatly expanded the range of variables relevant to culture by taking into account language knowledge and usage, familism and fatalism as cultural values, orientation toward modernity, and self-identification — the same cultural variables used in the analysis of ethnic identity in the preceding chapter. Our findings, however, are consistent with those of other research, for they provide little or no support for the proposition that culture directly affects the sharing of functions between husbands and wives.

To pursue the issue further, we then took the perspective that culture *indirectly* shapes role segregation between husbands and wives. From this perspective, culture is not relegated to a less important role. Rather, it is treated as playing an important role in shaping the meaning of socioeconomic variables which do directly affect role segregation. To develop the argument, we drew from Rodman's cross-national theory of husband and wife decision-making, expanded its focus to include the performance of household tasks and leisure activities, and then applied it to the two generations under study. The findings indicate the following: in the parent generation, the higher the husband's occupational status, the greater the sharing of decision-making; in the child generation, the higher the husband's occupational status, the less the sharing of decision-making. The findings are exactly what Rodman's theory would predict, thus suggesting the important indirect role of culture when the husband's socioeconomic status is the focus. Another set of findings, based upon the wife's education as the measure of socioeconomic status, indicates the following: the higher the educational achievements of the wives, the more the sharing between husbands and wives in both generations in the performance of household tasks, decision-making, and leisure activities. Thus, the weight of evidence affirms the important but complex interconnections between culture and marital relations in immigrant families.

Continuing the effort initiated in the preceding chapter, we then sought to examine whether there was selective continuity in spouse relationships and to identify continuity increases. Consistent with the pattern of pervasive discontinuity in ethnic identity, we found discontinuity in spouse relationships. Once again, we turned to the cultural context of early socialization and found that intergenerational continuity, with respect to the sharing of the three functions, is greater when the generations were raised in the same socialization context than when raised in different settings. When raised in the same socialization context, whether Puerto Rico or New York City, variations in the degree of role segregation in the parent generation were directly correlated with such variations in the child generation. Such correlations diminish when parents and children were not raised in the same setting. Then, to examine the impact of education upon intergenerational continuity in role segregation, we focused upon the wives' educational attainments because their education, more than any other variable considered in the preceding analysis, had a uniformly high direct correlation with the degree to which husbands and wives shared the functions: the higher the wife's education, the more the sharing. When the educational accomplishments of the wives in both generations were similar intergenerational continuity in role segregation was greater than when they were dissimilar. Intergenerational similarity in the wives' educational level increased intergenerational correlations in role segregation. Along with the cultural context of early socialization, education was found, once again, to increase our understanding of intergenerational continuity.

The findings in this chapter and our efforts to understand them parallel those in the preceding chapter. There we observed marked differences in the ethnic identity of the two generations, sought to identify variables affecting ethnic identity, documented pervasive intergenerational discontinuity in ethnic identity, and examined the conditions under which intergenerational continuity in ethnic identity increases. Here we observed marked differences in the degree of role segregation in the marital unions between the two generations, sought to identify variables affecting role segregation, documented pervasive intergenerational discontinuity in marital role segregation, and examined the conditions under which intergenerational continuity in role segregation increased. In comparison to the parent generation, the husbands and wives in the child generation had a substantially stronger bicultural ethnic identity and less role segregation or more sharing in marital functions. Chapter IV's first recognition of the puzzle of the lack of intergenerational continuity regarding ethnic identity, is further compounded by Chapter V's demonstration of the lack of intergenerational continuity in role segregation. But if the puzzle grows, the solutions proposed also attain strength. Intergenerational continuity is ruptured because the migration experiences sharply separate the two generations in the cultural settings of their early socialization while creating disparities between the generations in their educational attainments. The educational achievements of the child generation are the focus of Chapter VI.

REFERENCES

1. Fitzpatrick, J. P. 1971. *Puerto Rican Americans: The Meaning of Migration to the Mainland*. Englewood Cliffs, NJ: Prentice Hall.
2. Hill, R. 1970. *Family Development in Three Generations*. Cambridge, MA: Schenkman Publishing Co.
3. Olson, D. H. and R. E. Cromwell. 1975a. "Power in Families" in R. E. Cromwell and D. H. Olson (eds.), *Power in Families*. New York: John Wiley and Sons.

   Olson, D. H. and R. E. Cromwell. 1975b. "Methodological Issues in Family Power" in R. E. Cromwell and D. H. Olson (eds.), *Power in Families*. New York: John Wiley and Sons.

   Safilios-Rothschild, C. 1970. "The Study of Family Power Structure: A Review 1960-1969." *Journal of Marriage and the Family* 32 (November): 539-552.

   Safilios-Rothschild, C. 1972. "Answer to Stephen J. Bahr's 'Comment on the Study of Family Power Structure: A Review 1960-1969.'" *Journal of Marriage and the Family* 34 (May):245-246.

   Sprey, J. 1972. "Family Power Structure: A Critical Comment." *Journal of Marriage and the Family* 40 (May): 413-421.

   Bahr, S. J. 1972. "Comment on 'The Study of Family Power Structure: A Review 1960-1969.'" *Journal of Marriage and the Family* 34 (May): 239-243.
4. Fitzpatrick, see note 1.
5. *Ibid*.
6. Hawkes, G. R. and M. Taylor. 1975. "Power Structure in Mexican and Mexican-American Farm Labor Families." *Journal of Marriage and the Family* 37 (November): 807-811.
7. Richmond, M. L. L. 1976. "Beyond Resource Theory: Another Look at Factors Enabling Women to Affect Family Interaction." *Journal of Marriage and the Family* 38 (May): 257-266.
8. Blood, R. O. and D. M. Wolf. 1960. *Husbands and Wives*. New York: The Free Press.
9. Rodman, H. 1972. "Marital Power and the Theory of Resources in Cultural Context." *Journal of Comparative Family Studies* 3 (Autumn): 50-69.

   Scanzoni, J. 1979. "Social Processes and Power in Families" in W. R. Burr, R. Hill, F. I. Nye, and I. L. Reiss (eds.), *Contemporary Theories about the Family* (Vol. 1). New York: The Free Press.
10. Rodman, H. 1967. "Marital Power in France, Greece, Yugoslavia and the United States: A Cross-National Discussion." *Journal of Marriage and the Family* 30 (May): 321-324.

    Rodman, see note 9.

11. Rodman, see note 10.
    Rodman, see note 9.
12. Scanzoni, see note 9.
    Rodman, see note 9.
13. Cromwell, R. E.; R. Corrales, and P. M. Torsiello. 1973. "Normative Patterns of Marital Decision Making Power and Influence in Mexico and the United States: A Partial Test of Resource and Ideology Theory." *Journal of Comparative Family Studies* 4 (Autumn): 177-196.
14. Weller, R. H. 1968. "The Employment of Wives, Dominance and Fertility." *Journal of Marriage and the Family* 30 (August): 437-442.
15. Cromwell et al., see note 13.
    Richmond, see note 7.
    Tharp, R. G.; A. Meadow; S. Lennhoff, and D. Satterfield. 1968. "Changes in Marriage Roles Accompanying the Acculturation of the Mexican-American Wife." *Journal of Marriage and the Family* 30 (August): 404-412.
    Fitzpatrick, J. P. 1976. "The Puerto Rican Family" in C. H. Mindel and R. W. Habenstein (eds.), *Ethnic Families in America: Patterns and Variations*. New York: Elsevier.
16. Rodman, see note 9.
17. Cromwell et al., see note 13.
18. Rogler, L. H. 1978. "Help Patterns, the Family and Mental Health: Puerto Ricans in the United States." *International Migration Review* 12 (2) (Summer): 248-259.

VI

Socioeconomic Mobility

In Chapter III we demonstrated that before migrating from Puerto Rico the parent-generation men and women were in the vanguard of those who faced social changes which had been sweeping the island since before their birth. They came from families of higher socioeconomic status than that of the general population and from settings which were disproportionately more often urban. Moreover, women in the parent generation had more work experience than the female island population, and men in the parent generation were more often employed in middle-status occupations than was the male island population. Exceptional as they were in terms of such comparisons, socioeconomically, the parent generation at the time of their migration were quite similar to other first-generation Puerto Rican migrants of that period.

Sharply in contrast to the parent generation, however, was the child generation whose socioeconomic achievements notably surpassed the attainments of other New York City Puerto Ricans comparable to them. The percentage of the child generation who went to college, the proportion of child-generation females working, and the percentage of child-generation males employed in the two highest status occupational categories, professionals and managers, were more than double that of other Puerto Ricans of about the same age who were either born on the mainland or migrated at about the same age as those of the child generation.

Although the occupational accomplishments of the parent-generation males were modest after their arrival in New York City, their search for greater economic opportunities was strikingly realized in the educational and occupational achievements of their children. Chapter III placed the socioeconomic achievements of both generations in a historical context, but we did not compare the educational and occupational achievements of the child generation with those of their parents. We begin this chapter, as we did the chapters on ethnic identity and spouse relationships, with a detailed discussion of intergenerational differences, but now we focus upon the educational and occupational characteristics of the parent and child generations. Also, since we collected information on the education and occupations of the grand-parent generation, socioeconomic mobility will be examined from a three-generation perspective. Following the order of presentation established in the chapters on ethnic identity and spouse relationships, we will then examine intergenerational continuity. In those chapters we found a pattern of inter-generational discontinuity. We now will see if such a pattern is evident also for socioeconomic characteristics of the two generations. This chapter moves ahead to examine intergenerational continuity in education, not only because education is related to occupational attainment but also because education emerged as a major variable in our earlier analyses. Education, we found, affected the ethnic identity of the mothers, fathers, and children, as well as the degree to which the husbands and wives shared functions and activities in the two generations. In addition, the educational mobility of the child generation is an important condition affecting the process of intergenera-tional continuity in ethnic identity and spouse relationships. Thus, the examination of intergenerational continuity in education has far-reaching consequences. To provide a theoretical framework for the search for factors affecting achievement, we turn to the literature on status attainment. First, however, we describe the pattern of socioeconomic mobility characterizing the intergenerational families.

MOBILITY OF THE GRANDPARENT, PARENT, AND CHILD GENERATIONS

The educational achievements of the parent generation while in Puerto Rico, compared to that of their parents (the grandparent generation) showed considerable upward mobility. Table 6.1 indicates that a sizeable minority of the grandparent males, approximately one-quarter, never attended school. Among those who attended school, very few went beyond grammar school, and of those with grammar school education most terminated after only four years of schooling. In fact, more than 60 percent of the grandfathers had less than five years of schooling. The educational achievements of the grandparent females was even lower: close to one-half never had any formal schooling and about three-quarters had less than five years of grammar school education.

In contrast, almost all of the parent generation attended school: almost one-half of the parent males and 37 percent of the parent females completed eight years of grammar school and went to high school. While the parent

TABLE 6.1

Comparison of Grandparent, Parent, and Child Generations: Educational and Occupational Achievements*

	Grandparent Generation		Parent Generation		Child Generation
	Males	Females	Males	Females	
Schooling in Years	%	%	%	%	%
None	23.5	45.0	4.0	2.0	0
1-4	37.0	29.5	16.0	26.0	0
5-8	30.5	22.0	32.0	35.0	1.0
9-11	5.0	2.0	25.0	17.0	10.0
12	2.5	1.5	18.0	12.0	45.0
13-15	0	0	5.0	5.0	26.0
16+	1.5	0	0	3.0	18.0
Median Education	Yrs.	Yrs.	Yrs.	Yrs.	Yrs.
	3.4	2.2	8.3	7.2	12.4
Occupational Categories[a]	%		%		%
Professionals/managers	12.0		17.0		38.5
Clerical/sales/crafts	27.5		26.0		41.0
Operatives/laborers/service	18.0		57.0		20.5
Farmers/farm laborers	42.5		0.0		0.0
Median Occupational Status[b]	Score		Score		Score
	16.5		32.8		59.6

[a] For males only.

[b] Based on Nam et al. (1975). Scores can vary between zero and 100 and indicate the percentage of persons in the experienced civilian labor force who are in occupations having lower combined average levels of education and income.

*The information given for the parent and child generations shown in this table includes *all* the parent- and child-generation persons in the study group. This information, therefore, differs from the figures given throughout Chapter III which includes *only* the parent generation born and raised in Puerto Rico and the child generation born or raised in the United States.

Note: Differences between the grandparent and parent generations as well as between the parent and child generations are all statistically significant.

127

generation exhibited a pattern of sex differences in the median years of school, with the males completing more schooling than females, the difference was less than in the grandparent generation: the median level of education of the grandparent females was only two-thirds as high as that of the grandparent males, whereas the median level of schooling for the parent-generation females was more than four-fifths that of the parent-generation males. Compared to that of the grandparent generation, the educational attainment of the parent generation was high, reflecting upward mobility.

Compared to the educational attainment of the parent generation, that of the child generation, educated predominantly in New York City, also showed considerable upward mobility. In the parent generation only 23 percent of the males and 20 percent of the females finished high school, while 89 percent of the child generation did so. Moreover, a sizeable minority of the child generation went on to attend college. The lower educational achievement of women, compared to that of men, most notable in the grandparent generation and still evident in the parent generation disappeared in the child generation: both males and females in the child generation achieved the same median of 12.4 years of schooling. Like their parents before them, the educational attainment of the child generation was remarkably high, reflecting considerable upward mobility.

To compare the generations to determine which one experienced the most mobility, we examined intergenerational change using the seven levels of schooling shown in Table 6.1. The comparison revealed that those parents who were not upwardly mobile tended to complete the same level of schooling as their fathers; only 7 percent of the parent generation were downwardly mobile, completing a lower level of schooling than their fathers. Of the parent generation 75 percent completed at least one level of schooling more than their fathers. The child generation experienced even greater upward mobility than the parent generation, with almost 90 percent of the children completing at least one level of schooling more than their fathers; only 2 percent of the children had a lower level of schooling than their fathers. A substantial majority of both the parent and child generations were upwardly mobile, but the educational mobility of Puerto Ricans raised and educated in New York City exceeded that of their immigrant parents. This finding is consistent with Featherman and Hauser's analysis[1] showing greater educational mobility for the children of immigrant parents than for the immigrants themselves.

Not only did the parent generation show considerable mobility in education when compared to their parents, but the males of the parent generation experienced a notable improvement in occupational attainment. This improvement was clearly reflected in the comparison of the median occupational-status scores of the parent-generation males and that of their fathers. Looking more closely at the job changes that were responsible for this improvement, we note that a sizeable minority of males in the grandparent generation worked in unskilled farming jobs in rural Puerto Rico and the parent-generation males worked predominantly in semiskilled jobs in the manufacturing and service sectors of urban New York City. Semiskilled jobs are among the lowest status occupations in the urban labor market, but they represent an improvement in the required job skills and in salary above what was available to farm workers in rural Puerto Rico. In comparison to such intergenerational changes, there is very little difference between the males of the grandfather and parent generations in employment in the highest professional and managerial occupations or in the middle-status clerical, sales, and craftsmen occupations. Thus, the major job changes representing upward occupational mobility of the parent-generation males lie in the movement from rural farming jobs held by their fathers into semiskilled urban jobs in manufacturing and services.

When interviewed, the child-generation males were in their late 20s and hence still at an early stage of their occupational careers. Despite their younger age, the occupational attainment of the males showed considerable occupational mobility, as reflected in median occupational-status scores. A sizeable minority, almost 40 percent, of the child-generation males worked in the two highest status occupational categories of professionals and managers. The proportion of males employed in these two highest status jobs was more than double that of their fathers. Large numbers of child-generation males also were working in the middle-status occupational categories although they were more likely to be in clerical and sales jobs in contrast to their fathers who were more likely to be in skilled craftsmen jobs. The representation of child-generation males in the middle-status occupational categories, however, was 50 percent higher than that of their fathers. The major occupational changes representing upward occupational mobility for the child-generation males was in the movement away from the lower status, semiskilled jobs of their fathers toward the middle-status clerical and sales jobs and into the highest status professional and managerial jobs.

While both the parent and child generations experienced considerable occupational mobility compared to the previous generation, the greatest gains in occupational achievements were among the children of immigrant parents rather than among the immigrants themselves. The occupational movement of the parent-generation males, then, can be characterized as one-step mobility because the major shift in their employment was a one-step improvement of occupational level above their fathers. If the child-generation males had experienced comparable one-step mobility, the major occupational shift would have been out of the semiskilled jobs held by their fathers into the middle-status occupations. The mobility of the child-generation males, however, was greater than one step; a substantial minority went into professional and managerial jobs that were two steps higher than the major occupational achievements of their fathers. Thus, the growth in professional and managerial employment among the child generation supports the view that their occupational mobility surpassed that of the parent generation.

INTERGENERATIONAL EDUCATIONAL ATTAINMENT

Although education is a major mechanism affecting the socioeconomic integration of immigrant groups into American society, little has been done to identify the factors affecting the educational mobility of immigrants. Research on this topic has been mostly descriptive, relying on comparisons between unrelated first and second generations.[2] The assumption that studying first and second generations is the equivalent of studying immigrants and their children has been challenged.[3] We believe the measurement of intergenerational mobility among immigrant groups requires primary data from kinship-linked generational groups. The small number of studies relevant to this topic have relied predominantly on status-attainment literature as a framework for analysis.[4] The status-attainment approach, as originally formulated by Blau and Duncan,[5] highlights the family head's educational and occupational status as critical factors in understanding the educational achievements of individuals in American society. Studies on the general American population have consistently shown that the higher the socioeconomic status of the family of origin, the higher the offspring's educational attainment. Regardless of the level of educational opportunities in different historical periods, the socioeconomically advantaged families of one generation tend to pass on such advantages to the next generation.[6]

The importance of the family head's educational and occupational status in understanding the educational attainment of immigrants in American society has been substantiated in both Duncan and Duncan's and Featherman and Hauser's research.[7] Their conclusions, however, are based on two assumptions: (1) that the process of educational attainment is similar among different immigrant groups and (2) that this process is also similar among different generational groups. The scarcity of research on intergenerational change in education among national-origin groups makes it difficult to evaluate these assumptions. Nevertheless, scattered evidence is available. In regard to the first assumption on immigrant groups, Kobrin and Goldscheider's analysis[8] of several Catholic, immigrant national-origin groups in Rhode Island found that the father's occupation was not significantly related to the educational achievements of French-Canadians, Italians, and Portuguese, but was significantly related to the educational achievements of the Irish. In regard to the second assumption on generational groups, Peñalosa and McDonagh's study[9] of predominantly second-generation Mexican Americans in California found no significant relationship between their father's occupation and their own education. On the other hand, Hirschman's study[10] of first-generation Mexicans entering the United States through border stations in Texas found significant relationships between their education and their father's educational and occupational status. Contradictory findings of this type challenge the assumptions that the process linking parental socioeconomic characteristics to educational achievement is similar among national-origin and generational groups. Even within Featherman and Hauser's own work,[11] the uniqueness of the second generation is highlighted but not systematically analyzed: in comparing the educational achievements of first, second, and third (plus) generations, with all immigrant groups combined, Featherman and Hauser found that the second generation was more educationally mobile than either the new immigrants or the native population. In addition, the family head's educational and occupational status was less closely linked to the educational achievements of the second generation than that of the new immigrants. The small size of their sample prevented the separate analysis of first and second generations within specific national-origin groups. Only the Mexican group was large enough to justify reliable distinctions between first, second, and subsequent generations. Featherman and Hauser's analysis of the Mexican group assumes that the status-attainment process is similar among generations, thus ignoring the intriguing findings suggested by their own earlier generational analyses.

Our data analysis could yield three possible conclusions. First, it could be that the educational and occupational characteristics of the family of origin are related to the educational achievements of both the parent and child generations. Should this be true, then, for the first time there will be evidence in support of the selective continuity hypothesis in this study, because at the level of the 100 intergenerationally-linked families the pattern so far has been intergenerational discontinuity. Second, it could be that the socioeconomic characteristics of the family of origin are unrelated to the educational achievements of both generations. Such a finding would challenge the assumption that the process of educational attainment is similar for different immigrant groups. Factors relevant to intergenerational discontinuity in educational attainments would then have to be sought in those processes singularly affecting Puerto Ricans. Third, it could be that there are different intergenerational processes linking the parent generation to its family of origin and the married-child generation to the parent generation. The Mexican American research cited above and our own pattern of pervasive discontinuity between the generations lead to the following expectation: a pattern of continuity for the parent generation raised and educated in the same sociocultural system as their family of origin and a pattern of discontinuity for the married-child generation not raised in the same sociocultural system as the parent generation. Were such patterns to be found, the assumption that social mobility processes are the same across successive generations would be challenged and an invitation would be issued to examine closely how the migration experience of the parent generation disrupts intergenerational continuity in the education of their children.

Table 6.2 presents the relationship between the socioeconomic status of the family of origin and the years of schooling completed by the parent-generation females, the parent-generation males, and the child generation. In the parent generation, the educational and occupational status of their fathers shows a significant positive relationship with their educational attainment: the higher the father's level of education and occupational achievement,

TABLE 6.2

Partial Regression Coefficients of Educational Achievement on Socioeconomic Characteristics of the Family of Origin for Parent and Child Generations

Independent Variables[a]	Father	Mother	Child
Father's education	.34*	.29*	.06
Father's occupational status	.02*	.03*	.00
Mother's education	.07	.12	.07
Mother's employment	−1.59	−1.51	.55
Adjusted R^2	.18*	.21*	.03

[a]The terms *father* and *mother* used in the independent variable column are generic terms. Thus, the first-row and first-column coefficient, .34, refers to the partial regression coefficient of the education of fathers in the parent generation on the education of their fathers (grandfathers).

*$p < .05$

the greater the number of years of schooling completed by both males and females of the parent generation. Neither the education nor employment status of the women in the grandparent generation had an independent effect on the education of the parent generation once their interrelationship with education and occupational status of the father was controlled. The socioeconomic status of the family of origin, as defined by the father's socioeconomic achievements, was an important factor affecting the educational mobility of the parent generation. Thus, the pattern of findings for the parent generation is consistent with the status attainment literature, but the findings for the child generation, once again, are puzzling. None of the socioeconomic characteristics of the family of origin included in the analysis is relevant to the years of schooling completed by the child generation. The socioeconomic achievements of the parent generation do not help us understand the educational mobility of the child generation.

Since education is only one dimension of socioeconomic status, we also examined the correlations of two other commonly used measures — occupational status of the males and family income. The correlation of the son's occupational status with his father's was .04 while the correlation of the child generation's family income with that of the parent generation was .11. Neither correlation was statistically significant. Moreover, when no other variables were controlled, the correlations of the child generation's education with that of their mother (.16) and of their father (.11) confirmed the findings in Table 6.2 of no significant relationship. No matter what measure of socioeconomic status was used, the socioeconomic attributes of their parents had no direct effect upon those of their children, creating neither advantages nor disadvantages. The pattern of intergenerational discontinuity prevails.

Thus, we find that with respect to socioeconomic status there is intergenerational continuity between the parent generation, raised and educated in Puerto Rico, and their parents, but intergenerational discontinuity between the child generation, predominantly raised and educated in New York City, and their parents. These findings challenge the assumption of earlier researchers that the educational attainment process is similar for immigrants and the children of immigrants and invite analysis of the migration experience itself which, in this study, involved the movement of the parent generation from Puerto Rico to New York City.

INTERGENERATIONAL DISCONTINUITY REEXAMINED

Why was intergenerational continuity in socioeconomic status ruptured? The migration experience ruptures socioeconomic continuity from one generation to the next when differences in the educational and occupational characteristics of the immigrant parent generation do not coincide with the labor market opportunities of the new society. Between the early 1950s, when the parent generation migrated to New York City, and the subsequent two decades, the period in which the child generation was going to school, the employment situation in New York City changed dramatically. While total industrial and service employment in the United States between 1950 and 1973 grew about 50 percent, in the city of New York the absolute number of such jobs remained stable, growing less than 1 percent. This stability in overall number of jobs, however, hides important shifts in the types of jobs available. The number of unskilled and semiskilled manufacturing jobs that had played an important role for the earlier immigrant groups declined sharply. Puerto Ricans had been predominantly employed in blue-collar jobs and in sectors of the economy that were experiencing decline.[12] During this period, New York City lost about 38 percent of its manufacturing employment, primarily by the relocation of a substantial part of the manufacturing industries elsewhere. The jobs which grew to fill this void were primarily white-collar jobs requiring a high school diploma and facility in English. Among the industries experiencing notable growth in New York City were local government, business and financial services, and medical services.[13]

The shift toward a more educated labor force placed the parent generation in a seriously disadvantaged position because only about 20 percent of them had graduated from high school. Even beyond the parent generation, the educational achievements of the broader Puerto Rican community on the mainland had failed to keep up with that of the general population. The adult American population who were high school graduates increased from 34 percent in 1950 to 41 percent in 1960 to more than 53 percent in 1970. The percentage of adult Puerto Ricans on the mainland who were high school graduates was not only much lower, 15 percent in 1950, 17 percent in 1960, and 20 percent in 1970, but also increased at a slower pace.[14] The gap in education between Puerto Ricans and the general population of the United States became more noticeable in New York City where Puerto Ricans were still highly concentrated and the loss of low-status and semiskilled jobs made their educational disadvantage particularly acute. In the context of the high educational requisites of New York City's labor market and the historical trend of rapidly diminishing employment opportunities at the bottom of the stratification heap, the concentration of the parent generation at the lower end of the educational and occupational hierarchy did little directly to create advantages or disadvantages for the child generation. In contrast, such variations at an *even lower level* of the occupational and educational scales were consequential from one generation to the next in the traditional social structure of preindustrial Puerto Rico in the late 1920s and 1930s when the immigrant parents were going to school. Thus, the migration experience ruptures intergenerational continuity when differences in the socioeconomic resources of the parent generation do not coincide with labor market opportunities of the host society.

To examine the relevance of the foregoing argument we distinguish, once again, among our intergenerational families according to where the parents and children were raised. Table 6.3 shows that the educational achievement of the parent generation was lowest for those families in which both the parent and child were raised and educated in Puerto Rico and highest for those families in which both the parent and child were raised and educated in New York City. If the education of the parent generation must be evaluated in the context of available labor market opportunities, we would expect to find the greatest intergenerational continuity in education between parents and children when both were educated in Puerto Rico. Although parents' education was lowest for this group, the greater availability of low-skilled jobs in Puerto Rico makes meaningful the distinction between completing different levels of elementary school or some high school. Literacy, by itself, in this context has important job consequences. For the other two family types, the relevance of the parent generation's education must be evaluated in the

TABLE 6.3
Mean Education of Parents and Correlations of Education for Intergenerationally Linked Parent and Child Under Varying Conditions

| | *Mean Education* | | *Correlations* | |
| | | | *Mother* | *Father* |
Relevant Condition	*Mother*	*Father*	*with Child*	*with Child*
All Families	7.40	7.88	.16	.11
Socialization Context				
Parent P.R. raised	7.07	7.86	.14	.04
Child N.Y. raised				
Parent P.R. raised	6.18	6.18	.34	.55
Child P.R. raised				
Parent N.Y. raised	10.31	9.46	.17	.29
Child N.Y. raised				

context of diminishing low-skilled job opportunities in New York City. In this context, the parent generation educated in New York had an advantage over the parent generation educated in Puerto Rico. While the majority of the parent generation educated in New York did not have a high school education, they nevertheless had completed two and three years more schooling than those educated in Puerto Rico. Hence, among the intergenerational families whose children were raised and educated in New York City we expect greater intergenerational continuity in education when the parent generation's education was higher.

The data presented in Table 6.3 are consistent with our argument. The greatest intergenerational continuity in education occurred when the child generation was educated in Puerto Rico. Although their parents had the lowest level of completed schooling, minor variations in their level of schooling were meaningful in the context of the educational and occupational structure of Puerto Rico. Better educated parents in Puerto Rico were able to pass on this advantage as had their parents, to their children educated in Puerto Rico. Among the families whose children were raised and educated in New York City, greater intergenerational continuity in education occurred when the parents' education relevantly met what the jobs demanded in an increasingly more highly educated labor force, the situation in New York City during the decades when the child generation was growing up.

THE MIGRATION EXPERIENCE: A CLOSER LOOK

The pattern of intergenerational discontinuity in education was evident for the majority of our intergenerational families. Only among those families in which both the parents and children were raised and educated in Puerto Rico was continuity most clearly evident. If we are to understand the dramatic educational attainments of the child generation raised and educated on the mainland, it is necessary to broaden the search and consider variables other than those pertaining to the socioeconomic characteristics of the family of origin. To meet this challenge we return to the status-attainment literature with which we started earlier.

As originally formulated by Blau and Duncan,[15] the basic model for studying the socioeconomic mobility of individuals highlighted the family head's educational and occupational status. In studying the educational attainment of immigrant groups, they extended the model to include other characteristics of the family of origin, such as number of siblings, having been raised on a farm, and having been raised in a single-parent family. Duncan and

Duncan[16] and Featherman and Hauser[17] showed that when differences in such family background characteristics are controlled, the educational achievements of immigrant groups in 1962 and 1973 are similar to those of white, native-parentage Americans with the exception of Hispanics, in particular Mexicans and Puerto Ricans. The educational achievements of Mexicans and Puerto Ricans were considerably lower than those of other groups with similar socioeconomic background characteristics. Such findings make it evident, once again, that to understand the child generation's notable educational attainments, other carefully selected variables must be brought into the analysis.

Featherman and Hauser,[18] in fact, recognize the complexity of factors affecting the socioeconomic integration of national-origin groups. They state explicitly that there is a need to examine the "context" surrounding the immigration and the cultural characteristics of immigrant groups.[19] Their data set, however, did not allow the incorporation of other factors into the analyses. The reliance of the status-attainment literature upon data which derive from one generation reporting upon another has limited the consideration of family background characteristics to socioeconomic factors. Through in-depth interviews with both Puerto Rican immigrant parents and their adult children, our data provide direct information on the cultural characteristics of the family of origin. Although cultural factors have been repeatedly stressed as important determinants of the socioeconomic integration of immigrant groups,[20] field research on this topic is negligible. We propose to investigate two aspects of Hispanic culture – values and English language proficiency – that are repeatedly cited as explanations for their lower socioeconomic status.[21]

Two important cultural values stressed in both the literature on Puerto Ricans and the literature on Mexican Americans are the preeminence of the family and a sense of fatalism.[22] As indicated in Chapter IV, these values represent traditional modalities in Puerto Rican culture. Rosen,[23] in a general theoretical statement, sees such values as part of the individual's orientation toward achievement: persons who stress the importance of the family over concerns for individual opportunities or who believe in passively accepting their fate as opposed to actively shaping their future are less oriented toward the improvement of their social status. The parent generation in this study believed more strongly in familistic and fatalistic values than the child generation. Chapter III demonstrated, however, that the parents were in the vanguard of social change in Puerto Rico, and their migration to New York City attests to the motivation to achieve a better life. Thus, we wanted to see whether or not there is a relationship between the degree to which the parents endorsed such values and the educational achievements of the children. More specifically, is it true that the more the parents endorse the values of familism and fatalism the less the educational attainment of their children? To our knowledge, no study has empirically tested this hypothesis with immigrant parents.

The limited attention research has given to the role of cultural values in studying intergenerational mobility is reflected also in the neglect of the other cultural dimension present in our research, English language proficiency. This stands in contrast to the importance the theoretical literature has ascribed to cultural values and knowledge of English in the effort to understand cultural assimilation. Thus, Gordon[24] proposed that the initial adjustment process of immigrant groups involves learning the language of the new society. The English language is an important means through which the immigrants were exposed to a cultural system that stresses the importance of education for occupational success, thus giving direction and content to the achievement orientation of the parents. In addition, proficiency in the English language links immigrants to a new world of social contacts outside their ethnic group. Such contacts facilitate integration by providing the basis of trust, encouragement, and social support outside the extended family system.[25] We expect that the greater the cultural assimilation of the family of origin, that is, the weaker the adherence to the values of familism and fatalism and the greater the proficiency in the English language, the greater will be the educational attainments of the children. Before testing this hypothesis, there is a need, however, to examine a methodological issue.

Although the information on the cultural variables of the parent-generation males is derived from interviews with them, the cross-sectional design of the study raises the issue of retrospective validity. The issue relates to evidence indicating whether or not the cultural variables antedated the children's educational attainment. (The issue is not whether the measures of cultural variables are "right" in an absolute sense, but whether they systematically bias the relationship being examined.) To shed light upon the issue, we examined the cultural characteristics of the parent-generation males in relation to other critically important experiences in their life histories. Thus, we expected that the more English they knew and the greater their commitment to achievement values, the greater their occupational success since their arrival in New York City. Two measures of occupational mobility of the parent-generation males were used: the difference in occupational status between their present job and the last job they had in Puerto Rico, and the difference in occupational status between their present job and their first job in New York City. We found that parent-generation males who had experienced upward mobility after leaving Puerto Rico and during their lives in New York City had significantly greater proficiency in English and a significantly lower attachment to familism and fatalism than those who experienced little or downward mobility. The relationships are consistent with theoretical hypotheses linking the occupational success of immigrants to their cultural assimilation. Since the cultural variables were embedded in their occupational mobility experiences while the children were growing up, thus preceding the children's present educational attainments, the test demonstrates acceptable retrospective validity. Other cultural characteristics of the father did not meet this retrospective test and were discarded from the analysis.

In summary, previous status-attainment research on the educational achievements of immigrant groups has shown that the educationally disadvantaged position of Puerto Ricans in American society persists after adjusting for socioeconomic characteristics of the family of origin. Furthermore, the uniqueness of the second generation has been highlighted but not systematically analyzed within specific national-origin groups. Our major objective was to extend the socioeconomically based model of family background variables to include cultural characteristics of the parent generation. The analyses will elucidate elements in their migration experience which are useful in understanding the notably high educational mobility of the child generation.

We follow the procedure common to status-attainment research of focusing upon the father's experience to represent the family of origin, although a separate assessment of the mother's experience in no way altered the substantive conclusions of this analysis. Also, even though the father's educational and occupational status showed no relationship to the child's education in our earlier analysis, these socioeconomic characteristics were retained in the present analysis to determine if their effects were suppressed because of interrelationships with other variables in the status-attainment model. An additional socioeconomic variable forming part of the model was available, namely, the number of siblings in the household when the child generation was being raised. Other socioeconomic variables in the model were not relevant because the children were raised in intact families living in New York City.

The relationship of the parent generation's socioeconomic and cultural characteristics, on the one hand, to the child generation's educational achievements, on the other hand, is shown in Table 6.4. The greatest educational mobility in the child generation was evident among those coming from smaller families. Consistent with the findings of educational-attainment research, Puerto Rican children raised in large families had significantly lower

TABLE 6.4
Partial Regression Coefficients of Educational Achievement on Socio-economic and Cultural Characteristics of the Family of Origin for Child Generation

Family of Origin Characteristics	
Socioeconomic	
Father's education	.010
Father's occupation	−.001
Number of siblings	−.276*
Cultural	
Father's knowledge of English	.012
Father's familism values	−.401*
Father's fatalism values	−.380*
Adjusted R^2	.107

*p < .05

educational attainment than those raised in small families. One strategy available to parents with finite resources is to have fewer children. Decreasing the number of children increases the proportion of the family's limited economic resources available to each child. Here we see evidence that parents who limited the number of children in the family sharply increased the likelihood that their children would not only finish high school but would enter and complete college.

The pattern of findings is basically consistent with the theoretical argument that explanations of the children's educational attainment must incorporate much more than the parental socioeconomic variables by turning to components of the parent's migration experience. The immigrant fathers' commitment to familism and fatalism values was inversely related to their children's educational attainments; that is, the weaker the father's endorsement of familism and fatalism values, the greater the children's educational attainment. The loosening of such values focused the individual's attention upon status improvement and functioned to transform motivations directed toward excellence in performance to actual performance. The effect of fathers' values upon their children's educational attainment demonstrates the importance of cultural background in shaping educational careers.

SUMMARY AND INTERPRETATION

If we begin with the parents of the parent generation living in preindustrial agrarian Puerto Rico, we can shed light on the socioeconomic mobility of the two generations under study. The sequential pattern over the two-generation gap, from grandparents to parents and then from parents to married children, is one of clear, ascending social mobility, but with the child generation's mobility exceeding that of the parent generation. The two generations differ not only in terms of the degree of mobility they experienced, but also in the intergenerational processes in which their mobility was enmeshed: the grandparent generation was able to transfer to the parent generation its socioeconomic advantages or disadvantages, but the parent generation could not effect a similar transfer to their offspring. Parental socioeconomic characteristics contributed directly to the parent generation's mobility, but not to the mobility of the child generation.

The findings draw attention to two issues, one general, the other specific. In general, the assumption often made that mobility processes are the same, qualitatively, from one generation to the next must be subjected to testing through research in each national group. The mobility experiences of the children do not necessarily replicate those of their parents, not just in the degree of mobility but also in factors directly shaping the mobility. The socioeconomic legacies of one generation may or may not be transferred to subsequent offspring generations, depending upon the sociocultural circumstances impinging upon such intergenerational processes. In the context of this study, the socioeconomic characteristics of the grandparent generation directly shaped the mobility of the parent generation because they meaningfully coincided with Puerto Rico's preindustrial educational and occupational structure. In such a structure, small variations at the bottom of the educational scale, for example, the few years of education required to develop functional literacy, were consequential for the person and for his/her offspring. The intergenerational continuity in education between the grandparent and parent generations supported this proposition, as did the presence of intergenerational continuity in education when both the parent and child generations were born and raised in Puerto Rico.

The specific issue, on the other hand, pertains to the need to understand how the migration experience affects intergenerational processes; in this study, it did so by rupturing the socioeconomic continuity between the parent- and married-child generations. Such a discontinuity implies that socioeconomic legacies are not likely to be transferred directly from immigrants to their children when the host society's educational and occupational structure does not relevantly or meaningfully absorb the socioeconomic attributes of the newcomers. To increase our understanding of the child generation's educational attainment in the context of intergenerational educational discontinuity required the examination of variables not usually considered in the status-attainment model. However, one of the socioeconomic variables common to status-attainment research, namely, number of siblings, was relevant to the child generation's educational attainment: the fewer the siblings, the higher the educational attainments. This finding can be interpreted according to the allocation of the immigrant families' small and finite resources, concentrated when there are fewer children, dispersed when there are many.

Of the additional variables considered, one failed to add to the understanding of the child generation's educational attainments: even though plausible formulations supported its likely relevance, the parent-generation males' knowledge of English was unrelated to the child generation's educational attainments. Two other variables, the cultural values of familism and fatalism, are relevant. Culturally, the fathers' deemphasis of these values helped to channel mobility wishes into performance by increasing the child generation's educational attainments. In brief, even though discontinuity between the parent and married child generations prevailed in socioeconomic characteristics, as well as in other variables, the parents' cultural attributes influenced their offspring's educational attainments.

REFERENCES

1. Featherman, D. L., and R. Hauser. 1978. *Opportunity and Change*. New York: Academic Press.
2. Nam, C. 1959. "Nationality Groups and Social Stratification in America." *Social Forces* 37: 328-333.
   Lieberson, S. 1963. *Ethnic Patterns in American Cities*. New York: The Free Press.
   Glazer, N. and D. P. Moynihan. 1963. *Beyond the Melting Pot*. Cambridge, MA: MIT Press and Harvard University Press.
   Fitzpatrick, J. P. 1971. *Puerto Rican Americans: The Meaning of Migration to the Mainland*. Englewood Cliffs, NJ: Prentice-Hall.
   Macisco, J. 1968. "Assimilation of the Puerto Ricans on the Mainland." *International Migration Review* 2: 21-37.
3. Taeuber, A. F., and K. E. Taeuber. 1967. "Recent Immigration and Studies of Ethnic Assimilation." *Demography* 4: 798-804.

4. Duncan, B. and O. D. Duncan. 1968. "Minorities and the Process of Stratification." *American Sociological Review* 33: 356-364.
Featherman and Hauser, see note 1.
5. Blau, P. M. and O. D. Duncan. 1967. *The American Occupational Structure*. New York: John Wiley and Sons.
6. Duncan, O. D.; D. L. Featherman, and B. Duncan. 1972. *Socioeconomic Background and Achievement*. New York: Seminar Press.
7. Duncan and Duncan, see note 4.
Featherman and Hauser, see note 1.
8. Kobrin, F. E. and C. Goldscheider. 1978. *The Ethnic Factor in Family Structure and Mobility*. Cambridge, MA: Ballinger Publishing Company.
9. Peñalosa, F. and E. C. McDonagh. 1966. "Social Mobility in a Mexican-American Community." *Social Forces* 44: 498-505.
10. Hirschman, C. 1978. "Prior U.S. Residence among Mexican Immigrants." *Social Forces* 56: 1179-1181.
11. Featherman and Hauser, see note 1.
12. Bureau of Labor Statistics. 1975. *A Socio-Economic Profile of Puerto Rican New Yorkers*. New York: Middle Atlantic Regional Office, Report No. 46.
Wagenheim, K. 1970 (Second Edition). *Puerto Rico: A Profile*. New York: Praeger Publishers.
13. Sternlieb, G., and J. Hughes. 1975. "Is the New York Region the Prototype?" (pp. 101-137) in G. Sternlieb and J. Hughes (eds.), *Post Industrial America: Metropolitan Decline and Inter-Regional Job Shifts*. The State University of New Jersey, Rutgers: The Center for Urban Policy Research.
Greenberg, M. R. and N. J. Valente. 1975. "Recent Economic Trends in the Major Northeastern Metropolises" (pp. 77-99) in G. Sternlieb and J. Hughes (eds.), *Post-Industrial America: Metropolitan Decline and Inter-Regional Job Shifts*. The State University of New Jersey, Rutgers: The Center for Urban Policy Research.
14. Folger, J. K. and C. Nam. 1967. *Education of the American Population*. Washington, D.C.: U.S. Bureau of the Census.
Bureau of Labor Statistics, see note 12.
Bureau of the Census. 1953. U.S. Census of Population: 1950. Vol. IV. Special Reports, Part 3, Chapter D. *Puerto Ricans in the Continental United States*. Washington, D.C.: U.S. Government Printing Office.
U.S. Census of Population: 1960. 1963. Final Report PC (2)-1D. Subject Reports. *Puerto Ricans in the United States*. Washington, D.C.: U.S. Government Printing Office.
15. Blau and Duncan, see note 5.
16. Duncan and Duncan, see note 4.
17. Featherman and Hauser, see note 1.
18. *Ibid.*
19. *Ibid.*

20. Rosen, B. C. 1959. "Race, Ethnicity, and the Achievement Syndrome." *American Sociological Review* 24: 47-60.

Heller, C. S. 1969. "Class as an Explanation of Ethnic Differences in Upward Mobility" (pp. 396-402) in C. Heller (ed.), *Structured Social Inequality*. New York: Macmillan Company.

Kantrowitz, N. 1968. "Social Mobility of Puerto Ricans." *International Migration Review* 1: 53-71.

Featherman and Hauser, see note 1.

21. Gordon, M. M. 1964. *Assimilation in American Life: The Role of Race, Religion, and National Origins*. New York: Oxford University Press.

Tienda, M. 1981. "Sex, Ethnicity, and Chicano Status Attainment." (pp. 59-104) in *Socioeconomic Attainment and Ethnicity: Toward an Understanding of the Labor Market Experiences of Chicanos in the U.S.* Final Report submitted to the Department of Labor.

22. Fitzpatrick, J. P., see note 2.

Mintz, S. W. 1973. "Puerto Rico: An Essay on the Definition of National Culture" (pp. 26-90) in F. Cordasco and E. Buccioni (eds.), *The Puerto Rico Experience*. Totowa, NJ: Littlefield, Adams and Company.

Wagenheim, see note 12.

Grebler, L.; J. W. Moore, and R. C. Guyman. 1970. *The Mexican-American People*. New York: The Free Press.

Peñalosa, F. and E. C. McDonagh, see note 9.

Heller, C. S., see note 20.

23. Rosen, B. C., see note 20.

24. Gordon, M. M., see note 21.

25. Rogler, L. H. 1972. *Migrant in the City: The Life of a Puerto Rican Action Group*. New York: Basic Books.

PART 3

INTERGENERATIONAL INTEGRATION

Introduction

> When extreme gulfs form between generations in certain families, the loss of such a heritage [the family's] is a catastrophe from which recovery is usually slow. In general it appears that family disorganization, or even partial disorganization, affects not only a couple and their children, but also imposes some handicap that may remain for several generations. (*Faris, p. 164*)

Faris' article,* from which the cited quotation was taken, is of signal importance in calling attention to the need for sociological understanding of intergenerational processes. The argument presented in it is straightforward: the family is one of the most important institutions for transmission of a society's culture. When families function effectively, the process of intergenerational transmission is gradual and informal, the younger generation the unwitting beneficiaries of their parents' cultural heritage. Migration to a different society ruptures this transmission, with the catastrophic result of family disorganization and the likelihood of persistent handicaps through subsequent generations. The Puerto Ricans families under study, as migrants, have experienced a pervasive intergenerational gulf, clearly evident in the array of differences and discontinuities between the parents and their adult children presented in Chapters IV, V and VI. Have they become disorganized, thus displaying little intergenerational integration, as the argument would have it? How are they, in fact, integrated? Chapters VII and VIII turn to these questions.

---

*Robert E. L. Faris, "Interaction of Generations and Family Stability," *American Sociological Review*, Vol. 12, No. 2, 1947, pp. 159-164.

VII

The Prevailing Pattern: Parent-Benefactor Arrangement

Our repeated demonstration of the differences and discontinuities between the parent- and married-child generations in this study may well invite the interpretation that the two generations formed highly individualized or separate nuclear units and were disconnected and fragmented from each other, resembling perhaps Parsons' concept of the type of family which best fits urban industrial society.[1] To consider this interpretation we present data on intergenerational integration, one important factor in which is the frequency of intergenerational visits and reciprocal help exchanges. Although such frequency tells us very little about the specific ways in which the two generations of families were integrated, we have found that the ways in which they were integrated have a clear and definite shape. We discovered this shape inductively through successive examinations of family life. Some families exhibited intergenerational structures in which each nuclear unit enjoyed considerable autonomy. The linkage between these families was based largely upon mutual visitations and exchanges of gifts sometimes to meet emergent needs, but more often on ceremonial occasions such as birthdays, anniversaries, Mother's Day, Father's Day, and Christmas. Some families revealed an almost total dependence of the married children on their parents, the younger generation absorbed into and intensively nurtured in diverse ways by the older generation. Other families were organized as an intergenerational team with family roles differentiated and coordinated in the interest of a common goal. Still other families had an intergenerational matriarchal organization with an energetic parent-generation mother controlling and binding the family together. Following the presentation of data relevant to the degree of intergenerational integration, we will present case studies of specific families to illustrate the different types of integration. We will place each case study in a context of interfamily comparisons.

To discuss the relationship between generations presupposes the availability of comparative data on the degree of intergenerational interdependence

149

in specific settings. Fortunately, Hill's study[2] of three interlinked generations of families in Minneapolis/St. Paul, Minnesota, provides such data. Hill based his analysis of intergenerational interdependence on two types of data (p. 61): First, an assessment of kinship interaction using behavioral information on the frequency of intergenerational contacts through visits, telephone calls, and letters. Second, a help-giving and help-receiving inventory over a period of a year from ". . . all sources including immediate and extended kin, peers, church, social agencies, private specialists, and commercial sources," as reported by the women in the study. Hill concludes that the pattern of high frequency of visits and a "vast nexus of help-exchanges of mutual aid" (p. 78) justifies the appellation *modified extended family*. In this study we replicated with minor adaptations Hill's procedures for collecting data on the frequency of intergenerational visits and help-giving and help-receiving exchanges.

To make our data on visiting patterns comparable to Hill's, we focus only upon visits between children and their parents and only upon the responses of the women interviewed. Table 7.1 shows the results of the comparison. The columns designating the number of visitations between child and parents are comparable because the generations were at equivalent stages of the life cycle. In the Minneapolis/St. Paul families 69 percent of the child generation

TABLE 7.1

Comparison of Minnesotan and Puerto Rican Families: Intergenerational Visiting

(in percent)

Child-Parent Frequency of Visiting	Minneapolis/St. Paul Minnesota*	New York City Puerto Rican
Daily	21 | 69	23 | 77
Weekly	48 |	54 |
Monthly	25	21
Quarterly	6	2
Yearly	—	—

*Taken from Table 3.01, page 62 of Reuben Hill, *Family Development in Three Generations*, Schenkman Publishing Co., Cambridge, Ma., and London, 1970.

visited the parent generation at least once a week. In the New York City Puerto Rican families 77 percent of the child generation visited the parent generation at least once a week. Visiting among New York City Puerto Rican families, therefore, was more frequent than among the Minneapolis/St. Paul families. Such data provide the first step in demonstrating the degree of intergenerational interdependence among Puerto Rican families. A picture emerges of fastpaced repeated weekly contacts between parents and their married offspring.

The second step in examining intergenerational interdependence focuses upon help-exchanges. To make the data from both studies comparable, the source and recipient of the help-giving exchanges are categorized as in the Hill study and the focus upon generations in the Hill study was reduced to the parent and married-child generations in order to parallel the generational structure of our study. In examining Table 7.2 it is important to keep in mind that what is being classified is an *act* of help-giving or help-receiving, that is, an action, not a person. Table 7.2 has been organized also so that the row in each generation represents the source and recipient of help: other generations; all other kin; peers (friends, neighbors, and coworkers); agencies (religious groups, welfare agencies, professional specialists, etc.). From the top two rows to the bottom row, help-exchanges radiate outward from the family to peers and then on to the local community formal organizations. The transition is from social intimacy to social distance. The overarching structure of such help-giving and help-receiving exchanges is an important component of intergenerational interdependence.

In each row of Table 7.2 the "other generation" of relatives represents the main focus of help-giving and help-receiving. The movement of help, reciprocally, between generations is at the core of family transactions in both the Puerto Rican and the Minnesotan families. When the help-exchanges involving all other kin are added to help-exchanges across generations, the extraordinary dominance of the family as a supportive institution can be more fully appreciated. Among the Puerto Ricans studied, 73 percent of the help exchanges in the parent generation and 67 percent in the child generation centered upon the family. The percentage of family-centered help-exchanges among Puerto Ricans exceeded those of their corresponding Minneapolis/St. Paul generation. In comparison to their own parent generation, the Puerto Rican child generation appeared to be moving toward help-exchanges with peers: neighbors, friends, and coworkers. To this should be added that the Puerto Ricans were involved in a smaller percentage of help-exchanges with agencies or organizations than their generational counterparts in Minneapolis/St. Paul. If the percentage of help-exchanges is taken as an indicator, the

TABLE 7.2

Comparison of Minnesotan and Puerto Rican Parent and Child Families: Help Exchanges (in percent)

Source/Recipient of Help	Parent Generation Families		Child Generation Families	
	New York City Puerto Rican	Minneapolis/St. Paul Minnesota*	New York City Puerto Rican	Minneapolis/St. Paul Minnesota*
Other generations	56 ⎫ 73	47 ⎫ 63	35 ⎫ 67	35 ⎫ 61
All other kin	17 ⎭	16 ⎭	32 ⎭	26 ⎭
Peers	17	18	22	21
Agencies	10	19	11	18

*Taken from Table 3.03, page 66 of Reuben Hill, *Family Development in Three Generations*, Schenkman Publishing Co., Cambridge, Ma., and London, 1970.

Puerto Rican families of both generations focused their lives more upon the informal circle of family members, neighbors, and friends than did the Minneapolis/St. Paul families.

In the Minneapolis/St. Paul study, Hill used the term *modified extended family system* because of the strong familial interdependence in three-generation depth. In the absence of a three-generation family study it would be misleading, perhaps, to describe the Puerto Rican families with this term, but the degree of intergenerational interdependence of the Puerto Rican families, based upon the high frequency of familial visits and the heavy reliance upon the family in the giving and receiving of help, was stronger than that of the corresponding generations in the Minneapolis/St. Paul study. Thus, despite pervasive differences between the generations and little evidence of familial continuity, the Puerto Rican families were remarkably unified in a pattern of strong and viable intergenerational interdependence.

The strength of intergenerational interdependence in visiting and in help-exchanges was striking, in particular, when projected against the pattern of pervasive intergenerational differences and discontinuities. Yet the possibility remains that within this group of Puerto Rican families the strength of such interdependence varied according to variables relevant to intergenerational discontinuities. For example, we demonstrated earlier that similarities and differences in the place of birth and early socialization of the parents and their married children did influence intergenerational discontinuity. When the parents and their children shared a common place of birth and early socialization, whether in Puerto Rico or in New York City, intergenerational continuity among some variables tended to increase. We also demonstrated that, when the parents and their children had similar levels of education, intergenerational continuity among some variables tended to increase. Was the interdependence between generations affected by these seemingly important variables? The question is important because the place of birth and early socialization is an essential component of the migration experience, and education is an important measure of socioeconomic status. Thus, variations in the migration experience and in socioeconomic status could influence the strength of intergenerational bonds.

To answer the question the data were examined in a variety of ways, but no matter how examined, the answer was clearly and consistently negative: *there are no statistically important differences in intergenerational interdependence owing to differences in place of birth and of early socialization. Generational differences in education, also, do not affect intergenerational interdependence.* The bonds of intergenerational interdependence outweigh important components of the migration experiences and of socioeconomic status. In this way the Puerto Rican families retained their solidarity in the face of a new and different host society. Underlying such statistical patterns were deeply rooted norms binding the families into a unified whole. The norms include a set of rights and obligations in the relationships among relatives. In time of need the expectation is that relatives will receive help without having to plead. Thus, in the vocabulary of insults, most disparaging is "bad son," "bad father," "bad mother," indicating that the almost sacred duty to give family help in time of need has not been carried out. Such labels, imposed through gossip or angry confrontations, represented external forces which induce compliance with the familial normative system. The internal counterpart to the expressed insult is the feeling of guilt for refusing a relative in time of need. The double edge of criticism and guilt sustains the help-exchanges in the family.

Also relevant to intergenerational solidarity is the way persons viewed their marriage in relation to their expectations of marriage. To investigate this point, we asked the women in both generations about the degree to which they felt their marital expectations had been fulfilled; four alternative responses were provided, ranging from "not at all" to "more than completely fulfilled." We found proportionately fewer child-generation wives (43 percent) than parent-generation wives (62 percent) felt that their marital expectations had been "fulfilled." Aside from demonstrating the tendency of the younger women to be less satisfied with marriage than the older women, the important point for our purposes is the women's thoughts about marital fulfillment. To uncover such thoughts during the interviews we followed each answer to the question on marital fulfillment by open-ended prodding. In explaining the degree to which they had been maritally fulfilled, the younger women emphasized such thoughts as:

Some of my emotional needs are not fulfilled. . . . I have yet to be able to share my innermost feelings with my husband.

He is not sensitive about caring for the position I take.

Sexually I am satisfied and my husband cares for me.

Our love is something which grows with time. There is something always new.

He has been a good companion, friend, and father.

The older women, in contrast, emphasized such thoughts as:

I am fulfilled because I have my two daughters and my grandchildren.

He has always provided for his home. I wanted to have a family. I have only one son, but have grandchildren now.

I have my home and my children and a good man who respects me.

I wanted to raise a family and provide them with a good home, and I did.

The women of each generation agreed that marital fulfillment requires that the husband be a good provider and that he give them their own homes, but their statements revealed differences between the two generations in the very concept of marital expectations. The younger women's orientation toward marriage was more toward solidarity with their husbands, while marital fulfillment to the older women meant procreating and raising children. To the younger women, much of what is considered marital fulfillment rested upon their feelings of a satisfactory personal relationship with their husbands, usually a conjugal companionship. They yearned for the attainment of mutuality of affection, reciprocal understanding of personal feelings, and a sharing of experiences and activities in a context of a middle-class American life style. The older women could still point to the joys of motherhood and satisfying identification with their offspring as evidence of marital fulfillment even when they mentioned their husband's troublesome conduct, such as excessive drinking, violence, and philandering. The older women's alignment was vertical, toward lineage, while that of the younger women was horizontal, toward spouse. The intergenerational solidarity displayed by the families was indicated by the parents' reaching toward their adult children; it is consistent with the older women's sense of marital fulfillment and focus upon lineage.

The data presented in other chapters demonstrate unambiguously that the child generation exceeded the parent generation in attributes conducive to success in and adaptation to American life. They had a higher level of education, better occupations, larger annual family incomes, more ability to express themselves in English, and so on through a great variety of skills and values of functional utility in the host society. In the context of the host society, such differences indicate greater human resources in the child generation than in the parent generation. Inequalities in the distribution of human resources could invite the view that the flow of help, in the balance, went from the child to the parent generation, from those with greater to those with lesser resources. Although help was given by the younger to the older generation, the general pattern was quite the opposite: the parent generation helped the child generation significantly more often. Thus, during the year prior to the interviews with the families, 46 percent of the child generation *received* financial assistance from the parent generation, whereas only 22 percent of the child generation *gave* financial assistance to the parent generation. The statistics for help in the form of lend-a-hand services are 34 percent from the parent generation and 16 percent from the married-child generation. Parents more often counseled their children (15 percent) than the other way around (9 percent). The exchanges of goods between the generations was about even, but such goods were largely gifts given on ceremonial occasions, birthdays, anniversaries, and Christmas, for which the norms of reciprocity have specific, ritualistic meaning. We shall return presently to the significance of such ceremonial gifts in the context of the solidarity between the generations, but for now, the general aggregate pattern is clear: it was a parent benefactor arrangement; the parents were the donors; the children were the recipients.

The *parent-benefactor arrangement* represents the continuation of parental care and attention which started during infancy in the married-child generation. Having gone through stages of the life cycle to the point of adulthood, the child generation was focusing upon the establishment of its own nuclear family and household. The parent generation, having passed through the stage of the life cycle which their children were experiencing were acting the role of benefactors of their children, with perhaps a role reversal from donor to recipient of help as they grew older and became dependent upon their children. Thus, the parent-benefactor arrangement which prevailed in these intergenerationally linked families was based on the different stages of the life cycle of the parents and their married children. The arrangement outweighed the fact that the younger generation's human resources far exceeded those of the parents.

Although our main focus will be upon the objective aspects of intergenerational integration, it is important that we recognize the subjective component in ideas of what constitutes a need because it influences help-seeking and help-giving efforts. Help-giving exchanges between generations depended upon the subjective feelings couples in the nuclear units had regarding their needs. When nuclear units rigorously accommodated to their income level and adapted their aspirations to their resources, the occasions for dramatizing or even feeling the need for help diminished. One of the Puerto Rican families, the deeply religious Guevarras, provides a clear illustration of accommodation and adaptation. Fifty-eight-year-old Juan Guevarra in the parent generation worked in a shoe factory. Chemicals used in dying the shoes have damaged one eye and blinded the other, but Juan was proud of his 16 years on the job, perceiving it as a mark of his responsibility and seriousness as an employee. Since his wife, Manuela, did not work outside the house, the total family income was what Juan earned – less than $7,000 a year. Yet, at no time during the many days of interviewing did either of the Guevarras express a desire for something they did not have. In Manuela's words, "It is bad to wish for more than what you really should have. Going beyond your aspirations is bad. God may punish you." Juan repeatedly emphasized, "You must conform to what you have. You have what God wishes you to have."

In keeping with their fatalistic views, the Guevarras raised their children to look upon occupational success and affluent life styles as less important than being *gente buena* (good or decent people). According to the Guevarras' values, what you are as a person is important, more important than what you do or attain. Hernando, their son in the married-child generation, exemplified the parental values taught to him. A high-school graduate working as a truck mechanic, he was laid off from his job. Now he loads and unloads cargo from trucks, having recently been passed over for a job promotion that would have made his work substantially easier. He earned about $12,000 a year, all of the family's income which supported his wife Luz and their six children. Reflecting his parents' attitudes, he expressed no bitterness at the loss of the job for which he was trained or for not getting the promotion he felt he deserved. "Everything has been fulfilled," he says, "particularly because of my good job and the improvement in my own character. I am not a second-class person. I have friends, and good ones, too. No job or no friends leads to suicide."

In the little free time available to Luz, she did not look for additional family income, but worked as a volunteer in her children's school on yard duty, providing library help, and on the bingo committee. "That way," she explained, "the teachers can devote all their time to academic activities." The Guevarras accepted financial setbacks with equanimity and by adjustments in their expenditures. One of the interviewers of this family reports an incident:

The couple and their children reside in a federally subsidized apartment. Through meticulous budgeting and strict adherence to budgetary limitations, they are able to meet their $155 share of the rent. When the rent recently was increased sharply by $50 to $205 monthly, their budget was severely stretched. Their response to the crisis was to further trim their budget, cutting back on their food and postponing the purchase of a television set.

The parent and child generations of the Guevarra family have cordial relations with each other, spoke to each other on the telephone at least once a week and celebrated ceremonial occasions together, but they assiduously avoided either seeking or giving help to each other. In response to the question about receiving financial help during the preceding year, each couple replied almost indignantly, "Never! It is not our way of being." Thus, situations which some persons or families might view as requiring help were not seen as such by the Guevarras because their religious norms prescribed that they remain independent and self-sufficient.

Thus, if Hill's empirically based formulations are used, the Puerto Rican families, overall, fit the concept of a modified extended family because of the frequency of intergenerational visits and help-exchanges. Yet the concept discussed previously contains important variations in the ways in which families were integrated. We know there was substantial interdependence between the generations; the forms of integration tell us how such integration was organized. The most prevalent form of integration ranged from more or less delimited interaction between intergenerational nuclear units, each economically self-sufficient, to the almost total dependence of the child generation upon both parents in the older generation. When needs, whether transient or more enduring, arose in the child generation, the mother and father in the parent generation typically cooperate with each other in giving help. They worked jointly and cooperatively according to the organization of sex roles in the family: women leaned toward socioemotional help in social support, nurturance, guidance, and advice, while men leaned toward giving help from their activities outside the home, in their jobs, contacts with external organizations, or street activities.

Two other forms of integration, seen less often, differ qualitatively from the prevailing pattern just described. *Matriarchy*, one variant of the prevailing pattern of integration, weakens parental cooperation in giving help because it makes the parent-generation mother the central, sometimes almost exclusive, source of help while relegating the father to the edge of family interaction. The mother becomes the overwhelming central figure as, in attitude and behavior, the father's relationship to family affairs becomes passive and inactive. *Team effort*, the second variant, differs from the prevailing pattern of intergenerational integration when a strongly held objective influences and even alters both the customary organization of sex roles and the usual flow of help from parent to child. Family interaction in such efforts involves the collective mobilization of resources focused upon the attainment of an objective.

The identification of the prevailing pattern of integration and of the two variants in the form of matriarchy and team structure is based entirely upon the parent and child linkages which were studied and not upon other intergenerational linkages existing within the same family which were not studied. For this reason, the distinctions made between the forms of integration do not necessarily reflect the respondents' total family situation. Other research could have collected data directly from the parents of the daughter-in-law or son-in-law, or from the siblings of the husband and wives in the child generation to arrive at a more inclusive formulation of intergenerational patterns. Since this is not what the research set out to do, we limit ourselves to the intergenerational linkages which were studied directly: the specific parent- and married-child generations.

To determine whether families fit the prevailing pattern or were organized according to matriarchal or team structures, two researchers independently and systematically reviewed all of the interviews and observational reports of every intergenerational family unit according to the definitions of intergenerational integration already developed and drafted a report justifying the classification. The material which was most relevant to the classification was varied. The interviewers' observational reports were important: who gave help to whom was often so clearly patterned as to be seen over the course of several interviews with the interlinked families. For example, the interviewers were able to witness directly team efforts of family members reciprocally engaged in operating their own drugstore or in putting both spouses of the child-generation couple through medical school. However, the interview material was also important. Data relevant to the frequency of intergenerational family contacts were examined, as well as how such contacts were made. Helpful, too, were the data on the experience of each of the families of problematical life events during the year preceding the interviews. Once a serious problem was identified, data were collected on how the family sought to solve the problem, if at all, and, if they did, how they solved it and to whom they turned in their efforts to cope. In addition, the data on the help-giving and -receiving exchanges in the families, during the year preceding the interviews, were very relevant. Besides delineating the various types of help — financial, goods, lend-a-hand services, and counselling and orientation — the data reported who gave what to whom. Presently, we shall see that such exchanges were not random occurrences: they were structured and patterned according to identifiable configurations. The open-ended interview questions, following the identification of each instance of help given or received, provided information on whether the respondent perceived the norm of reciprocity to be relevantly involved. The other categories of information, income, life fulfillment, perceptions of the island-home in comparisons to the host society, and so on, provided ancillary or supportive material.

When the 100 intergenerationally linked families were classified, the pattern became clear: 10 percent of the families represent team structures; 9 percent represent matriarchies; and the remainder, 81 percent represent the prevailing pattern of intergenerational integration. The two researchers differed in the classification of 11 of the families ($p < .001$) which, in turn, were finally classified by reexamining the cases. To understand what these families were like, *in vivo*, we turn to case material which illustrates the forms of intergenerational integration and reveals new facets associated with the forms of integration. The remainder of this chapter focuses upon the most prevalent pattern of integration which ranges from weak to strong intergenerational integration with both parents jointly sharing help-giving responsibilities toward their children. The variant forms of integration, matriarchy and the team structure, are discussed in Chapter VIII.

Of the 100 intergenerational families, the Marín and Valdés families exhibited one of the weakest patterns of intergenerational interdependence. Pedro Marín, a 65-year-old, recently retired baker, had been married for 40 years to Sonia, who was employed as a paraprofessional assistant in a junior high school. The early years of their marriage were characterized by the traditional pattern of sex-role segregation. Pedro did not allow his wife to work or to visit friends or relatives unless she had his specific permission. He managed the family income, gave her a small allowance, and made all decisions from what was to be purchased daily to which friends they should have. Sonia refused to accept this arrangement and over the years had many arguments with her husband. Eventually Pedro began to change until there was a great deal of sharing between them, even to the point of his volunteering to do housework and permitting her to balance their financial accounts. Sonia explained that it was not just the fights that brought about the change but also that when their two daughters got married and left home, they found themselves alone. Marital discord, stemming from Sonia's unwillingness to accept the pattern of role segregation and husband dominance and the couple's realization of solitude, combined to create a more equal arrangement between them.

The admixture of the new and the old in such role changes reflects the view the Maríns had of themselves as part-Puerto Rican and part-American.

Both came from Mayaguez in search of economic opportunities which would enable them to surpass the economic attainments of their parents: a cigar-maker and washerwoman, and a carpenter's assistant and housewife. Both wanted to remain on the mainland and looked forward to Sonia's retirement when they would have more time to "enjoy life." But despite the split in their ethnic self-identity, both insisted strongly that their children keep Puerto Rican traditions. Sonia said, "I want my children to preserve the language, the hospitality, and the courtesy toward everyone which character-izes Puerto Ricans." To accomplish this and to help them avoid marital con-flict, she and her husband wanted their children to marry Puerto Ricans. Pedro added, "With other Puerto Ricans we can *desahogar*," meaning "get-ting things off our chest" through open, ingroup intimate talk.

The emphasis the Maríns placed upon the value of Puerto Rican traditions unexpectedly created in Andrea Valdés, their daughter, serious resentments toward her parents. Andrea, the wife in the child generation, completed one year of college and was working as a teacher's aide in a Head Start program. Her husband, Julio, was an independent trucker. They had moved to a town in New Jersey where they purchased a modern brick home. Andrea said, "When I was young, my parents were only interested in that I get married, have children, and become a housewife. They never thought of me as a person interested in a career and a profession, and not in children or a husband. If they had not taught me those values, I would not have gotten married at such an early age (21). I would have enrolled in a university and finished a career." This grudge against her parents was deep and persistent and had become part of the anger she felt toward her husband. Like her parents, who early in marriage fought over the performance of conjugal roles, she argued with her husband because of his irresponsible spending, his failure to consult her when changing jobs and making other decisions, and going out evenings unaccom-panied by her. When she found out that he was having an affair, she discussed it with an American friend who advised retaliation in kind, "a taste of his own medicine." However, her mother, drawing from her own marital experi-ences, advised Andrea to pressure Julio into more sharing of activities in the household and entertainment. They then began to share chores, Andrea shopping and cooking, Julio doing laundry and dishes. Following her parent's example, each partner contributed from their income to a common fund for family expenses.

Although the two generations, linked through Andrea, paralleled each other as economically self-sufficient nuclear units, there was intergenerational interaction, as seen in their writing and telephoning each other once or twice a week, visiting each other at least once a month, and celebrating ceremonial occasions. Conforming to the typical pattern, the parent generation was more often the giver of help, not only in the mother's counselling the daughter but materially as well: when Julio was laid off from work, Pedro loaned him money, gave him $150 to buy a car, and provided airfare to visit relatives in Colorado. The absence of urgent needs in the families and the distance between the parent- and child-generation residences kept them from more frequent interaction and help-exchanges, as did the daughter's continuing resentment toward her parents: "Some Puerto Ricans are good, but some try to hold you back from being yourself."

The Alarcón family, connected to the Bustelo family through their daughter Haydee, reveals, however, that intergenerational integration often is more complex than that exhibited by the Marín and Valdés families, the parent generation giving substantially more help to some offspring than to others. Anita Alarcón and her husband Claudio have been married for 36 years. Claudio is proud of his occupational achievement as a mechanic/welder in a trucking company and of his financial achievement in owning a two-story house in a "good" neighborhood of New York City. The history of their marriage may be divided into two phases. In the first stage the marriage was characterized by Claudio's dominance of his wife in issuing commands and making decisions, by frequent partying and drinking with friends, and by incessant womanizing. According to Anita, the marriage was on the verge of dissolving, but there was a turning point when Claudio suddenly converted into a "born again" Pentecostal. This conversion transformed the marriage and kept Claudio at home. Their relationship gained considerable peace and security, the sharing of decisions and activities, and the joint feeling of optimism that life would continue to improve. There is the suggestion that marital tensions and Anita's unhappiness in her marriage precipitated both Claudio's religious conversion and the subsequent solidity of the marriage.

This experience of successfully persevering and sailing through a stormy marriage had an impact on Anita and on her relationship with her twice-married daughter Haydee, who had a six-month-old son from her marriage to Eduardo Bustelo, a computer technician. Haydee also had two sons from a former marriage which had ended in divorce. After the birth of the third child, Haydee was sterilized because she did not want more children to prevent her from returning to work as a cashier. She and her husband shared in decision-making and household duties. Both were committed Baptists who gave hours of service to their church. Although Haydee repeatedly affirmed her marriage to be a good one, she revealed that during the preceding year she had considered divorce. The main focus of conflict between Haydee and Eduardo was his attitude toward Haydee's two children by her first husband.

Haydee felt Eduardo was too strict and unfair in disciplining his stepchildren; she admitted that she would always doubt his feelings about these children. The arguments between Haydee and Eduardo were bitter and extended to issues other than the disciplining of the older children.

Anita's contacts with her daughter were for the purpose of counselling. When Haydee and Eduardo had marital difficulties, Anita advised Haydee to control her temper and to be patient with her husband. Anita wanted Haydee to stay with Eduardo since it was her second marriage and, according to Anita, "it is the woman's responsibility to keep the marriage together." Anita's stress on this point reflected the pain she felt in the earlier phase of her own marriage and a criticism of her other two children. The Alarcóns were raising the child of an unmarried daughter and supporting and raising the two children of their son whose wife had died after an abortion.

Haydee was counselled on her marital difficulties not only by her mother, but also by the church pastor and by her best friend, Luisa. Haydee believed that the Bible commands the wife to be submissive to her husband, but she had trouble accepting this. Luisa advised her "to learn through prayer to become a submissive wife." The advice from the pastor, Luisa, and her mother was similar — she must learn to suppress her angry feelings toward her husband in the name of religion and in the interest of saving the marriage. Like the Alarcóns, the Bustelos had a marriage which appeared to survive through submission to religious standards, but because the tensions were more alive in the younger generation, Haydee seemed doubtful that she could adhere to religious standards. Meanwhile, Anita anxiously continued to give advice to Haydee. She felt overburdened and resentful at having to raise her grandchildren and, should Haydee's marriage to Eduardo fail, Anita didn't want the additional burden of raising those children. She was looking forward to the time when all the children would be out of the house and she and Claudio would have more time to themselves.

The Marín and Alarcón families were about equally involved with their offspring in the child generation in the frequency of visits, help-giving, and the celebration of ceremonial occasions. Both mothers in the parent generation were deeply committed to preserving their daughters' marriages, but the sharply different advice they gave their daughters reflects the ambivalence and contradiction in the marital unions of the Puerto Rican families. Sonia Marín focused her advice upon the negotiation of a more sharing, egalitarian conjugal relationship, conforming to intergenerational social change documented in Chapter V. Anita Alarcón advised acceptance of traditional patterns of conformity, prescribed in religious beliefs. The comparative effectiveness of such different advice cannot be determined, but it should be observed that Anita's daughter felt quite doubtful of her capacity to suppress her resentments toward her husband, even at the risk of her dissolving marriage. These words of advice were given and taken with unforeseen consequences, all in the general context of intergenerational integration. Though both families were economically self-sufficient, the Alarcóns, unlike the Maríns, had three grandchildren totally dependent upon them and were anxious about having to support even more grandchildren. While some parental families were giving comparatively little help to the child generation studied because there was no perception of pressing needs, they were fully supporting other offspring or grandchildren. Other persons in nuclear units not studied directly, offspring of the parent generation and siblings of the child-generation spouses, might have been relying entirely upon their parents for subsistence.

The prevailing pattern among economically self-sufficient intergenerational nuclear units, however, was one of substantially greater interdependence in help-giving than that exhibited by the Marín-Alarcón families. With the parents usually in the donor role, gifts of money or material goods were given to meet needs in the child generation. The birth of a child created such needs, as did an episode of unemployment or increase in rent. Few were the exceptions, indeed, to the pattern of gift-giving during ceremonial occasions. Such occasions inevitably were accompanied by some form of festivity, perhaps with some dancing and drinking, but practically always with the eating of traditional Puerto Rican dishes, but the festival was not just a matter of the participants' having fun. The intensity of interaction at such occasions provided an opportunity for releasing tensions through intimate talk and was a celebration of family bonds and a reminder of the family's enduring solidarity. The occasions served to symbolize the family as the primary source of help, a reservoir of potential help to be used in time of need.

When the potential for help-giving was put into full use, it assumed the form of the child generation's remaining or becoming totally dependent upon the parent generation. Of the child-generation families studied, about 6 percent were fully dependent upon their parents, although many more had siblings who were dependent. (No couple in the parent generation was fully dependent upon their children.) Such dependence varied in duration: sometimes it was temporary, a result of the child-generation son experiencing a period of unemployment, but sometimes it persisted or was likely to persist, thus affording the parents no relief from the heavy burden of supporting their married children. The Valencia family illustrates this point. Rafael, the 19-year-old son in the child generation, had gotten married 9 months before being interviewed, quitting his job at the same time because he felt that he was being given too much responsibility as a messenger distributing mail in an office building. He and his 17-year-old bride Lupe and their two-month-old daughter lived in his parents' home in a fully furnished basement apartment. Spending much of his time in the apartment, he talked about the future when he would be a professional musician playing a conga drum, and his daughter would become a fashion model. When they were first married he would not let Lupe go out alone or with her friends, but, recently, accompanied by him they began to visit her old neighborhood. As she reported, the visits were creating further conflict between them: "He argues with me because I have more male friends than female friends. When we go to visit my friends in my old neighborhood, he gets mad because my old boyfriends greet me and kiss me on the cheek." Visiting her old neighborhood, Lupe felt, affirmed her rights. However, Rafael's objections to the attention she received were seemingly satisfying to her: "He acts the way I like a husband to act." In general, she felt her main life objectives had been fulfilled, "I am happily married and I have a daughter. I am happy here; there will be no problem when I decide to get a job." As a teenage bride, a new mother, having an eleventh grade education, and no work experience, her optimism about future employment rested on doubtful assumptions. Her dependence upon her husband's parents would likely continue if her husband remained unemployed.

Although happy in marriage and optimistic about the future, Lupe observed that Rafael was angered easily by little things and had become progressively more tense. She attributed this to his unemployment and their total dependence upon his parents. She commented that his lack of skills would hinder his getting a job: "These days you need special education to get the kind of job you like." Both felt uneasy and worried about the burden they were placing upon his parents and the gifts of money they had received from her relatives. Specifically she was deeply concerned that out of desperate need for money, he might decide to start using drugs. When asked by the interviewer to describe what his life would be like ten years in the future, Rafael said, "I will try my best to do things better. By then I should have what I need: my job and money." This statement and others made by him suggest an underlying sense of disappointment, self-doubt about his competency to undertake the responsibilities of marriage and a family, and even a hint of remorse over personal deficiencies.

Humberto Valencia, Rafael's father, was proud of both his success in New York City and the solidarity of his family. A 39-year-old construction worker married for 20 years, he owned his mortgaged home, valued at $60,000, and lived with his wife Carmela, two younger children, aged 5 and 13, and a 5-year-old foster child, as well as with Rafael, Lupe, and their infant daughter in the married-child generation. The total annual family income on which these eight persons lived was about $22,000 — $17,200 from earnings as a construction worker, $2,100 from foster childcare payments, and the remainder from the rental of the second floor apartment in the house they own. Born and raised in one of San Juan's most oppressive slums, Humberto reported having lived, "like a savage." Through hard and often brutal labor in Puerto Rico's tropical heat, Humberto learned to work with cement and did some masonry and carpentry. The skills he acquired early in life were those he was using in construction work. He and Carmela felt that all their life objectives have been fulfilled in a good marriage, a family, and in the ownership of a house.

Neither parent begrudged providing Rafael, his wife, and infant with full economic support. In fact, over and above such support, they gave the young couple $25 per week for incidental expenses. At no time had there been outright parental reproaches directed at their son for not undertaking full responsibility as a husband and father, but their disappointment was evident during the interviews. Carmela explained her son's aimlessness: "He does not know what he would like to do." The father also was straightforward in discussing Rafael's situation. When asked about his aspirations for his children he said, "I would like my sons to be engineers. However, kids today don't know how to do anything. Look at this one here" (referring to Rafael). Humberto thought the younger generation looks down on hard work and lacks skills, but, however strong their disappointment, neither parent has threatened to withdraw support or make support contingent upon Rafael's efforts to get a job or get training for a job. Such feelings appeared to be inconsequential to Humberto's and Carmela's sense of parental responsibility and family stability; both were comforted by the presence of their children and newly acquired granddaughter.

In this case, Rafael had always been dependent upon his parents for support; his marriage and the birth of his daughter simply added two dependents to the family, but parent-generation families, as reservoirs of potential help, sometimes were activated for support when problems arose in the child generation. Thus, from time to time the two generations might have retained their nuclear autonomy within the delimited intergenerational interdependence already discussed, then have changed toward dependence upon the parent generation and back to autonomy again. Financial problems usually caused such changes, but marital problems, sometimes based on economic problems, might have increased dependence upon the parent generation.

The Labo family demonstrates this point. At the time we began interviews with the family, the couple in the married-child generation were undertaking a trial separation, the son Carlos returning to live with his parents, his wife Viola and 5-year-old daughter remaining in their apartment. Carlos, a college graduate, had gone from one sales job to another and had been unemployed for ten months. Every time he lost a job Viola considered divorcing him. She was a hard-working legal secretary who expressed frustration over her unfulfilled ambition to be a lawyer. Caught between what she would like to be but was not and a husband who had been an unreliable provider, she had little respect for him and blamed him completely for the failure of the marriage. She expressed disdain for his inability to find himself and felt he had lost face in his position of authority in the family. From her viewpoint, what made matters worse were his jealous accusations that she dated other men while attending social affairs related to her job. His move to his parents' home made him appear as a refugee from a bad marriage, seeking solace and understanding from his mother and father. His mother worked as an educational assistant in the city's school system, and his father was a general handyman. They had still at home three of their five children and an 8-year-old niece whose mother had died. They were proud of their family unity and expressed no misgivings about again supporting their adult married son. Through the pattern established by the child generation over the years of job-no-job and an on-again-off-again marriage, the parent generation remained a stable supportive system.

These families illustrate the prevailing range of intergenerational integration, from self-sufficient, largely independent units to a pattern in which the child generation depended entirely upon the parent generation. The following chapter takes up matriarchy and the family team structure as variant forms of integration, and concludes with points relevant to this chapter and the next.

REFERENCES

1. Parsons, T. and R. F. Bales. 1955. *Family, Socialization and Interaction Process*. New York: The Free Press, 3-19.
2. Hill, R. 1970. *Family Development in Three Generations*. Cambridge: Schenkman Publishing Co.

VIII

Variant Patterns: Matriarchy and the Team Effort

As demonstrated in the preceding chapter, parental help was, with few exceptions, a responsibility exercised jointly by the mother and father. The exceptions occurred among families ruled by a matriarchy or by family team efforts. We will illuminate important facets of these types of integration by discussing individual families we studied. In the matriarchal form of inter-generational integration the responsibility for helping was so strongly centered upon the mother in the parent generation that the relevance of the father's help was almost excluded or rendered marginal. Thus, matriarchy is a variant form of integration in relation to the prevailing patterns of inter-generational integration.

Devotion to the preservation of her family was already in evidence 28 years ago when Felicia Ivarra learned that her father in New York City was having an affair. A 19-year-old high school graduate and skilled typist, she left a good job in Puerto Rico because she felt obligated to go to New York and take some action to protect her mother who was living on the island with her. She failed to persuade her father to give up the other woman and was then burdened with the responsibility of supporting her mother. In New York City she found an unskilled job in a factory, of lower prestige than her former job in Puerto Rico, but one that paid more. As she became aware of other opportunities, she began to look upon her job as a stopgap. As the years passed, Felicia became involved in New York City's life, developing friend-ships, seeking contacts, and participating widely in civic activities. Later she became one of the founding members of an association of Puerto Rican organizations, the strongest social, civic, and political association of its type in her borough. Eventually, her knowledge of community resources and needs and her determination to succeed led to her present job as a paraprofessional community worker for a family planning clinic. "I think I have the potential to achieve anything I want to achieve," she said, confi-dent of her abilities.

Her husband, Eugenio, too, was proud of her accomplishments as he recalled his thoughts 24 years ago while courting her, "She is the one with whom to have a family." At the time of the interview Eugenio, 57, was 10 years older than Felicia. He was retired from the merchant marine and was working as a token-booth clerk for the transit authority. Their annual income was about $25,000. Both contributed their incomes to a common fund from which Felicia drew money for family expenses. Felicia and Eugenio expressed similar opinions on issues important to them: ethnic self-identification as Puerto Ricans; respect for each other and high self-esteem; pride in their disciplined habits of hard work; and a desire to improve their material conditions over and above what they had. Eugenio concluded, "I have been able to raise my family well;" then he added, "I do not owe money to anyone."

During Eugenio's long absences from the home while in the merchant marine, Felicia had assumed the sole responsibility for raising the children, worked full-time, and participated in civic causes. Looking back, she said, "I didn't think I was going to be able to hold a job and raise my kids, keep house, and be a good wife at the same time." The multiple roles she performed in the family, at work, and in outside activities consolidated her control over the children, provided her with knowledge about community resources, and gave her an independent income for her own use. A woman oriented toward institutional structures outside the family, she still looked upon her family bonds as the most vital of all: "Without families and their support, none of us could exist." Out of this context grew her role as the family's prime mover and matriarch.

Complementary changes were occurring also in Eugenio's relationship to the family because of the years he spent away. Retired from the merchant marine, he still found it difficult to get involved in family affairs after the many years of dissociation from such problems. He said that, whenever the family got together under Felicia's direction to discuss ways of helping each other, he withdrew because he found it difficult to adjust to continuous family life. Felicia reported that his tendency to withdraw emotionally from family affairs caused constant but inconsequential bickering between them. She stated, however, that she completely understood his uneasiness and allowed him freedom of movement away from the family.

The Ivarras have three children, two of whom lived at home. Felicia's guidance and financial assistance to them and to others in her extended family were so incessant and so extensive that they defied the possibility of a complete accounting. She had daily talks with her daughter about the importance of school work and planning a career and with her younger son, who was soon to be married, about the responsibilities of marriage and parenthood. In the year preceding the interview, she had given her daughter $1500 towards college tuition; she had begun to purchase housewares in preparation for her son's marriage; she had recently given her sister money to buy new furniture after a fire in her apartment; in addition, she was driving her mother-in-law to the doctor's office once a week.

However, the principal focus of Felicia's concern as a matriarch was her older son Mario, a troubled young man lacking the discipline in work and behavior so highly valued by his parents. As soon as he finished high school Mario had enlisted in the army but found himself unsuited for military life. After repeated infractions of the regulations he was dishonorably discharged. He returned to New York at age 19 to live with his parents, bringing with him Lisa, his newly acquired Chicana bride, but Mario found married life, like army routine, too confining. He was soon going to parties with old friends and running around with other girls. Lisa became less and less tolerant of his behavior and there were repeated arguments. Felicia saw that her daughter-in-law's complaints were justified. She intervened to settle their differences. While trying to quiet the arguments at home, Felicia found a job for Lisa, but the girl's working outside the home only served to complicate matters. Felicia heard through friends that Lisa had become involved romantically with a married man but she kept the information from Mario, while at the same time planning for Lisa's departure from the city. She arranged for Lisa to hide in the home of a distant relative until she could leave. Mario, realizing that his wife had left him, got a gun and went out to look for her. Fortunately, Lisa made it safely back to Texas without Mario ever finding her or learning of the circumstances associated with her disappearance.

Following Lisa's departure, Mario became addicted to drugs. Felicia counselled him every day, took him to spiritualists and, finally, for psychiatric consultations. After eight months of such intercessions, he returned to a state of normalcy. Then he met Yolanda who was 16 years old. Soon they were living together in a common-law union and became the parents of a daughter. Mario gave credit to his wife and the birth of the baby for inducing a change in his personality, a newfound sense of responsibility. Employed steadily in a furniture factory, he was earning about $8,200 annually. Without exerting her influence in the dramatic ways she had in the past, Felicia remained a highly visible and instrumental force in the lives of her son and his second wife. The other family members followed her example in extending help to the young couple. Eugenio spent one day a week in his son's small basement apartment, doting on his infant granddaughter, which was an exception to his reluctance to become involved in family affairs. After the birth of the baby, Mario's sister did household chores for them, and his brother gave them $80 to help cover the expenses of childbirth. While mobilizing the family's support of the young couple, Felicia provided direct help herself. Before the birth, she worked hours into the night preparing a bassinet and layette, she purchased nightclothes for Yolanda to wear in the hospital, and she ran in and out of their apartment cooking, cleaning, and helping.

As stated in Chapter III, the desire for a continuation of upward mobility was the motivation to leave Puerto Rico of most persons in this study and many other Puerto Rican migrants of that time. Felicia Ivarra was not typical in this sense. Her perception of opportunities in New York City was the unexpected result of her abiding commitment to family bonds. The evolution of her role as the family's matriarch coincided with and was reinforced by her upward occupational mobility, her ever-increasing participation and leadership in civic organizations, and her husband's long absences from home and subsequent marginal role in the give-and-take of family life. In Felicia's case, matriarchy was associated with the successful mobility and good citizenship themes in American society. Other forms of matriarchy appearing in the intergenerational families under study, however, differed from that of Felicia Ivarra's. Although matriarchy emerged, it arose as a result of significantly different social processes and life experiences.

The Tapia-Laboy interlinked families are a case in point. When the interviews first began with Miguelina Tapia, a 51-year-old housewife, she broke down and cried, plaintively recounting her many problems. The scene repeated itself several times during the interviews, leading the interviewer to observe that of all those interviewed, "Miguelina was the most pathetic and saddest parent-generation wife. Her face reflects much suffering; her eyes show a great sadness." Miguelina was suffering from diabetes, had inoperable cataracts, and feared going blind. Her 45-year-old husband, Luis, who seemed confused and disoriented during the interviews, worked as an unlicensed barber, earning about $5,000 a year, which was the total family income. By Miguelina's account, Luis was "crazy" and had beaten her in the past during fits of violence. "One of these days he is going to flip and kill us all," she stated, while explaining that to forestall such a possibility she had purchased a lock and had it installed on the door of her bedroom, which she has not shared with Luis for the past eight years. She said the beatings had become less frequent in recent years because of Luis' fear that their sons would retaliate against him in defense of their mother.

While seeking to withdraw from her husband almost to the point of isolation, Miguelina focused her attention upon her children; consequently, the full brunt of family troubles fell on her shoulders. Of the four children living with her, the three who were grown were unemployed: "They are out of school, and all they do is hang around in the street with the wrong crowd. They don't want to work." The youngest son failed sixth grade and had to be transferred to another school because his obesity had made him the object of taunts and ridicule among schoolmates. Miguelina walked him to school to protect him, but she was desperately fearful of crime in the neighborhood and would not leave the public housing apartment unless accompanied. During the year preceding the interviews, her daughter fell down the stairs breaking a leg, and a son was involved in a car accident, requiring stitches. Sometimes, when too many problems burdened her, Miguelina felt she would like to be alone or to get therapy. She had been going to a local community mental health center, but, ". . . instead of counselling me, they prescribe tranquilizers and sleeping pills which I do not take because I do not want to become addicted."

Her fear of addiction could stem from the experience of her eldest son, Jaime Laboy, a product of her former marriage, who is the intergenerational link in the study. Jaime, an ex-drug addict, was working in a drug rehabilitation program. Although he had overcome the drug problem, he had begun to drink heavily. He took $300 from his place of work and spent it dancing and drinking. (The stolen amount was later deducted from his paychecks.) Often violent when drunk, he once attacked his wife, Damaris, and bruised her. She retaliated by stabbing him, for which he needed to be stitched up at a hospital. Damaris began to reject his frequent sexual advances, but submitted twice a month, as she said, ". . . only to relieve myself." She reported telling him that he is not man enough for her and told the interviewer that she has him wrapped around her finger.

Damaris was a secretary, and, with her earnings included, the couple's annual family income was about $20,000. Little of the income was spent on common household needs because each claimed that the other should assume such responsibilities. There was little mutual control between them. Even though her husband forbade it, Damaris went out four nights a week to disco dance. According to Miguelina, when Damaris returned from her nights out, Jaime "almost kisses her feet." Sometimes to keep away from Jaime, Damaris stayed overnight with Miguelina. The interviewer reported:

She seems very bitter about her life in general, and her husband, in particular. After she had a miscarriage early in marriage, Jaime became a drug addict and she felt she had no future with him. She kept emphasizing how she was going to "make it," because she had the confidence and poise that other people lacked. She kept repeating this during the interview as if she were trying to convince herself. After an angry discourse against her husband, she would turn to her 4-year-old daughter Raquel and say, "Right, Raquel?" Raquel would obediently answer, "Yes, Mommy."

Almost all of the problems the young couple experienced were brought to Miguelina for solutions. The free spending of money during the year preceding the interviews put them into debt, and Miguelina had to lend them $750, even though her own family income was only one-fourth of theirs. Miguelina advised Damaris to stay at home more and improve the marriage. She counseled her son about his drinking. She moved forcefully to rescue her granddaughter, Raquel, from the harmful effects of her parents' stormy marriage by assuming full responsibility for raising her.

Unlike the rise of the matriarchy of Felicia Ivarra, Miguelina Tapia emerged as a matriarch as a result of the many intransigent family problems converging upon her. She confronted such problems largely isolated from her husband because she was fearful of his violence. Although seriously handicapped by diabetes and the loss of sight, she became the major focus of intergenerational integration, while attending to the needs of her offspring still in the household. She provided them with whatever help her limited resources allowed – money, services, counsel, or advice, contacts with hospitals, and even physical protection. Her performance went beyond the usual masculine and feminine tasks. Subject to frequent spells of uncontrollable weeping, she sought solace but could not find it either among her problem-ridden and self-preoccupied children and daughter-in-law or in the drug-oriented therapy of the community mental health center. Miguelina's matriarchy was a *matriarchy by default* because it arose from and functioned as compensation for the inability of others in the family to fulfill their role expectations or responsibilities or because they were distracted from them. In brief, her matriarchy was rooted in her solitary efforts to keep the family intact and to preserve in the family some minimal standards of civility and safety.

This same process was operative in the larger and more complex Echevarría and Toro families. Floripe and Lorenzo Echevarría of the parent generation lived in a consensual union for eight years from which they had two daughters. Both had marital histories of multiple partnerships, mostly consensual unions, in which Floripe had five children, Lorenzo four. Thus, the household consisted of 46-year-old Floripe and 47-year-old Lorenzo, their two daughters, two sons and one daughter from her former unions, and one son from his former unions. Lorenzo and Floripe had independent sources of income: she received Aid to Dependent Children for her five children, including food stamps and rent, and disability benefits because of a hypertension problem which forced her into complete bedrest, a total of about $9,000 a year. Lorenzo, who was unemployed, received about $2,300 annually, in disability benefits because of severe stomach ulcers and arthritis. Socially, Floripe focused her attention almost exclusively on her children, but she regularly attended meetings of a local organization which represented welfare recipients in confrontation with the welfare bureaucracy. Lorenzo, on the other hand, was a habitual gambler and spent much of his time with close friends. The arrangement did not displease Floripe; of the husbands she had had, she felt he was the best because he did not drink or philander. However, their separate sources of income and their independent use of that income and her focus on the home and his upon street life put him at the edges of the family interaction.

Floripe preferred and encouraged Lorenzo's peripheral family status so she could cope with sensitive issues and problems while preserving domestic peace. She feared that if he were to involve himself in the children's problems he would become violent toward them and create even more problems. The problems were many. Her eldest daughter who had a child out of wedlock with a man now in prison spent much of her time out of the house looking for a good time. Her 17-year-old son was involved in several violent incidents, suspended from school, and arrested. Her 15-year-old son regularly came home from school drunk and went to bed drunk. Floripe confronted one problem after another while striving for solutions. She counseled her daughter, babysat for her, gave her money; she scolded the 17-year-old, found him legal help, paid for bail; she reprimanded and counseled the younger son about his drinking problems. Her children acknowledged her influence by turning to her and not to their stepfather when problems arose.

Of the six children, however, it was Floripe's eldest son, 22-year-old Danilo Toro, who worried her the most. Danilo was the married child who linked the two generations under study. On parole at the time of the interviews, he had recently served two years for armed robbery. Eight months before he had married Elena after a 3-year common-law union. Both were unemployed, living on monthly welfare payments of $330 which Elena supplemented by babysitting. Feeling that Danilo's prison record impeded him from getting a job in New York, they planned to go to Puerto Rico. They felt in Puerto Rico there was less "social distance," meaning that the people there are friendlier, more intimate, more supportive, and more forgiving; they thought his mother exemplified these attitudes. Danilo often took Elena and his 3-year-old daughter to Floripe's house, but then went out to the street. Elena said, "I expected he would be another kind of man."

Floripe worried that Danilo's unemployment would make him turn to crime once again. She gave him a weekly allowance of $25, bought clothing for her granddaughter, and frequently invited the young couple to dinner. Referring to this problem, she said she was compelled to "stay on top of things" and expected Danilo to stay out of trouble. In brief, she had become her son's custodian: "I have to help them as much as I can, so that through my efforts and his wife's efforts, Danilo will follow the right course."

In her efforts, Floripe followed a pattern not unusual to matriarchy, that is, enlisting her daughter-in-law as a collaborator to control a wayward male — a pattern which was seen also in the matriarchy of Felicia Ivarra. Through such collaborative efforts, the matriarch's influence was reinforced, extended, and likely to be projected into the future through the training given to Elena on coping with such problems. Matriarchies centralized influence and control within one person, the parent-generation mother. In contrast, family teams required the sharing of coordinated responsibilities. Collectively held goals resulting from the interaction of family members gave rise to the team structure. As they marshalled and directed their activities in the pursuit of their goals the team members were committed to attain, the family took on the organizational shape of a team. A family-based organizational structure arose to interact in a variety of ways with the usual organization of intergenerational family roles. Roles were differentiated and coordinated as a means of attaining the goal. In some family teams it was difficult or impossible to distinguish between donor and recipient, the specific peculiarities of this form of intergenerational integration often rendering such distinctions inapplicable.

An example of this process was the Padrón and Crespo families. They owned and operated a non-prescription discount drugstore. Dalia, the Padrón daughter, was the intergenerational link between the parent generation and the married-child generation. Her husband, Geraldo Crespo, 33 years old, was the main figure in the business venture by virtue of experience and background. Since the age of 18, when he first migrated to New York, he had worked as a drugstore clerk. With the passing of time, he assumed more and more responsibility in the store until he felt he had enough experience to embark on an enterprise of his own. Through hard work, careful planning, and the input of his in-laws, particularly his father-in-law who shared ambitions similar to his own, Geraldo achieved his goal and more: he not only owned the drugstore, modeled after the one in which he had acquired his experience and business acumen, but also owned the 18-family tenement building in which the store was located.

Geraldo was devoted to his wife's family, especially his father-in-law Ruben whom he described as his best and only friend. Ruben, 47 years old, had been a sugarcane cutter in Puerto Rico. For 24 years he had worked in one of the large New York City hospitals, first as an office clerk, then in the pharmacy which dispenses serums and drugs to other departments in the hospital. In this job Ruben had seniority, a good salary, and good benefits. He applied his knowledge of pharmaceuticals acquired in the hospital to the drugstore he owned with Geraldo where he worked as a clerk in his spare time and also acted as caretaker in the tenement building Geraldo owned.

The team effort in running the drugstore was based upon a division of labor: the parent-generation father was the buyer and general salesman; the parent-generation mother was the cashier and bookkeeper; the child-generation spouse was the general administrator and salesman; the child-generation daughter helped out in whatever needed to be done. Coexisting with this division of labor were three strong dyadic relationships and one other which appeared to grow less harmonious with the passage of time. The two men had much in common, sharing pharmaceutical knowledge, entrepreneurial ambitions, and their deeply felt love for Puerto Rican traditions and the island-home. Both identified exclusively with Puerto Rico, preferred to speak only Spanish, and planned eventually to return to live in Puerto Rico. Both missed the tropical weather and yearned to be with relatives they had left on the island. There was a common base in experience and feelings uniting the men in this intergenerational family-team effort.

The second strong dyadic relationship was the conjugal union in the parent generation. Celenia, the 50-year-old parent-generation wife, worked full-time in the drugstore, deriving satisfaction from the financial solvency the venture offered and pleasure from her 20 years of marriage to her husband and workmate. She was proud of Dalia, her daughter, who was working part-time at the drugstore and full-time toward a master's degree in social work. Dalia was Celenia's child from her first marriage which ended after one year when Celenia was abandoned by her husband. With Ruben, she had a 12-year-old son she described as a happy, studious, and obedient seventh-grader. Ruben did not restrict Celenia's activities in any way, but she reported that if he were to do so, it would make no difference to her. He was supportive of her many civic activities and of her monetary donations to church, community organizations, and relatives. They banked her entire income in a joint savings account, and they used his income for their living expenses. They did most things together; they went to movies, parties, and dances together, and visited relatives and friends together. She summarized the marriage: "We have matured together with understanding and respect for each other. We have a solid fulfilling relationship."

Mother and daughter comprised the third solid dyadic relationship in the team effort. Celenia considered Dalia to be her best friend, and this feeling was reciprocated by Dalia. They confided fully in each other. Celenia talked over with Dalia her desire to cut down the long hours she worked in the drugstore; Dalia talked to Celenia about problems with her children and conflicts with her husband. Whatever advice each got, it was invariably from the other. Through the years Celenia stood as a model for her daughter of a person devoted to community service. Before she began working in the drugstore Celenia had been employed as a community worker and she was still doing volunteer community work. Dalia had previously worked in a neighborhood Youth Corps Program and then went on to graduate school. To help her educational efforts, Celenia gave her $25 a week for school expenses and occasionally babysat. Through example, friendship, and overt acts of support the relationship between mother and daughter was reinforced through the years.

Considerable strength and harmony were evident in the dyadic relationship between son-in-law and father-in-law, husband and wife in the parent generation, and mother and daughter. The daughter and father and the son-in-law and mother-in-law had relationships that were warm, cordial, and appropriately respectful. It was in the child-generation marital relationship that there was growing unrest, even though the couple had strong points in common. Geraldo and Dalia shared deep ideological convictions about the need for Puerto Rico's independence and the establishment of a socialist state in the island. They belonged to the Socialist Party and made financial contributions to it (in contrast to Celenia, whose strong community orientation took the form of participation in "mainstream" organizations). They believed the United States had a deteriorating economic system and a political system that discriminated against minorities such as Puerto Ricans. Socialism, they felt, would make Puerto Rico sovereign and eliminate vestiges of American colonialism from the island.

The problem was that Geraldo had been devoted to the drugstore at the expense of his marital and familial obligations. Geraldo and Dalia were married when he was a 30-year-old widower with a son and daughter who were 13 and 8 at the time of the interviews. They had together an 18-month-old daughter. Dalia took her duties as a stepmother as seriously as her duties as a mother. Sometimes she was overwhelmed by the demands on her time and effort in graduate school. She thought Geraldo's involvement in the business had caused him to abdicate family responsibilities and relegate them to her. Among the children, it was the 13-year-old who required much of Dalia's attention. In an effort to understand the boy who was mentally retarded and to learn how to cope with him, Dalia consulted a private organization specializing in the problems of retarded children. At her prodding, Geraldo attended an orientation session of this organization twice a week for eight weeks. When she sought to reach some compromise with him by talking openly about the problem, he promised to give more time to the family. However, he soon reverted to the heavy schedule of work at the store. Her marital expectations continued to be unfulfilled. The intimacy of marriage was missing, and she had yet to share her "innermost" feelings with Geraldo. The companionship and mutuality of shared sentiments, and the joining together in reciprocal efforts to uncover and understand each other's feelings — a procedure which was so much a part of the mental health ethos of her graduate studies in social work — were superceded in importance by the division of labor which progressively alienated her from him. She turned to her mother for consolation and advice, but she said she would not marry the same person again and had entertained thoughts of divorce as a step toward self-realization.

As a result of the friction between the demands of two social organizations, the business and the family, conflicting expectations had intruded into the life of this couple. Nonetheless, the overarching pattern was one of cohesion and reinforcement between the two structures based upon a set of solid dyadic relationships and criss-crossing relationships of respect and affection between family members. All were committed to the success of the drugstore, and all, even the disgruntled Dalia, were proud of their economic attainments. Two recent incidents symbolized the integrity of each of the interrelated systems. On the family side, the drugstore recently was closed for an entire day so that everyone could attend the sixth grade graduation of the mentally retarded boy. To the consternation of the family members, one by one the children received diplomas and awards, but their child was left out. Painful embarrassment gave way to bitterness. They found the incident discriminatory against Puerto Ricans because the other children were not Puerto Rican. With the family's backing, Dalia complained to the school and was told an error had been made. Subsequently, the boy received a diploma and a certificate for penmanship. The other incident occurred in the summer of 1977 when the study's data were being collected. The entire city was blacked out by a power failure. Almost instantly, gangs of looters appeared. The innercity area where the family's store was located was particularly hard hit, but the drugstore escaped damage. When the lights went out, the family members drove their two cars on the sidewalk to block the store's two doors. The family remained there guarding their property until the afternoon of the following day when electricity and order were restored.

The family team was, in effect, a small corporate structure requiring the performance of roles in the business through the recruitment of persons performing family roles. Thus, a clear and comprehensive distinction was made between the corporate and the family structure, but team efforts in the service of family-derived collective goals were not always of a corporate character. In the Del Valle-Mantilla families, the team effort resulted from the focusing of the more or less usual family roles upon the attainment of a collectively beneficial objective — the medical education of both the son-in-law and daughter in the married-child generation. It is worthy of notice that the team effort in this family encompassed three generations to include the mother of the mother in the parent generation.

The daughter, Magdalena, aged 25, was completing a medical internship. Her husband, Daniel, 24 years old, was a third-year medical student. A year before they were interviewed they had been married and were living in an expensive studio apartment in Manhattan. They began to have difficulties in budgeting finances and time. Quickly and willingly, Magdalena's parents moved out of their apartment to rent a large house so they could all live together. Efrain, the 49-year-old father, was a stock clerk earning $200 weekly; Isabela, the 40-year-old mother, a billing clerk, earned $185 weekly; and the widowed grandmother received Social Security payments. The Del Valles put their earnings into a common fund for the entire family's expenses, delegating almost all of the housework to the 71-year-old grandmother who had lived with Isabela for 22 years and had helped raise the children. This division of labor made the parent generation the breadwinners for the family and relieved the married-child generation of financial and time-demanding household problems. Isabela said, "All I want is for them to be good students." An unmistakable feeling of pride of accomplishment suffused the family's collective efforts.

This parental pride and assistance extended to their other children. A 16-year-old daughter was finishing high school in Puerto Rico where she lived with relatives, receiving $100 monthly from her parents; a son who lived outside the home and was preparing to enter law school had recently been given a used car by his parents so he could commute to work. Over and above the daily support given to Magdalena, the Del Valles gave her $1000 to pay for tuition, and, upon her marriage a year before, $2000 as a wedding gift. Isabela said, with much delicacy, that the family also made an attempt to give the young couple as much privacy as possible, since, after all, they were practically newlyweds and liked to be alone. The young couple, in turn, helped in the housework whenever they could. Magdalena vowed that when she began to earn money as a physician she would always look after her parents' welfare and see to it that they would have a more comfortable life in the future.

The Del Valles did not restrict their help-giving to their own children. For years their household had been a launching pad for numerous nephews and nieces newly arrived in New York City from Puerto Rico. The new arrivals were given a headstart, with room and board, cash gifts, counseling, and orientation until they could find jobs and apartments and get out on their own to continue their education. Some who were helped in this fashion had become college students, pursuing career goals. Mindful of the help her relatives would give her children if the need should arise in the future, Isabela summarized her attitude, "The doors of my house are always open for the needy." She added emphatically, "Especially if they are relatives."

Two elements were evident in this family's team structure. First, the underlying theme in most of the help they gave was furthering the education of their offspring and relatives. The recipients were socially mobile, attempting to move up through educational means. Help-giving became an investment, not with the promise of returns specifically to benefit the parent-generation couple, but returns which enhanced the collective welfare of the larger family. Second, the team structure was an expeditious way of attaining the difficult, long-range objective of the children's full medical education. It should be noted that Isabela went through the eleventh grade and Efrain was a high school graduate. Going to college was not a family tradition; the medical students represented, in fact, the first generation ever in their family lineage to go to college. It was seen as the principal way of fulfilling mobile aspirations in the host society, the same aspirations which had uprooted the first-generation Puerto Ricans from their island-home and brought them to New York City. The team effort, both in this family and in the Padrón-Crespo family, was a social construction built out of the family in the service of mobility objectives, whether profits accruing from business success or the eventual symbolic and tangible rewards associated with the prestigious and lucrative practice of medicine. Through highly disciplined, rigorous budgeting, with expenditures made only on the bare essentials of family life, these team efforts were succeeding.

Team structures developed not just to serve the upward mobility goals of family members. Sometimes the issue was family survival, and the accompanying structure which emerged to serve the goal of survival was fluid and flexible. Survival, in turn, was not symbolized in the form of an external, distant goal but in the form of proximate, almost daily, goals of resolving problems which threatened the fabric of the family and the welfare of its members. The team configuration was reactive as opposed to the sustained purposeful behavior characteristic of the upward mobility-oriented team. The Roque-Espinel family exemplified the survival-oriented team pattern.

Fifty-three-year-old Joaquín and 38-year-old Tomasa Roque in the parent generation, had been married for 22 years and had six of their seven children living at home along with Joaquín's sister Leonor. The intergenerational link was the eldest child, Gabriel Espinel, the only offspring of Tomasa's prior common-law union. Gabriel considered Joaquín to be his father. He lived with his wife and two children in an apartment in the same building as his parents. The nine persons in the parent-generation family subsisted on disability payments, Aid to Dependent Children, and welfare, an annual total between $7,000 and $8,000. No one in the household was employed.

Joaquín had had several operations on his spine because of an injury sustained when he was in the army; he was partially deaf and had had several heart attacks. The problem worrying him the most, however, was that his father had never carried out a religious promise to recite prayers and sing spiritual songs. Joaquín believed he was experiencing the burden of a spiritual test (*prueba*) designed by evil spirits. He thought he would not have rest and tranquility until he finished what his father had left undone. He had consulted several spiritualist centers, said special prayers, and took baths with aromatic herbs. In the year before the interviews, Joaquín went to Puerto Rico to fulfill the promise made by his father, but according to Tomasa he was possessed by the presiding spirits and became crazy. Joaquín believed that spiritual forces told him what to do. He thought his deafness was the result of poison that someone was sprinkling in his ears. When he thought this was happening, he got violent. Tomasa thought Joaquín's problems were more than spiritual and once forced him to go to a hospital, but Joaquín would not return for his second appointment. Since he believed that his problems were of a spiritual nature, he would go only to spiritualist centers for consultation. Tomasa felt helpless and said the only thing she could do was "wait to see what will happen." Meanwhile, she accompanied him to the spiritualist centers, even though she believed that he should be hospitalized for treatment.

Joaquín's behavior created an array of episodic problems for the family. (He repeatedly asked the interviewer to speak more loudly because the spirits were talking to him at the same time, interfering with the interview.) Family resources had to be marshalled to cope with each bizarre episode, although the heaviest burden fell upon his wife. Joaquín helped out to his ability by doing family chores, but Tomasa managed the money and considered herself the main authority in the house. The couple no longer participated in many activities together, although Joaquín was still active, visiting friends and relatives, going to the movies, sporting events, and parties, watching television, and listening to music. Tomasa believed that a husband and wife must be tolerant and accepting of each other's faults but she had thought occasionally of leaving her husband because she did not feel she could control him. Tomasa stated that if she had to do it over again she would not marry him because of the many problems she had with his illness.

Despite their difficulties, the Roques provided help and services to their relatives. They were involved heavily in the marital and legal problems of Leonor, Joaquin's sister, who was living with them. They gave her $100 for her plane fare to New York and willingly took her into their house because "we knew that she needed us." On another occasion, they took in Tomasa's aunt for three months when this aunt had trouble getting along with her son-in-law. Tomasa also took in a cousin, a recent migrant from Puerto Rico. Unable to support another dependent, but not wanting to leave the cousin homeless, she took her to the welfare office for assistance. When funds were approved by the city agency, Tomasa helped her cousin find an apartment and settle in. She also provided counseling to her godchild when the girl's mother died, advising her to return to Puerto Rico and try to get along with her relatives there. All of this help came from a household with a family of nine living on an income of less than $8,000 annually. Tomasa expressed her hopes about the future: "Right now we are receiving welfare and we can get only the things we need, but that doesn't mean we don't want to prosper."

Both Roques believed in the value of education for personal advancement and had high aspirations for their children, but they expressed bitter disappointment at the fact that most of their children dropped out of school; not one had finished high school. Joaquin expressed guilt at the academic failure of his children and blamed himself for not providing them with what they needed. He asked the interviewer in this study to speak to his children to encourage those who were in school to continue and those who had dropped out to enroll again. Appreciative of the interviewer's interest, Joaquin took his address so he could invite him to a son's wedding.

Gabriel and Nydia Espinel, the child-generation family, were married for five years, and interacted daily with his parents since they lived in the same building. She was a housewife and he a school-crossing guard. She was still receiving Aid to Dependent Children for her two children, which began when she and Gabriel were separated for six months. That assistance, combined with his salary, made the family income about $13,000 annually. Their marital problem had been caused by Gabriel's infidelity. Gabriel said, "The man is for the street while the woman is for the house." He claimed his infidelity was a legitimate expression of masculinity.

Nydia had mixed feelings about her in-laws, the Roques. On the one hand, she liked having them live in the same building because they could help easily if any problems arose. On the other hand, Nydia told Alicia, her future sister-in-law, that Tomasa was very nice, but "meddlesome," and that Tomasa liked "to tell people what to do." She advised Alicia not to get too close to Tomasa when she got married, and that if she had a problem, "she should solve it with her husband." Despite the ambivalent attitudes Nydia harbored toward her mother-in-law, the young couple was heavily involved with the Roques. Gabriel and Nydia were very concerned about Joaquín's illness, and had taken him to spiritualists and helped pay for his herbal cures. Since they believed the problem was a spiritual one, they did not seek other types of assistance.

Direct observation indicated the incessant help-giving exchanges between the generations: Nydia habitually lent Tomasa money for the groceries until Tomasa's welfare check came in. She also accompanied Tomasa to the doctor for a cataract operation. Tomasa babysat for Nydia's children. She was constantly in and out of Nydia's apartment, using the washing machine and cooking dinner for them. The help-giving exchanges moved not just across generations but within generations as well. When a sister and brother-in-law were unemployed, Nydia took them into her apartment. When this same sister could not decide whether to marry her common-law husband legally, she came to Nydia for advice. Nydia also accompanied this sister to the hospital for an operation. And so it went in the Roque-Espinel families. Inter- and intra-generational help-giving exchanges were so frequent, so fast moving, and so spontaneous as to defy accurate monitoring. The family members themselves were often unaware of the help they were giving or receiving.

The problem-ridden lives of these families projected the image of a landscape with flash fires erupting everywhere with bewildering rapidity. The fires had to be extinguished; the family's problems had to be solved. The team structure of this family attempted to solve such problems, and the cumulative impact of the solutions was to enable the family to survive and the members to experience momentary relief from the repeated stresses of life events.

The team function in the first two families discussed, was a purposeful reaching out to the future to attain an objective relevant to upward mobility. In addition, the family members were in more or less stable relationships with their corresponding team roles. In the Roque-Espinel families the person's team role shifted quickly over time: one day's help-giver was the next day's recipient of help, or both roles were performed simultaneously. Who played what role depended upon who was experiencing the problem and who, at that moment, commanded resources relevant to the problem. The team functioned in a reactive manner to the stimulus of problems. Therefore, the objectives as well as the team structures of the first two families differed from that of the third family.

SUMMARY AND CONCLUSIONS

The diversity of actions presented in the case studies should not becloud the fact that overall the families displayed substantial intergenerational solidarity. If criteria established by Hill's research[1] are taken as a standard, the families more than fulfilled the conditions of a modified extended family when considered in two-generational depth. Moreover, the families' strong inter-generational solidarity remained uninfluenced by other life conditions impor-tantly involved in the continuity between generations. Thus, earlier chapters demonstrated that commonalities between the parents and their adult children in their place of birth and early upbringing and similarities in their educational levels did affect, in some important ways, the continuity between generations. When there were such commonalities, continuity increased, but commonalities in place of birth and upbringing between the generations and the similarities in their educational levels had no effect whatsoever on the frequency of intergenerational visits or help-giving exchanges. *Intergenera-tional family bonds retained their strength despite the possible divisive influ-ences associated with the migration experience and the many disparities between the generations.*

The portrait of intergenerational solidarity became even more compelling when seen in relation to the pervasive and statistically significant differences between the parents and their adult children, differences which were reported in detail in earlier chapters. Although the parents were upwardly mobile in relation to their own parents in Puerto Rico, their adult children far exceeded them in upward mobility. This signified that the adult children more than their parents substantially possessed human resources of functional impor-tance in the new host society, from a better mastery of the English language to a higher level of education, and on to larger incomes. Yet, even though the children commanded greater human resources, the balance in the flow of help was from the parents to adult children. The life-long, continued dependence of the adult children upon their parents, which is likely to diminish in the future as the parents begin to retire from work, coincided with the older women's vertical orientation toward marital fulfillment – the self-realization they experienced through identification with their offspring.

There was a subjective component in the views of what constitutes a family need which caused variable responses to objective conditions of deprivation. However, when a need was perceived and dramatized it became linked to that almost sacred familial norm supporting help-giving familial exchanges. This process contributed to the prevailing pattern of intergenerational integration. The pattern ranged from economically self-sufficient, somewhat autonomous, interlinked nuclear units to one of complete dependence of the adult children upon the parents. Among the self-sufficient families, the celebration of ceremonial occasions served as an expression and a reminder of the family's solidarity. Even when not immediately needed, the family still stood as a reservoir of potential help in time of need. For this reason, it was not unusual for the adult children to oscillate between self-sufficiency and complete dependence upon their parents, depending upon the vicissitudes of the employment situation and the stability of their marriages.

Matriarchy and the team structure represented variant forms of intergenerational integration which sometimes emerged in family life. Some general features of matriarchy can be identified: The matriarch represented the major focus, indeed, the dominant focus, of family interaction and intergenerational interdependence. She was the most important vehicle in the service of family solidarity. Her profile of involvement in the family made it appear as if she had undertaken an almost full-time job in responding to family needs. Her help was varied. Accompanying her numerous family activities and multiple help-giving acts was her capacity to influence other family members. Her voice carried greater weight and credibility than that of other family members. Without neglecting the possible ambivalent attitudes of other family members toward her position of centralized authority, we found the overt responses to her by such family members generally were admiration, respect, and affection. Her actions and the other's reactions to her created in her a confident sense of authority which allowed her to intervene to solve problems on her own, without having been invited to do so. (In this regard, notice Felicia Ivarra's decisive actions in getting her son Mario's first wife a job; then, after discovering the wife's infidelity, sequestering her to avoid the prospect of a tragedy.)

The development of a matriarchy required that the patterning of marital and parental roles relegate the husband-father to the periphery of family concerns and activities. This occurred as a result of the man's *de facto* absence from the home or because of habits of non-familial involvement acquired in interactions with family members and with persons outside the family. Many of the things the man would have done as a husband and father, the matriarch did herself as a wife and mother. Thus, she was afforded the opportunity to combine in her familial activities both elements of the traditional roles of women and men: the customary nurturing, socioemotional function of the women of binding the family together, and the customary instrumental functions of the men of linking the family to institutions external to it. Thus, matriarchy embodied both feminine and masculine functions.

There was a common axis that cut across matriarchy and the team structure as variant forms of intergenerational family integration. Both can be viewed as oriented toward either social mobility or social survival. When mobility oriented, the matriarch premised her actions upon the gains made in the host society while directing the family toward even greater gains. Survival-oriented matriarchs, on the other hand, crystallized their roles as a result of their almost incessant reactions to family problems and the need to resolve them. Team structures also exhibited the two orientations, but the actions toward mobility and survival goals were collectively based; team roles were coordinated so as to enable the incumbents to share in the making of direct contributions toward the goals. Whereas some team efforts involved a corporate structure, thus making it possible to distinguish between it and the family system, others involved the shaping of usual roles to attain objectives. In either case, the team structures were being adapted to the attainment of distant, social mobility goals. Survival-oriented teams, in contrast, were flexibly structured to enable rapid change among the incumbents.

REFERENCE

1. Hill, R. 1970. *Family Development in Three Generations*. Cambridge, MA: Schenkman Publishing Co.

PART 4

INTERGENERATIONAL PROCESSES

Introduction

We have approached the families in our study in a variety of ways. We have approached them personally in our encounters and visits with them during the course of our work in the neighborhoods of greater New York City. We have approached them demographically by comparing their sociobiographic characteristics at different periods of their lives to appropriately selected groups. We have approached them historically by trying to understand the convulsive social changes they experienced from the time of their birth in Puerto Rico to the time of their migration and then during the almost three decades of their life in New York City. We have approached them analytically by focusing upon explanations of their ethnic identity, marital relations, and social mobility in the context of intergenerational processes. We have approached them through the use of qualitative case studies to understand the forces which integrate them intergenerationally. What have we learned from this effort? The final chapter answers this question.

IX

Summary and Interpretation

Before summarizing and interpreting our findings, we want to repeat the focus and limitations we set for this study. The 400 persons we studied were part of 200 nuclear families, which in turn were combined into 100 intergenerational families. The persons were all Puerto Rican by birth or parentage, and they all lived in New York City or adjoining areas, but mostly in the borough of the Bronx. The families were not selected by methods of probability sampling. Instead, we used census tracts of the Bronx which were at the top and at the bottom of a rank order developed according to the percentage of Puerto Ricans with a high school education, as reported by the 1970 Census. We visited schools, Catholic and Pentecostal churches, spiritualist centers, and Puerto Rican ethnic and civic organizations, and we approached households in door-to-door visits in selected neighborhoods. A 13-step screening sequence was required to fulfill the study's intergenerational family model. In terms of their greater residential and marital stability, these families differ from other Puerto Rican families wherever they may reside.

The parent generation was, in many important ways, typical of the large number of Puerto Ricans who were migrating to New York City. In the vanguard of the social transformation taking place in Puerto Rico from the Depression of the '30s to the industrialization of the '50s, they had a relatively high educational level and exposure to the conditions of urban life. Improving conditions on the island generated aspirations for a better life for themselves and their children, and to realize these aspirations they migrated to a sociocultural setting different from their own. Arrival in New York City formed the initial phase of yet another set of changes, this time experienced in the host society. The changes were economically troublesome but, in the long run, gratifying. The married-child generation became highly successful both educationally and occupationally. Their success represented a remarkable fulfillment of the aspirations which prompted their parents to migrate.

We knew very little about the lives of these families when we first met them. Although all of us in the field spoke Spanish and shared with them the many features of our Hispanic culture, we found that many of the parent generation in our study resisted the interviews, displaying more distrust than their adult children and their children's spouses. Still more marginal to the culture and with more modest educational attainments and jobs than their children, the parent generation was understandably less trusting of us as strangers during initial contacts. Thus, our field methods very early in the study had to take intergenerational differences into account. Because of the fundamental differences between generations, even within the same family lineage, our field workers had to make use of different techniques in interviewing the two generations. In shaping our efforts to collect data, therefore, we recognized at the very beginning of the study the importance of the main object of the research – intergenerational processes in immigrant Puerto Rican families.

The intergenerational differences between the parents and their married children were remarkably pervasive and strong. Originally, this pattern was revealed during the analysis of ethnic identity, a topic of compelling importance because of the study group's bicultural experience. The scope of our analysis was broadly conceived to include diverse elements of ethnic identity: mastery and use of Spanish and English; the extent of adherence to traditional Puerto Rican values and modernity scores; and subjective views of the self and the person's individualized preferences for aspects of both cultures. When educational and occupational characteristics were incorporated into the analysis, the same pattern of striking differences was evident: the married-child generation had substantially outdistanced their parents in terms of socioeconomic attributes.

The socioeconomic generational differences, taken in conjunction with the diverse items comprising ethnic identity, indicated, however, that intergenerational change was variable. The greatest intergenerational change occurred in socioeconomic status, then in the language used, then in values, and, finally, the least change occurred in the subjective elements describing self-concept and bicultural preferences. Immediately, the inference is that external elements, pragmatic in character, which were relevant to the immigrants' objective integration into the host society, were more susceptible to intergenerational change than the internal elements, subjective in character but of substantial symbolic importance. (Presently we shall reconsider these elements according to their "instrumental" and "expressive" meanings.) Both generations experienced the erosion of much that was associated with their lives as Puerto Ricans but internally, in the symbolisms linking them to the island, they experienced less change. Despite their remarkable upward mobility in the host society, the married-child generation still retained symbolic bonds with Puerto Rico, a place hardly known to them from direct experience.

We then turned to the important task of explaining variations in ethnic identity in each generation. Why were some persons more than others allied to their Puerto Rican heritage and cultural experiences? Rather than drawing up an *ad hoc* list of independent variables to explain ethnic identity, the choice of such variables, we believed, should reflect the person's receptivity to influences shaping ethnic identity and/or the degree of exposure to such influences. Although those we interviewed were all Puerto Rican by birth or parentage, they differed from each other in their receptivity and exposure to the bicultural environment in which they lived. The complexity of this problem required that we depart from the usual procedure of simple bivariate analysis and turn to multivariate techniques which would allow us to identify the independent sources of influences affecting ethnic identity. Two variables of signal importance emerged in the analysis: the age at arrival in New York City and the level of education. Once these variables were taken into account as determinants of ethnic identity, the other independent variables added little or nothing to our understanding of ethnic identity.

Age at arrival in New York City and level of education, however, played sometimes similar and sometimes different roles in shaping ethnic identity, depending upon which elements of ethnic identity were being considered. Thus, each variable had an independent effect upon the language component of ethnic identity. As education increased the knowledge of English and Spanish increased, but the daily use of Spanish decreased. Moreover, regardless of level of education, age at arrival was related to language ability and usage, with those who arrived at an older age reporting less ability and use of English than those who had arrived at a younger age. In turn, those with more years of education were less familistic, less fatalistic, and more modern than those with fewer years of education; age at arrival had no effect upon such variables. On the other hand, age at arrival was an important influence on ethnic self-identification, whereas education was not. The discovery of the importance of the sociocultural context of early socialization and of education programmatically shaped the way in which subsequent topics were examined. As used to examine ethnic identity, the variables provided the first clues as to how the experiences of migration and adaptation affected intergenerational family processes.

Before we discuss our analysis of the ways in which migration-induced changes were related to intergenerational continuity, we want to point out once again the meaning we have assigned to this concept. Simply put, inter-generational continuity refers to the presence of a statistically significant correlation between the parents and their children with respect to some characteristic chosen for analysis. The correlation is the operational counter-part to the concept of intergenerational continuity. It should be mentioned that the use of measures of association with less stringent assumptions than those of Pearson's product-moment correlation – which was used in this study – did not alter the pattern of findings relevant to intergenerational continuity. Nonetheless, in a cross-sectional study such as this one it is usually impossible to identify reliably and in detail the specific processes, including the intergenerational direction of influences, which create continuity. Our formulations regarding such processes represent informed speculations.

Early in the study we adopted the selective continuity approach because it left open to empirical demonstration the possible unevenness of intergen-erational continuity. This approach, we believed, would have heuristic value but, as we proceeded to analyze the data with the objective of uncovering ways in which migration-induced change was related to intergenerational processes, the findings began to puzzle us. When the 100 intergenerationally linked families were analyzed, little if any evidence of intergenerational continuity was apparent. The ethnic characteristics of the children were unrelated to the corresponding ethnic characteristics of either parent. We began to wonder if the two generations, even though connected through family lineage, were utterly disconnected in terms of continuity. Perhaps the wrenching change produced by migration from one sociocultural system to another attenuated or dissolved the type of linkage which continuity entails. The puzzle prompted more refined questions: Are there conditions which underlie continuity that strengthen it under some circumstances and weaken it under others? Are some of the characteristics used to evaluate intergenera-tional continuity more likely to produce continuity than others? Findings relevant to intergenerational change in ethnic identity and to the determi-nants of ethnic identity provided a point of departure for re-examining the puzzle.

We began with the assumption that age at arrival in New York City signi-fied the cultural context of the person's early socialization. If born in New York City or arrived before the age of 15, the context was New York City; if arrived at 15 or older, the context was Puerto Rico. With such distinctions, the intergenerationally linked families could be classified according to whether or not the parents and their children had a common cultural context in their early socialization. Thus, what was first taken as an attribute of persons, *age at arrival in New York City*, in the explanation of ethnic identity, was recast in broader terms as a joint attribute of the parents and their children. The logic of this procedure was applied to the other major determinant of ethnic identity, *education*. Parents and their children were classified according to similarity of educational level, with graduation from high school as the dividing point. Thus, in answer to our first question, the sharing of an early context of socialization and similarities in educational level represent the two underlying conditions thought to be relevant to intergenerational continuity.

Previously we made the point that even though intergenerational differences were strong and pervasive, the differences themselves were variable: they were greater with respect to elements which are external and pragmatic and less among elements which are internal and subjective. This distinction between elements, suggested to us by Hill's intergenerational research,[1] needs to be further developed as we turn to the second question of whether some characteristics are more conducive to intergenerational continuity than others. In this regard, Bales' distinction between "instrumental" and "expressive" acts[2] is pointedly relevant. He takes this distinction from our common everyday habits of speech but argues, at the same time, that the two types of acts are not sharply separable, their differences being a matter of the "proper weight of emphasis." Customarily, some activities are viewed as *goal-directed, the person performing the acts "in order" to realize an end*. These are *instrumental* acts, for they are directed toward some objective in the future. *Expressive* acts, on the other hand, are not explicitly directed toward an objective; rather, they are reactive to, or signs of, a person's "immediate pressure, tension, or emotion." Not being explicitly harnessed toward the attainment of an end, expressive acts are produced "because" of some internal emotion or feeling. Bales summarizes the differences between the two types of acts as resting upon "the degree to which anticipated consequences enter as a steering factor." Some of the elements used to evaluate intergenerational differences and continuities do not lend themselves clearly to the instrumental-expressive distinction because they represent an admixture of meanings or do not fit. Other elements clearly do, and it is upon them that we shall focus in order to complete our formulations regarding intergenerational continuity.

In the lives of the Puerto Rican immigrants and their children, the acquisition of the English language had instrumental significance to their adaptation to the host society. The acquisition of English presents an instrumental element *par excellence* because in a multitude of ways it determines the attainment of a multitude of objectives. Without it, the migrants' life space would have been constricted largely to the ethnic in-group, thereby preventing them from realizing the aspirations which led them to migrate.

As we move through the many elements we have used to demonstrate intergenerational differences, and away from those which are instrumental, such as the mastery and use of English, we come to elements designating subjective feelings. The rise of such feelings was not immediately or explicitly linked to the anticipation of future goals. Rather, they were the psychological residuals or by-products of the migrant's bicultural experience which came to be suffused with expressive meaning. They reflected preferences as to place of residence, maintaining Puerto Rican traditions, or the language of use. Subjective elements of even more evident expressive content were the person's views of himself/herself as Puerto Rican or North American in terms of the corresponding cultural values and the perceived degree of closeness to Puerto Ricans or North Americans. To recall Bales' definition of the expressive, such feelings arise "because" of emotions or sentiments rather than of explicit organization "in order" to attain external goals. The distinction between expressive and instrumental elements, nonetheless, is still a matter of degree.

When the answers to the two basic questions previously posed are brought together, many of the complicated findings on intergenerational continuity can be brought into order. In response to the first question, we found there are underlying conditions which promote intergenerational continuity: when parents and their children were socialized in the same culture or when they were similar in educational level, intergenerational continuity increased. The distinction between expressive and instrumental elements, although a matter of degree, is relevant to the second question because it serves to identify the elements likely to form part of intergenerational continuity. We found that when the parents and their children were socialized in the same culture, intergenerational continuity appeared among both instrumental and expressive elements: there was intergenerational continuity in the mastery and use of English and in the subjective bicultural preferences just discussed. When the parents and their children were similar in educational level, intergenerational continuity did not appear among the expressive elements but did appear among those which were instrumental such as the mastery and use of English. Selective continuity was operative but must be qualified according to both the underlying conditions linking the generations and the character of the element used to evaluate continuity.

The general effect upon continuity of parents and children sharing their early socialization in the same culture is understandable. Such sharing involved a total cultural environment, whether Puerto Rico or New York City, not preselected exposure to a narrow band of cultural stimuli. It occurred early in childhood, allowing the learning to take hold in diverse ways from the development of personality to the shaping of world views, attitudes, and skills. The shared learning, in brief, was so pervasive and wide-ranging as to provide a backdrop for intergenerational continuity without favoring instrumental over expressive elements or the other way around. When parents and children experienced such sharing, their level of acquisition of the English language was directly correlated. Also directly correlated was the strength of their respective preferences for things either Puerto Rican or North American. The sharing of a common cultural environment early in life enabled intergenerational transmissions to produce continuity in both instrumental and expressive elements. To answer a question posed in Chapter I, one of the most notable consequences of migration-induced changes is that in about three-fourths of the families migration itself kept the parents and their children from having a common culture during their early socialization. Among these families, there was no intergenerational continuity in either instrumental or expressive elements. Put metaphorically, the children were orphans to family legacies which, for better or for worse, were truncated by migration.

We have seen that the sharing of educational levels between the two generations had a more specific impact: it promoted intergenerational continuity in instrumental but not expressive elements. Again, this finding can be rendered understandable if we keep in mind that educational similarities were instrumental in character, and thus narrowed the focus of intergenerational transmissions to other similar elements, purposively oriented, such as the acquisition of the English language. Against the backdrop of similar education for the two generations, the transmissions decisively favored instrumental elements, but in most of the families, in fact, in about two-thirds of them, no such similarities were found, since the child generation's upward mobility created sharp dissimilarities between the generations in education. In these families there was no continuity in either instrumental or expressive elements. To use the same metaphor, the child generation was rendered an orphan to family legacies, this time because of its own extraordinary socioeconomic success in adapting to the host society.

The pieces of the puzzle previously discussed now fall into place. The pervasive absence of intergenerational continuity at the level of the entire study group, with no subdivisions, is the result of the preponderant number of families in which the parents and their children did not share the culture of their early socialization and were strongly dissimilar in their educational levels. Migration and social mobility, therefore, play a significant role in shaping the important intergenerational processes of continuity.

Extending the pattern of intergenerational findings already presented, notable intergenerational differences were demonstrated once again in the examination of spouse relations. This analysis focused upon the sharing of household tasks, decision-making, and leisure activities. We found that in each generation there was more sharing in decision-making and leisure activities than in the performance of household tasks. The overall thrust of change from parent to child was, however, in the direction of stronger egalitarian relations. Our data, for the first time, resoundingly confirm what other observers of stateside Puerto Ricans have speculated, but the specific meaning of this change must be taken into consideration. Thus, of the three functions mentioned above, the greatest intergenerational change toward egalitarianism occurred in the sharing of household tasks, resulting from the wife taking on traditional male tasks and not from the husband performing traditional female tasks.

Our findings, based upon a more comprehensive set of cultural elements than had been used in prior research on spouse relations in immigrant families, are consistent with the findings of others: culture does not directly affect the sharing of household functions. However, we did not conclude from such findings that culture is irrelevant. Rather, we undertook the challenging task of uncovering the role culture plays in shaping factors relevant to the sharing of functions. Rodman's cross-national theory[3] of spouse decision-making was singularly useful even though we focused upon cultural differences in the generations and not upon the culture of nations at different levels of economic development, as Rodman had done. In the parent generation, which was still demonstrably enmeshed in the cultural norm of a modified patriarchal society, the higher the husband's occupational status, the greater the sharing of decision-making. In the child generation, which adhered to the cultural norms of a transitional egalitarian society, the higher the husband's occupational status, the less the sharing of decision-making. The different cultural norms the generations represented conferred different meanings upon the husband's occupational status, thus showing the important indirect role culture plays in shaping husband and wife decision-making. Another set of findings strikingly revealed the general importance of the wife's education: in each of the two generations, the higher the wife's education, the less the role segregation in each of the three functions.

The distinction between expressive and instrumental elements, so useful to the understanding of intergenerational continuity with respect to selected elements forming part of ethnic identity, was not applied to the analysis of intergenerational continuity in the three spouse functions. We believed it would be difficult, indeed, to decide how the functions reflect the meaning of the expressive-instrumental distinction and concluded it would be logically inappropriate to attempt the distinction. Thus, the analysis of intergenerational continuity of the three functions used only the two underlying conditions stipulated before: sharing of a common culture by parent and child during their early socialization, and the similarity of their educational attainments. One modification was introduced, namely the use of the wife's education instead of the husband's, because the strength of the findings indicated the general importance of the wife's education in influencing the spouses' sharing in the performance of the three functions. The findings followed the predicted path. A common context of early socialization was conducive to intergenerational continuity with respect to the sharing of household tasks, decision-making, and leisure activities. The other underlying condition, namely, similarity of educational attainments, was also conducive to intergenerational continuity with respect to the three marital functions. Once again, such continuity was wiped out at the level of the entire study group, with no subdivisions, because most of the parents and children in the families were not socialized in the same culture and because of dissimilarities in their education. We should bear in mind that the factors used to evaluate intergenerational continuity represent the degree of sharing between husbands and wives in a complex set of marital functions. This highlights the powerful influence of migration-induced changes in early socialization and social mobility in shaping intergenerational continuity, even when such continuity involved the husbands and wives negotiating their own special marital arrangements.

Historically, the parent generation, in comparison to the total Puerto Rican population, enjoyed at an early age a set of advantages which favored them in the context of modernization occurring on the island, but they were more or less comparable to the many other migrants in the 1950s who came to New York City. However, their children's socioeconomic success in the host society far exceeded the success of an appropriately designated comparison group. Socioeconomic success was examined also from the perspective of family lineage, tracing back to the parents of our parent generation, the grandparents. The movement across the three generations, from the grandparents to the parents, and from the parents to their married children, described a clear sequence of upward mobility. Intergenerational upward mobility, however, has been uneven: although the parent generation was upwardly mobile, their married children's upward mobility was substantially greater. Tracing mobility through lineage also revealed another important facet of the generations' experiences: there had been intergenerational continuity in socioeconomic status between the grandparents and the parents, but no such continuity between the parents and their married children. The pattern of findings for the parent generation fit the status attainment model which affirms intergenerational continuity in socioeconomic status. Indeed, one of the most consistent findings of research on social mobility in the United States indicates that the educational attainments of children are directly related to the socioeconomic characteristics of their parents. The parents transfer their socioeconomic advantages or disadvantages on to their children. Moreover, an earlier study of Puerto Ricans demonstrated intergenerational continuity in socioeconomic status between the parents of first-generation migrants and the first-generation migrants themselves,[4] but the findings pertaining to the child generation strongly departed from the model. Once again we found ourselves in an intergenerational puzzle: the substantial educational attainments of the child generation were unrelated to the socioeconomic achievements of their parents.

Intergenerational continuity in socioeconomic status is shaped by the setting in which it occurs. Years before, in pre-industrial Puerto Rico, even small variations in socioeconomic resources at an even more modest level had been sufficient to create intergenerational continuity between the grandparents and the parent generation. The migration experience ruptured intergenerational continuity in socioeconomic status because of the increasingly higher educational requirements of New York City's labor force, with accompanying rapid erosion of employment opportunities at the bottom of the occupational hierarchy. The parent generation did not transmit their socioeconomic advantages or disadvantages to their children because the variations in their humble socioeconomic resources did not meaningfully coincide with the more elevated labor market opportunities of the host society.

To develop this point further, we turned once again to one of the underlying conditions which the preceding data analysis had shown to be relevant to intergenerational continuity, the sharing by parent and child of the same culture in their early socialization. The pattern of correlations substantiated our expectations. Although the educational attainments of the parents were at their lowest in families where both the parent and child generations were born and raised in Puerto Rico, intergenerational continuity was higher among them than among families in which the generations did not share an early context of socialization or shared it in New York City. The higher educational attainments of the latter two types of families must be seen in the context of decreasing opportunities for low-skilled jobs in New York City. Thus, the impact of migration upon intergenerational continuity is complex. It creates a sharp change in the context of early socialization between the immigrant parents and their children. Additional differences are introduced by the children's upward social mobility. Among immigrants with marginal labor market skills, intergenerational processes are further complicated because the parents are unable to draw upon their labor market skills to advance their children's achievements. Research on the impact of migration upon intergenerational continuity must be sensitive to the degree of congruity between the migrants' socioeconomic resources and the labor market structure of the host society.

In sum, the extensive application of the status attainment model to the study's data revealed new and unsuspected findings. Continuity can occur in one generational sequence but not in the next generational sequence. Migration had a critical effect upon such transmissions, operating through the disjunctions it induced. The parents' socioeconomic attributes were not helpful in understanding the exceptional upward mobility of the younger generation we studied. One variable forming part of the status-attainment model, namely, the number of siblings, was inversely related to the child generation's educational attainments, thus suggesting its influential role. If the migration experience serves as a necessary qualifier to the status-attainment model, other findings compel an expansion of the model. The parent generation's degree of adherence to the traditional values of familism and fatalism also was inversely related to the child generation's educational attainments. When released from the force of such values, the parents were able to induce in their children greater educational achievements. The role traditionally derived cultural factors played in the child generation's educational attainments foreshadowed the need to incorporate the relevance of culture into status-attainment models of social mobility.

One point which we have not discussed previously should be mentioned here. In our analysis, we were sensitive to the possible importance of gender in the parent and child generations. In general, we found that there were more differences between husbands and wives in the parent generation than in the child generation. We also divided the 100 intergenerational families into two groups: in 56 families the daughter was the connecting link and in 44, the son was the connecting link. There were no differences between these two groups with respect to the three major components of intergenerational processes: intergenerational differences and similarities, continuities and discontinuities, and the degree of integration. In sum, none of the intergenerational processes we analyzed was influenced by whether the married child was a son or a daughter.

We then turned to the examination of another major component of intergenerational processes: intergenerational integration. This analysis was based upon the statistical patterns of visitations and reciprocal help exchanges between the parents and their married children. The use of such patterns has the advantage of rooting the concept of integration in objective measures which had been used in another major study of intergenerational processes.[5] By replicating the measures, a basis for interstudy comparisons was established. The comparisons amply justified the use of the concept of a modified extended family in characterizing our Puerto Rican families, that is, if the strength of intergenerational integration is taken as the deciding criterion. The human picture underlying such integration was one of almost incessant interaction between the parents and their married children.

Once we combined the findings demonstrating strong integration with the other findings pertaining to intergenerational differences and discontinuities, we were then able to focus upon a major conclusion of the intergenerational research literature, that of Troll and Bengtson: ". . . high levels of intergenerational cohesion do not necessarily reflect high levels of similarity. . . ."[6] Our findings require that such a concluding statement be followed by the emphasis of an exclamation point, since it states weakly the decisive and preponderant pattern we found. Step by step, our study has demonstrated a strong and pervasive pattern of intergenerational differences and discontinuities among the 100 families taken as a whole. It found also that the two underlying conditions inducing discontinuity, intergenerational differences in the settings of early socialization and in educational attainment, had no effect upon the strength of intergenerational integration. Metaphorically, it seems as if the parents and their married children, having come through the vicissitudes of a rapidly modernizing pre-industrial Puerto Rico, the migration experience, and almost three decades of a changed life style in New York City, were still bound together in an almost-sacred agreement: "No matter what potentially divisive elements and influences may impinge upon us, we shall retain our unity." In this context, the portrait of intergenerational solidarity was of compelling importance.

Such findings, taken together, led to an important implication. Intergenerational transmissions which created continuity were no more inducing of family solidarity than were those interactions between generations which failed to produce continuity. The implication can be more clearly focused if early socialization context is taken as an example. When the parents and their children shared the early context of their socialization, intergenerational continuity in education was greater than when there was no sharing. The parents' educational advantages or disadvantages were transmitted to their children, which could lead one to suppose a greater intergenerational solidarity, but that supposition is patently erroneous. Erroneous, too, would be any inference that the magnitude of educational differences between the generations affected intergenerational integration. Whether or not such transmissions occurred, and no matter the degree of educational differences, intergenerational solidarity was uniformly retained, almost as if there had been a primitive bonding between the generations.

At first, the findings surprised us. Upon reconsidering them, however, our surprise diminished. To examine the issue we focused upon intergenerational differences, although a similar argument could have been developed with respect to intergenerational continuity. From the very moment of the child's birth and on through his/her socialization into adulthood, differences between parents and children were intrinsic to the relationship. Though bound together into complex reciprocal patterns, the parents and children were enmeshed into a partnership of persons who necessarily and habitually differed in a multitude of ways but, no matter the differences between them, the Puerto Rican value of familism strongly sanctified and reinforced the mutual commitment of the parents and children to their enduring familial bond. Suffused with an almost sacred character, the commitment underlies the statistical patterns demonstrating strong intergenerational integration. Thus, the intergenerational integration observed in the present, which has retained solidarity in the face of so many pervasive differences, is an up-to-date instance of a life-long acceptance of differences in the interest of parent-child unity.

A further observation should be made. Many of the differences between the parents and their children derived directly or indirectly from the child generation's superior educational attainments. Their higher education, in turn, led to better occupations and larger incomes. Upward social mobility was viewed as desirable by both generations. Instead of being divisive to intergenerational integration, the children's exceptional social mobility was the object of parental pride. It also buttressed parental feelings that the sacrifices and hardships they endured in leaving the island were now being recompensed.

Intergenerational differences, or the "gulf" between generations, are often taken to signify the loss of family heritage, as the quotation introducing Part 3 would have it. The view is that something of considerable value has been lost, but an alternative view should be advanced if the issue is one of determining that the direction of intergenerational change fits many of the requirements of the sociocultural environment where the change occurred. In this study, the married children's socioeconomic attributes exceeded those of their parents. The general pattern of intergenerational change, which created such a wide gulf between the generations, at the same time enabled the children to function more effectively and successfully in the host society without the loss of intergenerational family solidarity.

The prevailing pattern of intergenerational integration varied from one extreme in which the child generation was fully submerged into the parent generation's household, totally dependent upon it, to the other extreme of distinctly separate, economically autonomous nuclear units. Although the children commanded more human and economic resources, the prevailing flow of help still moved from the parents to the children as a continuation of previous life-cycle experience. The matriarchy and the team structure represented variant forms of intergenerational integration. In the matriarchal structure, the husband-father was relegated to a marginal role while the wife-mother dominated help-giving transactions at the sociometric core of family life. Team structures entailed the mobilization of the entire family in the interest of a common goal; sometimes, this involved the construction of a new set of corporately organized roles; other times it involved the extension and reshaping of usual family roles. Each variant form of intergenerational integration can be viewed as oriented toward social survival or social mobility.

It is important to note that the role changes associated with the development of a matriarchy paralleled intergenerational changes in the roles of husband and wife in the performance of household tasks. In those exceptional cases where a matriarchy did arise, the direction of intergenerational family change was congenially related to the rise. Consistent with this interpretation is the finding that not one intergenerational family, out of the 100 studied, had a husband-father performing both socioemotional and instrumental functions while relegating the wife-mother to a peripheral family role. The woman's family role was bound and locked into socioemotional functions which were not easily relinquished to the man and, culturally, the husband's performance of traditional women's tasks was tinged with stigma. The inverse of this pattern carried with it no culturally induced stigma. In combination with such cultural factors, the intergenerational social change the Puerto Rican families experienced through urbanization, migration, and increasing levels of education consistently and decisively favored the acquisition, by women, of competency in areas of performance customarily associated with the male role or representing an extension of it.

The prevailing patterns of intergenerational integration and their two variant forms revealed how the Puerto Rican families are organized and how they functioned while making their way in the society to which they migrated in the face of pervasive intergenerational differences and discontinuities. We believe their strong intergenerational integration and the stability of their intact marital unions enabled them to confront the problems of social change from yesterday's Puerto Rico to today's New York City and buttressed the younger generation's drive toward success.

REFERENCES

1. Hill, R. 1970. *Family Development in Three Generations.* Cambridge, MA: Schenkman Publishing Co., p. 386.
2. Bales, R. F. 1950. *Interaction Process Analysis: A Method for the Study of Small Groups.* Cambridge, MA: Addison-Wesley Press, Inc., pp. 50-51.
3. Rodman, H. 1967. "Marital Power in France, Greece, Yugoslavia and the United States: A Cross-National Discussion." *Journal of Marriage and the Family* 30 (May): 321-324.
4. Rogler, L. H. 1972. *Migrant in the City: The Life of a Puerto Rican Action Group.* New York: Basic Books, Inc., pp. 212-225.
5. Hill, R., see note 1.
6. Troll, L. and V. Bengtson. 1979. "Generations in the Family," in Wesley R. Burr et al., (eds.) *Contemporary Theories about the Family*, Vol. 1. New York: The Free Press.

Index